# The
# EVERYTHING®
## Grant Writing Book

Dear Reader:

Your reasons for wanting to learn more about grant writing probably vary, ranging from expanding your services to clients to taking on a new task at work. Or perhaps you're simply looking for a way to increase your income.

Whatever your motivation, we're delighted that you have *The Everything®* *Grant Writing Book.* We know you'll find it full of valuable information on how to write winning grant proposals, how to become an entrepreneur, and even how to set up and expand your grant writing business. We're excited about being able to share our professional grant writing expertise.

Bringing this information together in a comprehensive publication that addresses the public and private sectors has been a pleasure. We're also pleased to bring you one of the most accessible and readable grant writing books on the market.

As an added bonus, we've provided samples of components of grant proposals throughout the book. You'll also find complete proposals for a federal and a foundation grant that together brought nearly $1 million to our community.

But there's no substitute for experience. So read the book and dive into what you'll find can be a challenging, rewarding, and creative new career. Here's to your success!

Judy Tremore                Nancy Burke Smith

# The EVERYTHING® Series

## Editorial

| | |
|---|---|
| Publishing Director | Gary M. Krebs |
| Managing Editor | Kate McBride |
| Copy Chief | Laura MacLaughlin |
| Acquisitions Editor | Bethany Brown |
| Development Editor | Karen Johnson Jacot |
| Production Editor | Khrysti Nazzaro |

## Production

| | |
|---|---|
| Production Director | Susan Beale |
| Production Manager | Michelle Roy Kelly |
| Series Designers | Daria Perreault |
| | Colleen Cunningham |
| Cover Design | Paul Beatrice |
| | Frank Rivera |
| Layout and Graphics | Colleen Cunningham |
| | Rachael Eiben |
| | Michelle Roy Kelly |
| | Daria Perreault |
| | Erin Ring |
| Series Cover Artist | Barry Littmann |

**Visit the entire Everything® Series at everything.com**

# THE
# EVERYTHING®
# GRANT WRITING
# BOOK

### Create the perfect proposal to raise the funds you need

Judy Tremore and Nancy Burke Smith

Adams Media Corporation
Avon, Massachusetts

An Everything® Series Book.
Everything® and everything.com® are registered trademarks of F+W Publications, Inc.

Published by Adams Media, an F+W Publications Company
57 Littlefield Street, Avon, MA 02322 U.S.A.
*www.adamsmedia.com*

ISBN: 1-58062-877-X
Printed in the United States of America.

J   I   H   G   F   E   D   C

**Library of Congress Cataloging-in-Publication Data**
Tremore, Judy.
The everything grant writing book / Judy Tremore and Nancy Burke Smith.
            p.      cm. (An everything series)
                    ISBN 1-58062-877-X
1. Proposal writing for grants–United States. 2. Grants-in-aid–United States.
3. Fund raising–United States.  I. Smith, Nancy Burke. II. Title. III. Series.

HG177.5.U6 T73 2003
658.15'224–dc21

                                        2003000372

*This book is available at quantity discounts for bulk purchases.*
*For information, call 1-800-872-5627.*

# Contents

## 10 Planning for Letters of Support / 101

## 11 Writing a Statement of Need / 111

## 12 Writing Goals, Objectives, and Outcomes / 123

## 13 Writing Action Plans and Timelines / 135

## 14 Designing an Evaluation Plan / 147

## Top Ten Reasons to Learn Grant Writing

1. People who write grants are highly valued by employers and clients.

2. Grants bring money to your community and to the causes you believe in.

3. Grant writing helps develop your skills as a writer, a small business person, and/or an administrator.

4. Whether the economy is good or bad, grant writers can easily find work. In fact, when the economy is bad, the need for services increases.

5. Securing grants for important organizations and projects helps you effect positive change in society.

6. Grant writing expands your network of professional and personal associations.

7. You can build your knowledge base of your community: who's who, who's doing what, what's important, what needs to be done, and how things fit together.

8. Grant writing skills are transferable to private-sector work.

9. Grant writers can write full-time for attractive earnings or part-time for additional income.

10. Writing a grant exercises both your left and right brain—you can be creative and practical simultaneously.

# Introduction

▶ The simple fact is that there are now more options for funding than ever before. But how do you get the money that's out there? It's often left to busy executive directors of nonprofits to identify, track, and write grants for just a portion of the billions of dollars available annually from foundations and government departments. And that can be overwhelming, but it doesn't have to be.

*The Everything® Grant Writing Book* is a comprehensive "how-to" book that draws on the expertise of grant-writing professionals. You'll receive advice throughout the book from foundation program officers, grant reviewers, and a number of experienced grant writers. You'll read success stories, and you'll read stories about failures so you can learn to avoid the pitfalls. In this book you'll get the know-how you need to effectively complete grant proposals to get the funding you need, or to establish and build a thriving freelance writing business, or to qualify for a full-time paid staff position as a grant writer in a large nonprofit organization.

You'll learn that in grant writing you especially need to cultivate two abilities: meeting deadlines and following directions. If these are qualities you have to cultivate or improve, you'll get help along the way.

You'll learn about the components of grant proposals: letters of intent and inquiry, letters of support, statements of need, goals, objectives, and outcomes. *The Everything® Grant Writing Book* will teach you how to write project descriptions, action plans, and timetables. You'll learn how to design evaluation plans, develop budgets, write budget narratives, and find partners or other nonprofit agencies that will collaborate on your project.

*The Everything® Grant Writing Book* is filled with tips about going to grant-seeker workshops and conventions, on getting to know officers in your local foundations, and for increasing your expertise and your value to clients. It has practical advice about what to include in proposals and what to leave out, how to fill out forms, and how to write, proofread, and package your proposal.

*The Everything® Grant Writing Book* is filled with samples, charts, and letters that were written for successful grant proposals. You'll also find a complete government grant proposal and a complete foundation proposal that you can refer to when you're writing a proposal.

The rewards in writing successful grant proposals are not only monetary. You'll reap the satisfaction of knowing you've helped your organization reach its goals in providing services to families and children—your neighbors.

*The Everything® Grant Writing Book* can help you write a successful grant proposal and increase your chances of getting the funding you desire. Good luck!

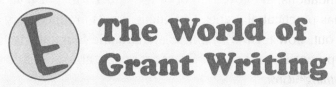

## Chapter 1

# The World of Grant Writing

The first thing you try to learn when you intend to live in another country is the language. The same is true of venturing into the world of grant making: You'll need to learn the language. Key terms are listed in Appendix B, but you'll come to understand the "flavor" of the language as you read through the book. This chapter provides the foundation for your learning more about grant writing.

## What Is a Grant Proposal?

Most people think of grants as those monetary awards you get to help with college tuition. Unless you are involved in the nonprofit sector, you are not likely to have encountered the world of grant writing for charitable causes. Grants for tuition are made based on the individual's need and the goals of the government or the educational institution providing those educational grants. Charitable grants are monetary awards by a grantor, usually the government or a charitable foundation, that pay for a prescribed activity or project. Grant proposals are submitted as requests for that funding.

Grant proposals come in two forms: as a response to a Request for Proposal (RFP) or as a submission for funding made to a philanthropic organization. In both cases, the grant proposal is formulaic. That means you must follow the instructions and the outline provided in either the RFP or the funder's guidelines. You also must use the accepted language and the approach set forth by your reading audience.

Grant proposals are most often written to seek funding for a specific project within a larger organization. Projects may be capital (for construction of buildings) or based on a program (to support staffing, equipment, and other items that are necessary to launch a special project). Sometimes grants are made for operations (utilities, ongoing staffing costs, etc.), but sources for operational funding are very rare.

**FACT**

Few funders want to award grants for sustaining (operational) funding, even though this is the most critical need for most nonprofit organizations. Look carefully to find funders interested in sustaining good work.

## Grant Writing versus Fundraising

A grant writer is most often a writer with a specialty, though he or she may also do fundraising. A fundraiser may write grants as part of his or her job. But most often a fundraiser is a person on staff who is assigned to general fundraising duties.

Fundraising duties can include such things as nurturing long-term donors, developing candidates and plans for bequests, planning and executing fundraising events or speaker series, managing a database of donors, developing year-end and mid-year letter campaigns, and other similar responsibilities. Larger organizations usually have someone on staff assigned to fundraising, and often that person is called a development director.

While many development directors can and have written grants, they become so busy with the other requirements of their jobs that grant writing becomes a sideline for them or something they seek from an outside source, such as a professional grant writer.

## What Kinds of Projects Get Funded?

Maggie is a freelance grant writer who works for various nonprofits helping them get grant money. In the early 1990s, Maggie received a call from a potential client in her state who wanted to meet with her to share his ideas and enlist her help writing grants to fund the project. He had already purchased a building and was in the process of renovating it into a hospital/orphanage for children born with AIDS.

As part of Maggie's interview with the client, she asked him why he had chosen this particular project. He responded that two of his primary reasons were that funders like projects that benefit children, that AIDS was a priority social/health issue of the time, and that the two together seemed a natural way for him to launch his new career in human services.

There's a reason that a "statement of need" comes first in a grant proposal—all projects should identify and respond to a proven need in the community. Be wary of projects that are one individual's idea of what's needed. Make sure the need can be supported with testimony or data before you write grants for funding.

Maggie didn't like any part of his answer. The project seemed opportunistic, manipulative, and motivated more by self-interest than interest in others. She did some research and learned that other long-standing service organizations had also discussed similar programs until they learned that a children's AIDS center was not necessary. One executive director told her, "We thought it might be an important contribution to society, but we learned that there are thousands of foster families that are more than willing to take in children with AIDS. We believe those children would be far better served in a family environment than an institution, so we simply scrapped the idea."

## There Must Be a Real Need

Maggie turned down the client. "Funders are not stupid. If I could learn with a few telephone calls that this was a 'phantom' need, they either already knew that or would learn it just as quickly."

Projects that don't address a real and pressing community, state, or national issue are not fundable. They might be creative. They might have strong possibilities for collaboration with potential partners. They might appear to address the priorities of a funder. But even with all these earmarks of a fundable proposal, they fall short unless the need is documented with supporting data.

## Fundable Projects

What are the attributes of "fundable" projects? A project and/or the organization proposing a project must have most of the following:

- Strong and recent data to support the need for the project.
- An experienced project manager or other lead person such as the executive director of an organization.
- A history of fiscal responsibility (or, if a new organization, comprehensive plans for fiscal oversight).
- A response (project description) that clearly addresses the identified need.
- Collaboration with others in the community.
- Community member involvement in identifying the problem and the solution.

Collaboration is important to most funders, but it must be an efficient and cost-effective means of addressing the problem. So keep that in mind when you are seeking cooperation from other agencies.

## Trends in Funding

There are "trends" in funding priorities among both government funders and charitable foundations. During the 1980s and early 1990s, children's issues (child abuse and neglect, early childhood education, etc.) were important criteria for projects. While that focus has not disappeared, the trends have shifted somewhat to new priorities.

In the mid- to late-1990s, closing the digital divide became a new funding priority, particularly at the federal government level. Other recent trends include projects that support professional staff development, projects that develop skills in chronically unemployed adults, and projects that identify the potential for violence and work to prevent it, especially among teens. Since September 11, 2001, projects that address safety and security issues in communities throughout the United States have become especially important.

## Planning Is Critical

All Requests for Proposals (RFPs) have a deadline. Foundations, which most often issue guidelines rather than RFPs, frequently have deadlines as well. Sometimes the deadline is months away, but more often you'll find that it's approximately thirty days after you hear of an RFP to its final deadlines. You have a lot to do in a very short time.

Short deadlines are sometimes deliberately designed as a sort of "natural selection" process. If the organization has not already planned for a project that responds to the focus of the RFP, they won't have time to plan, convene meetings of key partners, write the proposal, complete the forms, and send off a strong proposal in thirty days.

## The First Steps

Develop your schedule by putting down a "ship by" deadline—not the actual due date. Then work backward. If you plan overnight shipping with next-day delivery, your ship deadline will be the day before the actual due date. If you plan to use the post office, shorten your deadline by three to five days. If you can hand-deliver grants to local foundations or drive to your state capital if that's the final destination, you may be able to work closer to the actual due date. But be absolutely certain you'll be able to meet the deadline.

Remember, you have to allow enough time for first and second drafts, final "tweaks" to the narrative, completing forms, having forms signed, and developing and justifying budgets. Also, critically important, be sure to leave enough time for planning the project and identifying and securing commitments from community partner agencies.

**ALERT!**

Before September 11, 2001, the federal government discouraged overnight shipping of grant proposals by not providing all the information necessary for such shipping (such as a street address, phone number, etc.). Since mail delivery, particularly in Washington, D.C., has slowed for new inspection processes, the government now encourages overnight shipment and discourages the use of the postal service for time-sensitive materials.

Some RFPs indicate that they will accept a postmark date for the deadline. Be sure to read the instructions carefully and note whether it states "must arrive by" the date or "must be postmarked by" the date. If the project must be postmarked by a predetermined date, you must use the U.S. Postal Service for the postmark. Marks made by other delivery providers will not fulfill this requirement.

Following is the schedule for a typical grant-writing project. Let's say that it is due March 10, four weeks after you've received it.

| Completion Date | Activity |
|---|---|
| 2/2 | Download RFP from Web site and review instructions. |
| 2/3 | Identify partnerships, plan program, and plan meetings, if necessary. |
| 2/4–2/6 | Draft brief (two-paragraph to one-page) proposal summary for partner meeting. Call State Single Point of Contact, if required. |
| 2/8 | Hold partners' meeting: present information, discuss roles of partners, secure commitments. |
| 2/9 | Write and distribute sample support letters from each partner. Request printout on agency letterhead and signatures by 2/24. |
| 2/15 | Submit first draft narrative for review by colleagues. |
| 2/18 | Review grant and fill in blanks. |
| 2/20 | Submit second draft to partners for review and meet to discuss issues (also discuss financial needs for partner services). |
| 2/24 | Partner meeting to review draft two. |
| 2/26 | Finalize narrative based on partner input, check against rubric or evaluation criteria. |
| 2/28 | Meet with financial officer to develop final budget. |
| 2/29 | Write budget narrative, if required, for review by CFO. |
| 2/30 | Complete all application forms and tag for signatures. |
| 3/3 | Compile grant package and check against instructions. Proofread again. Make list of any outstanding letters of support or other items and schedule time to take care of these things. |
| 3/5 | Compile final grant package with original signatures on all forms. Make requisite number of copies. Include copies for State Single Point of Contact if required. |
| 3/6 | Package original and required number of copies. Send USPS for arrival 3/10 in Washington, D.C., and at State Single Point of Contact, if requested. |

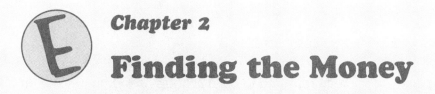

## Chapter 2

# Finding the Money

W here do you find the money for the projects you're looking to fund? Maybe you already know of some sources, but it's also the case that you may be overlooking some less obvious options. You'll soon learn the philanthropic land-scape in your community and state. You want to know who gives out money, how much, and what for.

# Brief History of U.S. Philanthropy

The United States is unquestionably the most philanthropic nation in the world. Our long-standing tradition of caring for others and sharing our blessings dates back to Native Americans in the New World who were willing to share their harvests and knowledge with new settlers. The early religious leaders also brought a tradition of caring for others and sharing their blessings as they colonized the land, staked out farms, and populated early settlements.

For the most part on their own, those early settlers banded together to plant and harvest crops and to build schools and churches. When one family had a need, others pitched in to help, knowing that if they were ever in the same position, the community would respond in a like fashion. That ingrained willingness to help lives on today throughout our land.

## The Federal Government's Role

With passage of the Federal Tax Act in 1913, the federal government established an income tax program through which it collected money, then redistributed it throughout the United States to wherever it was most needed. Today, our government predetermines the types of projects and programs that need public support and then, through its various federal agencies, identifies exactly where the funding should go. The process starts when those agencies issue Requests for Proposals (RFP) to nonprofit and governmental agencies in each of the states.

## Private Philanthropy

The federal government encouraged local philanthropy when it passed the Federal Tax Act of 1969, which provides tax incentives to individuals and businesses for charitable giving.

But even before tax incentives were enacted, individual, family, and community philanthropy, which preceded government philanthropy, flourished. Ben Franklin was one of the earliest philanthropists, both with his time and his money. He gave to causes that would provide equal opportunities for community members and volunteered at his local hospital, library, and fire department. Andrew Carnegie was among the first of the turn-of-the-century industrialists to promote "giving back."

Subsequently Carnegie was joined by such notables as John D. Rockefeller and Margaret Olivia Sage, wife of wealthy industrialist Russell Sage, who channeled his bequest to her into programs that strengthened education and encouraged social reform. These early millionaires established formal philanthropic foundations modeled after their successful business practices. The new foundations took the place of and provided more flexibility than the charitable trusts that had preceded them.

## Government Funding Sources

The federal government issues RFPs to determine which of the various local and state programs that meet its predetermined requirements should be funded. That money is allocated from the government to its federal departments, such as the Department of Housing and Urban Development or the Department of Education, to be used in each department's various grant programs.

While you may be tempted to put the grant writing off for a year if the deadline is rapidly approaching, knowing that the program will likely be offered again, it's often a good idea to submit even before you are entirely ready. You may request reviewer comments for failed proposals and use these suggestions to strengthen next year's proposal.

Often the funded programs are available year after year, especially during a presidential or congressional election year. When there's a change in leadership, priorities shift and money is often allocated to new priority categories and departments. For example, when President Bill Clinton was in office, funding technology-infrastructure improvements ("Closing the Digital Divide") was a priority. The emphasis shifted when George W. Bush came into office, particularly after September 11, 2001. Then police and fire department projects became the focus in an attempt to strengthen "homeland security."

Often government programs go on for years, so you will have more than one opportunity to submit a proposal for funding or to resubmit a failed proposal.

## Where Do You Find RFPs?

You, or the executive director of your organization, may already be on a mailing list for appropriate RFPs. For instance, school districts receive most announcements issued by the Department of Education; large mental health agencies are notified by the Department of Health and Human Services; and police departments will be given notice of grants available from the Department of Justice. As you develop these larger nonprofits as long-term clients, they'll begin to send you the RFPs and ask your opinion about whether they are qualified to pursue the grant program or if the proposed program is appropriate for their needs.

**FACT**

**If you are working as a freelance grant writer, you can review RFPs on your own and call your clients and potential clients when you think one of the RFPs matches their requirements.**

RFPs are published by each federal department and can be found on their individual Web sites. You can also go to your local congressional representative's office and ask for time to review the office copy of the National Register.

The National Register contains all proposed grant opportunities for the upcoming year, regardless of which federal department is issuing them and regardless of whether it's secured funding or the actual levels of funding listed.

The Register is published or updated annually, but is not distributed widely. Instead, a one- or two-page announcement is mailed to pre-established mailing lists approximately 90 to 120 days before the grant deadline. The announcement contains a brief description of the program, its Federal Register number, the requesting department, a list of legal entities that may apply (and those that may not), the URL of the full RFP, and an application or a telephone number so you can request an application package. It also contains information about any grant-seeker workshops or conferences that will take place and where they will be held. (See Chapter 6 for more information on these.)

**FACT**

Sometimes announcements of available grants are made and the RFPs are issued before the money is actually allocated by Congress to the department. And sometimes the grant program is funded at a smaller dollar amount than the department sought. Things can change during the review process, and there's nothing you can do about it except to be aware that these things happen.

# Philanthropic Organizations

Besides the government, philanthropic organizations, such as local foundations or the United Way, are a rich source of grants. Occasionally, in addition, people of wealth bestow grants without using a formal philanthropic organization or a grant-seeking process. A good grant writer is aware of these individuals in his or her community, but, because the needs and interests of these individual philanthropists vary widely—as do the best ways to approach them—they are not the subject of this book on grant writing. Suffice it to say that, in cases of individual donors, it matters who approaches them more than it matters what they are asked to fund.

## Getting to Know the Funders

In Maggie's community, a midsized city in the Midwest, there are three major foundations: a large family foundation, a corporate foundation, and a community foundation. She has a local United Way agency and knows of several individuals who make large grants without using foundation governing boards. There are also numerous smaller foundations and corporate donors in her hometown. Maggie considers it a part of her service to clients to know what each of these local funders is interested in, what their program areas are, who is on their boards, and how often and when they meet to make decisions about grants.

Maggie got her information by meeting with funders, reviewing catalog listings of local funders, researching foundation 990s (tax statements indicating charitable gifts and their amounts), and talking with other clients about their experiences in local grant seeking. Her conclusions are not likely to be 100 percent applicable in your community, but they are worth sharing so you can look for similar patterns.

## What Has Maggie Learned?

By doing her research beforehand, Maggie knows the following things:

- When the United Way changes board composition (annually), it also seems to change priorities for grant making.
- The three major foundations have regular meetings in which they discuss projects and their planned portions of giving.
- Many of the smaller foundations wait to see what the corporate foundation does. They've come to understand and respect the staff person's approach to review and due diligence.
- When there's a really large capital project (such as an arena, convention center, or large university installation) that requires full community support, it becomes more difficult to get other special projects funded from the traditional sources.
- Staffs of foundations can't make promises or assurances on behalf of their boards.
- Changes in staffing (especially at the director levels) and trustee board membership can affect grant-making decisions and/or can delay decisions.
- The foundations publish their values (what's important to them) and mission statements (what they hope to accomplish through grants) and expect you to address the ways that potential projects fit with their vision and values.
- Most local deadlines for proposal submissions fall within a month of each other. Maggie also has learned that it's best to submit to all the major foundations during the same funding cycle.

# Requests for Proposals

Although foundations sometimes issue RFPs, these instances are rare. Foundations usually issue RFPs only when they are planning special programs and need to identify appropriate grantees for their program. For instance, Pew Charitable Trusts in New York issued an RFP to midsized American cities requesting proposals to participate in a leadership training program for nontraditional leaders. The RFP requested a description of the city leadership as it was, a process for identifying potential participants, and the means for ensuring long-lasting benefits to the participating communities.

The State Single Point of Contact is assigned responsibility by the federal government to monitor grant applications in his or her state or region.

In another example, some states distributed money from the tobacco settlement to community foundations, which, in turn, invited proposals from appropriate local agencies addressing tobacco use. In most cases, however, RFPs are issued by governmental agencies and departments. Each RFP contains the following information:

- Purpose
- Issuing agency/department
- Criteria for the program
- Total grant funds available and range of prospective grant awards
- Eligibility criteria for applicants
- Statements that must be signed by the applicant (regarding the enabling legislation, nonsupplanting, public comment requirement, etc.)
- Deadline
- Mailing instructions
- Outline of proposal content
- Points available for each section of the narrative
- Rubric (a chart of judging criteria and scoring) or other selection criteria for judges

- An application kit containing budget forms, cover sheets, and assurances
- Appendices/documents such as State Single Points of Contact, resources, call for reviewers, etc.

As a grant writer, you are most concerned with four sections:

- The eligibility criteria. You want to check it first to ensure that your employer (or client, if you are working as a freelancer) meets all criteria for applicants, or that, with partners, they can meet the criteria.
- The deadline. You want to identify the deadline and develop your plan working backward from it.
- The outline of content. This third section is the most critical part of the RFP. Think of the outline of content as the writer's instructions. Pay close attention to these instructions, and don't deviate.
- And last, the review criteria. When you've completed your draft, you'll want to have it reviewed by peers and others both within and outside your organization. You do this to ensure that the narrative meets the highest level of the rubric scale.

**ALERT!**

You may not deviate from the outline in the RFP. Ever! If you don't follow the outline to a "T," you can be assured that a grant proposal will be awarded funding, but it won't be yours.

## Grant Source Searches

Since RFPs, or at least announcements of their availability, are generally sent to qualified applicants, it's likely that your clients or employer will identify these grant sources for you. But when it comes to compiling lists of other fund sources for your own files, you have a big job ahead of you.

To find foundation and other grant sources, you must check catalogs, software databases, and/or the Internet. As you begin to build your own knowledge base by asking for guidelines for various projects, you'll be smart if you start putting those foundation sources and the focus they have in a file cabinet.

**FACT**

You may want to plan ahead by organizing information about fund sources in ways that make sense to you. Then block out time on your calendar for annual or biannual updates to these files.

# Regional Associations of Grantmakers

Catalogs and CD databases of foundations are available through organizations called the Regional Associations of Grantmakers (RAGs). Different RAGs cover different regions of the United States; for instance, the Council of Michigan Foundations (CMF) has members from Michigan and northern Ohio. You'll have to pay a fee to get these resources from your RAG, but they are worth it when you consider the time it would take you to hunt down every individual grant source on the Internet.

RAGs publish catalogs that list only those foundations that are members of the organization. The listings contain the following information:

- Name and address of foundation (usually in alphabetical order)
- Contact person
- Donor
- Purpose of the foundation
- Limitations (what the foundation will not fund)
- Fiscal year (the time in which the foundation must pay out its 5 percent)
- Assets
- Typical annual expenditures (includes grants and foundation operations)
- Grants made in previous year by focus area
- Range of grant funding
- Deadlines for submission and/or decisions about grants (grant cycles)
- Means of approach (letter of inquiry, request guidelines, submit full proposal, etc.)
- Typical grant size
- Officers and trustees

**XYZ FUND**
P.O. Box 1
Somewhere, USA        123-456-7890
Contacts: John Doe, Foundation Manager

*Donor(s):* John Smith
*Purpose and Activities:* Support for health-care agencies, humanities, human service agencies, public benefit, and religious organizations.
*Fiscal Year Ended:* 12/31/04
*Assets:* $1,234,567
*Expenditures:* $75,975

|  | TOTAL | SOMEWHERE, USA |
|---|---|---|
| *Grants* | $65,000 | $25,000 |
| *Number of Grants* | 50 | 18 |
| *Humanities* | 5.00% | 4.26% |
| *Education* | 2.50% | 4.26% |
| *Health Care* | 11.33% | 16.17% |
| *Human Services* | 32.83% | 30.64% |
| *Public Benefit* | 13.33% | |
| *Religion* | 35.00% | 44.68% |

*Grant Range:* $1,500–$15,000
*Typical Grant Size:* $3,500
*Application Procedure:* Initial approach with letter describing purpose of grant and tax-exempt status verification.
*Funding Cycle:* Grants made in January of each year.
*Officers and Trustees:* USA Bank
*EIN:* 123456789

▲ Sample entry in a RAG catalog.

**ALERT!**

In some catalog entries, the foundation states that it "gives to preselected organizations only." They are not open to reviewing unsolicited requests, so do not submit your grant proposals to them.

The RAG catalogs (which may also be published and cross-referenced in an interactive CD) include such additional information as lists by geographical area of giving or lists by subject- or focus-area for giving.

You'll also find lists from the Council on Foundations, or on special CD/DVD research programs, such as those published for universities or medical research facilities that may be of use.

## How to Begin Your Search for Grant Opportunities

To narrow your search in any of these resource materials, refer first to their index of subjects or areas of interest. For instance, if your client or employer is a women's health service, refer to the index of grant makers in medical research, mental health, or general health and also to the index of foundations that focus on women's issues.

Next, refer back to the individual foundations listed in those subject areas. Look at their limitations.

If a foundation generally limits its giving to a specific city or region that your agency is not a part of, cross that foundation off your list of possible prospects. If they are listed as giving to "preselected organizations only," find out if your organization has any connection either through friends, staff, or previous funding. If not, cross these foundations off your list, too.

Now look at the range of grant funds and the allocation to health or women's issues to get an idea of what each foundation might do to assist financially. Look up the best prospects, in terms of shared focus and size of awards, on the Internet or by using the contact information. Then write to request guidelines from each of your final prospects.

Once you have all the information about appropriate foundations and the size of the grants they tend to give, develop a plan for approaching them. Be sure to note such things as means of approach. (For instance, will you stress that your organization fills a health-care gap in your community or that it addresses critical women's health issues?) Also note deadlines for submission and decision-making and the amount you can or should request.

# COMMON GRANT APPLICATION FORMAT

*Please provide the following information in this order. Briefly explain why your agency is requesting this grant, what outcomes you hope to achieve, and how you will spend the funds if the grant is made.*

## A. NARRATIVE

### 1. Executive Summary
- Begin with a half-page executive summary. Briefly explain why your agency is requesting this grant, what outcomes you hope to achieve, and how you will spend the funds if the grant is made.

### 2. Purpose of Grant
- Statement of needs/problems to be addressed; description of target population and how they will benefit.
- Description of project goals, measurable objectives, action plans, and statements as to whether this is a new or ongoing part of the sponsoring organization.
- Timetable for implementation.
- Who are the other partners in the project and what are their roles?
- Acknowledge similar existing projects or agencies, if any, and explain how your agency or proposal differs, and what effort will be made to work cooperatively.
- Describe the active involvement of constituents in defining problems to be addressed, making policy, and planning the program.
- Describe the qualifications of key staff and volunteers that will ensure the success of the program. Are there specific training needs for this project?
- Long-term strategies for funding this project at end of grant period.

### 3. Evaluation
- Plans for evaluation, including how success will be defined and measured.
- How evaluation results will be used and/or disseminated and, if appropriate, how the project will be replicated.

- Describe the active involvement of constituents in evaluating the program.

### 4. Budget Narrative/Justification
- Grant budget; use the Grant Budget Format that follows, if appropriate.
- On a separate sheet, show how each budget item relates to the project and how the budgeted amount was calculated.
- List amounts requested of other foundations, corporations, and other funding sources to which this proposal has been submitted.
- In the event that we are unable to meet your full request, please indicate priority items in the proposed grant budget.

### 5. Organization Information
- Brief summary of organization's history.
- Brief statement of organization's mission and goals.
- Description of current programs, activities, and accomplishments.
- Organizational chart, including board, staff, and volunteer involvement.

## B. ATTACHMENTS

**1. A copy of the current IRS determination letter** indicating 501(c)(3) tax-exempt status.

**2. List of Board of Directors with affiliations.**

**3. Finances**
- Organization's current annual operating budget, including expenses and revenue.
- Most recent annual financial statement (independently audited, if available; if not available, attach Form 990).

**4. Letters of support** should verify project need and collaboration with other organizations. (Optional)

**5. Annual report,** if available.

INFORMATION INCLUDED IN A COMMON GRANT APPLICATION

Date of Application:

Legal name of organization applying:
(Should be same as on IRS determination letter and as supplied on IRS Form 990.)

Year Founded:                          Current Operating Budget: $

Executive Director:                    Phone Number:

Contact person/title/phone number
(if different from executive director):

Address (principal/administrative office):
City/State/Zip:

Fax Number:                            E-mail Address:

List any previous support from this funder in the last 5 years:

Project Name:
Purpose of Grant (one sentence):
Dates of the Project:                  Amount Requested: $
Total Project Cost: $
Geographic Area Served:

Signature, Chairperson, Board of Directors     Date
Typed Name and Title

Signature, Executive Director                  Date
Typed Name and Title

## GRANT BUDGET FORMAT

Below is a listing of standard budget items. Please provide the project budget in this format and in this order.

A. Organizational fiscal year:

B. Time period this budget covers:

C. For a CAPITAL request, substitute your format for listing expenses. These will likely include: architectural fees, land/building purchase, construction costs, and campaign expenses.

D. Expenses: include a description and the total amount for each of the budget categories, in this order:

| | **Amount requested from this organization** | **Total project expenses** |
| --- | --- | --- |
| Salaries | | |
| Payroll Taxes | | |
| Fringe Benefits | | |
| Consultants and Professional Fees | | |
| Insurance | | |
| Travel | | |
| Equipment | | |
| Supplies | | |
| Printing and Copying | | |
| Telephone and Fax | | |
| Postage and Delivery | | |
| Rent | | |
| Utilities | | |
| Maintenance | | |
| Evaluation | | |
| Marketing | | |
| Other (specify) | | |

D. Revenue: include a description and the total amount for each of the following budget categories, in this order; please indicate which sources of revenue are committed and which are pending.

| | Committed | Pending |
|---|---|---|
| 1. Grants/Contracts/ | | |
|   Contributions | | |
|   Local Government | | |
|   State Government | | |
|   Federal Government | | |
| Foundations (itemize) | | |
| Corporations (itemize) | | |
| Individuals | | |
| Other (specify) | | |
| 2. Earned Income | | |
|   Events | | |
|   Publications and Products | | |
| 3. Membership Income | | |
| 4. In-Kind Support | | |
| 5. Other (specify) | | |
| **6. TOTAL REVENUE** | **$239,956** | **$607,952** |

This sample guideline was developed by a Regional Association of Grantmakers (RAG) for use by any foundation within the geographical area of the RAG. Common grant applications generally have every question you will ever be asked to respond to in other grant proposals; therefore, it's smart to do one of these first so you have text for subsequent proposals to other funders.

You're finally ready to begin preparing your submissions. We suggest you take the most complex proposal outline first. In it, you'll create responses to sections that you can use again and again on the other proposals, such things as the need statement, program description, evaluation plan, and other sections that only have to be tweaked slightly to fit the focus or emphasis of the other foundations.

**ALERT!**

As with RFPs, when applying for foundation funds, you must follow the instructions for submission (the outline contained in the guidelines) to the letter.

## Foundation Grant Guidelines

Grant guidelines are issued by most larger foundations and are available by request or by search. They contain critical information for framing your grant proposal, including the following:

- Background/brief history of foundation
- Categories for funding/focus areas, with brief descriptions of types of programs
- Means of approach (such as letter of inquiry, meeting with funders, arrangement for site visit, full proposal requested)
- General requirements for funding
- Instructions for submission (outline of required sections)

## "Cold Calling" versus Responding to Requests

There are two basic approaches to seeking grants: responding to requests for proposals or "cold calling" on foundations. In the former instance, you receive a request for proposals that clearly outlines the types of projects the funder is seeking and the requirements for each project. Then you work with your employer or client either to develop a new program that responds to the requirements or to modify an existing program to meet the requirements in the RFP.

Most often, the programs described in the RFP are those that have been found to work in other communities or those that the funder wants to explore through several demonstration projects because they show great promise for systemic change. In these cases, you must design a program that is similar to or exactly like the one the RFP describes.

A "cold call" is when you go to a foundation, describe the need you've identified in the community that is not being met by any other agency, and tell what your organization would like to do about it.

When you cold call you can be more creative. You can create a program that responds to an identified need in your community. For instance, and purely hypothetically, let's say data indicate that a large number of Polish immigrants have moved to your community recently. To help them resettle, you decide to call together partners, such as an established refugee settlement organization, a Polish society hall, the Red Cross, a community education program which teaches English as a Second Language (ESL), and several other local organizations, to establish a comprehensive resettlement program. You want it to include English-language tutors, housing assistance, furniture and clothing banks, job-skill development, job-placement services, and other assistance needed by new residents.

The chance that an RFP comes out that exactly describes this sort of program is very slim. You might find a couple of them seeking to fund resettlement programs in general, but they probably wouldn't include Polish refugees as a target population. The best way to launch a program that responds to this specific need then is to cold call on foundations.

A cold call is an opportunity for you to educate local foundations about a new need in your community and to position your client as a responsive, engaged participant in coalition-building and program activities.

You'll find that area foundations are keenly interested in learning about new needs in their geographic areas and in responsive, creative programs that can help meet those needs. Cold call grants can be extremely successful, and you'll feel great that you helped launch a program that's sure to be positively evaluated. (E)

Chapter 3

# Government Grants

Government grants are tax dollars redistributed to programs in your community. As such, they can be made by any entity that collects taxes: federal, state, and even local city or county governments. In general, the larger the government, the larger the fund available for grants and the larger the individual awards for projects.

# Local Government Funds

Local governments are your city, township, county, regional coordinating body—a water district or a planning commission, for instance—or other such mechanisms. Local governments rarely have grant opportunities and those that do provide only limited programs. But they do issue RFPs.

## Two RFPs That Aren't for Grant Programs

Local governments are more likely to issue requests for proposals that are actually for work they wish to have completed. For instance, the city council or similar unit of local government might decide they need to build a new parking lot. They will send the job out for bids and call the process a "request for proposals." But of course, this is not a grant program.

On occasion, local governments may issue requests for proposals for public art projects. These types of requests equalize for-profit and nonprofit applicants. A small group of independent artists belonging to a nonprofit group may apply, as well as artists of national repute (and cost). But even though some applicants may be nonprofit organizations, this too is not technically a grant program. Again, it is a request for bids.

## Local Grants with Pass-Through Money

Don't cross local government off your list of grantors, however, because sometimes they issue grants using someone else's money. When a local government entity does issue an RFP for grants, it's because there is pass-through money available.

**FACT**

Pass-through funding comes from some source other than the local tax base. Usually it's state or federal money.

Pass-through grant programs are often broad in scope and cover broad issues, such as housing, elder care, child welfare, and health. In addition, these programs are very likely to be offered annually and can be used as a source of operational funding for nonprofits that meet the criteria.

One advantage of this local government funding is that sometimes it can be used to cover ongoing expenses. What this means for your nonprofit organization is that once you have received one program grant for a successful community improvement effort, you may go back again, year after year, to request continued operational support.

## State Government Funds

Grants from the state are among the easiest to apply for and to receive. You'll find that your state is close enough to communities to have an understanding of what's going on and the problems they are having, yet large enough to provide grants in sufficient amounts to address the problems that have been identified.

You can find state grant opportunities in very nearly the same way as you find federal government grants: by going from department to department. Most states have a Web site that lists departments. Pages within each department contain information about upcoming RFPs.

Some grants are awarded on what appears to be an "it's-your-turn" basis rather than merit. For example, a state department of education might give funding to different school districts on a rotating basis. When that's the case, it's better not to apply for the funding every time it becomes available. Instead of putting in a lot of effort, you'd be better off to wait four or five cycles, then try again. Then you can be assured of being successful.

## Pass-Through Funds

State or federal governments occasionally will provide pass-through funds to a nonprofit organization in your community. In these instances you'll discover that the pass-through agent is likely to be your local government or one of the local nonprofits, such as Family Independence Agency, United Way, or your community foundation.

When this happens, the local agency usually receives some compensation for reviewing the grant proposals, distributing the grant dollars, and ensuring that all reports and evaluations are submitted on time to the granting agent.

**FACT**

Pass-through government grants include such programs as Community Development Block Grants (CDBG). Pots of money are provided to larger metropolitan areas that can identify the programs and nonprofits that best exemplify the goals of the CDBG program. Other CDBG money might be retained at the state level for application from rural areas or small towns that do not have a local office for monitoring grant funds and evaluation.

## Pass-Through Funds Are Specific

Pass-through funding is always granted for a specific purpose and made to a local agency because that agency knows more about needs in the community. A local agency also is much better aware of the reputation of various service providers than any federal or state government could be.

Community Development Block Grants (CDBGs), for example, are meant to be spent locally and used to develop projects that respond to specific community needs. Block grant money generally is passed from the federal to state government. The state awards some grants to rural or smaller communities, and then, in turn, passes the rest of the money to larger city governments and lets them administer their own programs.

Another good example of pass-through grants came when states received money as a result of the large tobacco settlement. The money was earmarked for prevention and stop-smoking programs. Some states actually administered the tobacco-settlement funds. Other states, however, passed it through to local agencies, such as community foundations. The foundations, in turn, passed it on to local nonprofits that had programs in place that addressed the targeted tobacco-use issues.

## A Foundation Example

In Maggie's state, the tobacco settlement money first went to the local community foundation. The foundation then invited approximately twenty organizations to apply for the grants, knowing they either already had programs in place or were capable of putting one together in short order.

Technically if an organization didn't receive an invitation to apply, in this instance, it couldn't. But Maggie made a strong case for getting one of her clients added to the list.

"I had a client that had a strong program for educating teens about advertising and helping them use that knowledge to produce commercials that rebutted claims in the ads. Their program, however, was not well known." While her client had not specifically addressed smoking as an issue, she knew that eventually they would.

"I heard about the fund because another of my clients had been invited to apply. So I called the community foundation and told them about my other client's program. They were very nice about it. In fact, they welcomed the idea of teaching teens how to evaluate ads. They invited my agency to submit a proposal. It turned out that both of my clients got their grants, and the one that I had brought to the foundation's attention was awarded twice what they asked for."

## Federal Grants

You will find that federal government grants are where the money is and where the work is! Federal government grants are meant to launch big programs. That's why awards can range from very small grants of less than $10,000 to grants of several million dollars.

A writer's work on a federal grant proposal can range from twenty pages of text and forms to literally hundreds of pages.

Federal government requests for proposals are published in the Federal Register and are announced at various department sites on the Internet. In addition, qualifying organizations often get advance notice of grants appropriate for their agency.

**ALERT!**

As a grant writer you will want to surf the Web frequently looking for special opportunities for your clients or employer.

There are also "watchers" who tag educational grants, technology grants, health-care grants, and other opportunities, then share that information with their constituents.

## Ongoing Federal Programs

Some federal grant programs have been offered for decades—year after year—and are provided to designated agencies based on their progress reports and annual reapplications.

For instance, health-care clinics for the indigent may apply for a "330" designation by the federal government. Once they have that designation, they qualify to apply for ongoing funding through the aptly titled 330-program grants, which come up every year. While the 330 grants don't entirely support these clinics, they do provide a relatively stable source of ongoing funding.

## New Grant Programs

Other grant programs are relatively new. Think about the new funding that became available once Congress passed the Homeland Security Act of 2002. This program increased funding that already was available to qualifying law enforcement agencies through grants made by the Department of Justice. For the first time ever, firefighting units were also eligible to receive federal funding so that they could build up their capacity, purchase equipment, or receive additional training.

**FACT**

When the federal government opens up a new grant program, such as the Homeland Security Act, it often means that fewer dollars are available for other grant programs. Some grant programs may even be phased out as money is redistributed to new programs.

## Why You Should Watch Trends

Unless you are applying for designation and annual funding that is relatively stable, you should watch these trends. That way you can learn which government departments are receiving congressional allocations and in what amount. When there is a large allocation made to one federal government department, you can be certain that large grant opportunities will be coming up within the year.

## One-Time Opportunities

There are many one-time grant opportunities available from the federal government. These are usually multiyear awards—often of more than $1 million—that are awarded to demonstration projects throughout the nation.

A good example occurred when the federal Departments of Education, Justice, and Health and Human Services combined funds in response to the shootings at Columbine, as well as other school violence. Their program funded multimillion dollar, three-year grant projects known as "Safe Schools–Healthy Students."

The grant called for the school district applicant to work in tandem with a mental health agency and the local police or sheriff's department to address the entire life cycle (from birth to seniors) in its programs. The school district and agencies also had to develop a coherent program for using these tools to reduce school violence and improve the mental health of students and families.

Many of the districts funded under this three-year grant used the one-time money to purchase equipment or to develop materials that they could use again and again. They also had to develop new programs and partnerships. At the end of three years, the school districts were ineligible to reapply for new grants under the program. If they wanted more funding to sustain the programs and partnerships they'd launched under the grant, they had to look elsewhere.

**The success of a new program funded by a large grant award can be short-lived if you don't plan for the continued funding you'll need to keep the project going after the grant funds are spent.**

Multidepartment grants like "Safe Schools–Healthy Students" are very difficult to write. Not only must the writer respond to all the requirements in the joint RFP, but he or she also must meet the individual requirements for each department. Those additional requirements are generally append-ed to the RFP.

# Federal Register

The Federal Register contains all requests for proposals, from all federal departments, that are issued in a given year. It must be voluminous, but most writers have never seen the entire Register. Instead, you will receive or download individual RFPs for individual grant programs.

If you receive an RFP package, it is usually bound and saddle-stitched as a small booklet. It contains all the information found in the Federal Register about that particular grant program, including the following:

- Program number
- Enabling legislation
- Purpose of the grant program
- Outline for your narrative
- Evaluation criteria judges will use to select the programs that are funded
- Forms and assurances (that the organization practices equal opportunity or has an environmental policy, for instance)
- Listing of State Single Points of Contact
- Instructions for forms
- Instructions for appendices
- Mailing instructions and addresses

Sometimes the booklet also includes frequently asked questions and responses and/or government contact information so that you may ask questions by e-mail or telephone.

When you go online for an RFP, don't forget to download all the related forms and other information pertinent to your grant application. They will be in separate files.

More often, nowadays, you can download RFPs from the department's Web site. However, the package is not complete as a single downloadable file. You must download the RFP (usually listed by program title), as well as the forms (usually called "application package") separately. You also may choose whether or not you want to download additional pieces of information, such as frequently asked questions or other background information. These are provided as separate documents.

# Other Sources of Information

Most reputable nonprofits are on mailing lists to receive notification of upcoming grant opportunities. They also are often contacted directly by the local, state, or even federal department with which they work. But you can also search for government programs and RFPs on your own.

## How to Go about It

A good search engine is the grant writer's best friend. Key words that will help you find government grants include the following:

- The purpose of your program or project (for example, "lead hazards," "school violence," "prosthetics").
- The name of the department (be sure to specify "U.S." or name of state first to avoid getting a long list).
- The name of a similar program you know that has received funding. (When you search this way, you are likely to find out the name of the grant program they used and which department issued it.)

If your Web-surfing skills are weaker than you'd like, you might start out with some of the Web sites set up especially for grant writers. In addition to listing private, corporate, public, and community foundations, they often include federal agencies that have issued RFPs. Usually you can search these sites by categories or topics, so if your agency would like to reduce lead poisoning in your community, you can search under children, health, and environment and get a list of possible funders.

There's no guarantee that a site will have links to all possible grant sources, but until you get a feel for what you can find on the Web, they may be a good place to start your search. At the very least, you won't be wasting time filtering through a lengthy list of grant topics pulled up by a search engine, only to discover that half the sites only contain news releases while the other half list grants with deadlines that expired a month or more ago. These portal sites that may be helpful in your search for funders:

- ✑ *www.lib.msu.edu*
- ✑ *www.mickeys-place-in-the-sun.com*

Other Web sites that may be helpful in your business can be found in Appendix A.

## Bookmark Your Results

It can take a while to locate different departments and agencies that issue RFPs. So be sure to bookmark sites that you know you'll want to return to again and again (such as the state and federal departments of Education if you work for a school district). Also bookmark sites where you downloaded an RFP, so you can check it again and again throughout the writing process.

Why do you want to do this? Sometimes deadlines are extended, and the only way you will have of finding this out is to watch the Web site for updates. For your own good, however, never count on a deadline being extended. Meet your own timeline.

Check the Web site where you downloaded the RFP once or twice during the month you're writing. This is where you'll find late-breaking news such as an extended deadline, clarification of the RFP based on questions from others, or changes in the level of funding since the RFP was issued.

## Another Valuable Source

Your local representative's office can help keep you informed about upcoming RFPs. Members of Congress often have a local office as well as a Washington, D.C., office, and your hometown staff is there to assist constituents. They will be willing to put you on a mailing list or a computer listserv so that you can receive important announcements. Ⓔ

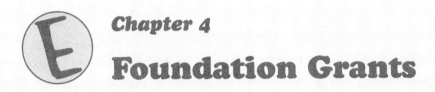

*Chapter 4*

# Foundation Grants

A private charitable foundation engages in charitable giving from its "corpus," which is money endowed to the foundation by a wealthy person, family, or corporation. You'll learn more in this chapter about how charitable foundations invest those funds and, depending on the kind of foundation they are, how they use the proceeds to make grants to nonprofit organizations like yours.

# Funding from a Foundation

Charitable private foundations are required by tax law to pay out, through grant making, 5 percent of the total corpus (endowment plus earnings) each year. They usually invest their endowment funds. In years that the stock market does well, they earn more than the 5 percent payout requirement and are able to build the corpus of the foundation. In years that their investments, overall, earn less than 5 percent, they must dip into the corpus to meet the payout requirements. Poor earnings in a single year won't affect a foundation's corpus or its ability to award grants, but if the market continues to decline in subsequent years, those foundations that have no means of income other than earnings from investments will suffer, and so will the nonprofits that they fund.

While there are variations in type and size, in general, charitable-giving foundations are founded as corporate, family, or community foundations.

# Corporate Foundations

There are slightly more than 2,000 corporate foundations in the United States, and they hold approximately $13 billion in assets. Although they are often linked with the founding corporation, corporate foundations actually are a separate, legal organization subject to the same rules and regulations as other private foundations.

Profit-making businesses, usually large corporations, establish corporate foundations to enable them to support projects in communities where they operate manufacturing plants, retail outlets, and other direct business. They are most interested in helping organizations in the communities where their employees live, though sometimes they expand grant making into communities where their customers live as well. Their missions may state that they want to improve the quality of life for all citizens in a community as a means of improving their own employees' lives. Corporate foundations have a board of trustees usually composed of current and retired corporate leaders. Staff often includes an executive director who reviews grants and makes recommendations to the board.

Some corporations have direct-giving programs instead of or in addition to a corporate foundation. An office furniture manufacturer, for instance, will give a nonprofit a gift of desks and chairs for its offices; a mill might make a gift of lumber to be used for capital construction. Cash grants also may be awarded directly to selected charities or applicants. Whether the company gives a gift of merchandise or money, the donation comes out of the company's annual budget for charitable giving, not from a separate endowment.

**FACT**

Direct-giving programs do not accept grant applications, and they are not part of the endowment entrusted to the corporate foundation. Gifts of money and goods are allocated out of the annual budget.

Most of the time, direct-giving program funds are committed in the budget at the beginning of the company's budget cycle. For instance, the company may allocate money annually for purchasing Christmas gifts for needy local children.

# Family Foundations

There are nearly 19,000 family foundations in the United States, and collectively they give approximately $7 billion annually to charitable causes. These private foundations can range in size from very small (such as a $10,000 endowment) to those with hundreds of millions of dollars in assets.

Family foundations are generally established by one or two donors, typically an entrepreneur, siblings, or a married couple. Family foundations have been founded to ensure that future generations continue to practice philanthropy. They are set up so that the endowment upholds values the donors believe are important. Most founders are successful entrepreneurs who want to use their fortunes to support the communities in which they and their families live. In return, they receive substantial tax benefits from the federal government.

## Who Runs It?

Family foundations may be operated by a local bank, by the founder, or by a staff hired for that purpose. When a bank is in charge, grant proposals are mailed to a contact person at the bank. Staffed foundations will have an executive director and, as the corpus grows, will hire additional program staff. The board of trustees, which makes decisions about grant making, is usually composed of family members and sometimes includes third- and fourth-generation descendants of the donor. There also may be representatives from the community who were asked by trustees to serve on the board.

## Pass-Through Foundations

Some family foundations are established initially as "pass-through" foundations. This means that the donor has selected charities that he or she wishes to give annual support. A pass-through foundation generally does not accept grant applications from those organizations that have not been preselected for funding. Some family foundations serve as pass-through foundations for only a couple of generations. Then they become so large that they must broaden their grant-making focus or endow the preselected charities directly.

# Community Foundations

Community foundations are a great example of strength in numbers. Usually established by one or two major donors in a community, these foundations broaden their effectiveness by approaching other successful individuals and getting them to contribute to the foundation's corpus through direct donation, legacy gifts, or annual donations.

## Major Players

Because many community foundations were founded decades ago and have grown with continued donations and investments, they have built up their corpuses to the point that they are now some of the largest foundations in their communities. The Cleveland Foundation is the oldest community foundation in the United States; the New York Community Trust is the largest in terms of assets.

**ALERT!**

Do not apply for a grant from a community foundation that is in a different geographic region or city than that of your nonprofit client. These foundations are set up by individuals who want to restrict their grants to organizations within their own communities.

There are more than 500 community foundations in the United States, all of which restrict their giving to the community in which they were founded or, at most, to the state in which they were founded. Their boards are composed of community leaders who often include representatives of the major banks and law firms in the city. A new trend is to include some representatives from area nonprofit organizations. Community foundations work hard to keep their boards a diverse mix of individuals who reflect the composition of the overall city or region.

## Foundations Within Foundations

One of the operational hallmarks that separates a community foundation from family, private independent, and most corporate foundations is that a community foundation both raises funds and makes grants. They also hold, administer, and grant money through separate minifoundations, funds that were donated by a small family foundation or trust account.

**FACT**

You need to submit only one grant proposal to a community foundation to access funds held in a small foundation or trust. Part of the job of community foundation staff is to match your needs with the interests of donors and make recommendations for funding either through the community foundation and/or a fund held within the foundation. Sometimes you can get two grant awards with one proposal.

The grant-making process for these minifunds is separate from the programs operated by the community foundation. Different boards and different values guide their giving. These smaller "foundations within the community foundation" benefit from having the community foundation staff provide fiscal and grant-making oversight.

Family foundations and large independent foundations often have set amounts of discretionary funds—grants that can be awarded on the decision of one person, rather than an entire board—for program officers, presidents, and some board members. Read their annual reports or call the foundation to learn who has control over discretionary funds and how you can request them. These smallish grants can sometimes be quite easy to get (a letter or visit often suffices) as you only have to convince one person of the value of your proposed project.

## Private Independent Foundations

Though often started as a family foundation, private independent foundations are no longer controlled by the original donor or his or her family members. Instead they are administered by a board of trustees that represents past and present leaders in their fields of interest. They are often the largest foundations in the United States, and their scope often includes making grants throughout the world.

Private independent foundations can have billions of dollars in assets and make grants totaling millions of dollars each year. They are staffed with numerous program officers and often have communications departments, presidents, vice presidents, financial officers, and other departments and staff similar to that of a large corporation.

While the programming of a private independent foundation is often the most sophisticated of all charitable foundations, that can make the private independent foundation more difficult to reach, especially if the geographic or social reach of a program or activity is narrow. You would not, for instance, ask a large private independent foundation in New York City to fund construction of a youth center in Iowa. But if the youth center was first-of-its-kind and likely to change the youth-center "industry" worldwide, you might get the attention of a foundation that wants to help children. Depending on how "cutting edge" the mission is, the large private independent foundation just might want to hear about that youth center.

# Requesting Guidelines

A good way to identify foundations in your area is to request a catalog from your Regional Association of Grantmakers (RAG). RAGs provide services to all the foundations within a region and develop catalogs that list them, often by city, alphabetically, and/or by type, and sometimes also by program area.

Once you've identified the foundations that operate in your area, you should request guidelines from each of them. If you just want to learn more about the foundation for future reference, request the guidelines by telephone. If, however, you have a particular project you intend to propose, you should write a letter. Briefly—preferably two paragraphs or less, but no more than one page—describe the project you hope to submit, then close by requesting a copy of their guidelines. In this way, the foundation can help you assess whether they'll be interested in receiving a proposal to learn more about the project. And—a big bonus—they sometimes even send a small donation without your ever having to submit a full proposal.

One format that identifies the project and also asks for guidelines follows.

Date
Name of Executive Director
Foundation
Address
City/State/ZIP

Dear Name:

ABC College, a liberal arts college founded in 1886, and DEF Theatre, a fifty-year-old performance and production theatre company, have joined together in your community to build a new performance complex on the ABC College campus. The complex will feature a 500-seat theatre and several classrooms/rehearsal halls, and will represent a new direction for education through the arts. The shared vision for the partnership is to enrich, educate, and entertain the community with dramatic arts that are innovative, creative, and accessible to all.

Both partners in this undertaking must grow to meet "customer" demands. In ABC's case, it must expand its curricula in dramatic arts, arts education, and arts management, and will be strongly positioned to do so with a performance arts complex and its long-term collaboration with DEF Theatre. DEF Theatre operates a children's performing arts program, a full-season theatrical production house, and hosts numerous visiting performances for a range of ages. Its current facility, Arts House, has seating for only 300 and cannot be expanded further despite consistent sell-out performances. In addition, DEF is limited by the owners of the current facility to providing theatrical productions only from May through September. A school operates in the theatre off-season, and it too could improve programming in a facility dedicated to only one purpose. DEF Theatre and ABC College are also planning collaboratively with the Children's Museum, city public schools, member schools of area Intermediate School District, and other arts organizations in the community to develop curricula, joint programming, audience-engagement strategies, and future presentations.

The partnership between arts and educational organizations reflects a national trend toward cooperative efforts of nonprofit organizations to build audiences and help develop in individuals a deeper, richer involvement in the arts. When the facility is complete, ABC students—as well as the members of the larger community—will be afforded opportunities to participate in various aspects of dramatic arts production or attend arts presentations that are relevant to and enrich their classroom learning. In addition, ABC and DEF Theatre plan teacher and student-teacher workshops with guest artists and staff to build parent/child relationships, incorporate the arts into the curricula, encourage creativity, and celebrate multiculturalism.

In January, the partners launched a joint $5.6-million capital campaign to construct and equip the performing arts center and provide seed money for collaborative projects. At the close of year one of the campaign, the local community, including major donors, DEF Theatre patrons, and ABC alumni, has committed more than $2.2 million. Architectural renderings are complete, and site improvements preparatory to construction have begun.

ABC College and DEF Theatre are eager to tell you more or to answer specific questions about a project that promises to be one of the first of its kind in the United States—one that reaches new audience segments, engages them fully in lifelong learning and the performing arts, and provides a national model for organizational and community learning. We respectfully request that guidelines for a full grant application be sent to our president, ABC College, 1600 Main Road, your town and state. Thank you in advance for your assistance.

Sincerely,                                     Sincerely,

College President                      Theatre Director

▲ Sample request for guidelines.

Guidelines provide some or all of the following useful information:

- Name of a contact person and telephone numbers
- Description of program areas (the types of projects the foundation is interested in hearing about)
- Restrictions, or those projects, geographic areas, or types of organizations the foundation does not fund
- Range of grant awards and average grant award
- Assets of the foundation
- Previous projects the foundation has funded
- An application form
- An outline for a proposal narrative
- A list of required attachments for the grant proposal
- Deadlines for submission
- General indication of the time it takes from submission to approval or denial
- Foundation history, mission, values, board roster, or anything else that will help you learn what motivates their giving

## Other Sources of Information

While you are exploring the range of foundations in your area, you may also be interested in learning more about foundations throughout the

United States. A great source of information to help you explore is the Council on Foundations (COF), a national organization that supports philanthropy throughout the United States and provides services and publications to member foundations.

**FACT**

COF is located in Washington, D.C. Though some areas of its Web site are restricted to members only, the COF has a wealth of information about philanthropy in the United States. Its Web address is ✍ *www.cof.org.*

You may also wish to use the Internet to download the guidelines of your targeted foundations, but do so only for information gathering. If you have a project in mind, you really should request guidelines to make sure you aren't wasting energy. If the foundation is not interested in receiving a full proposal, they will say so. That keeps you from wasting your time on behalf of a project the foundation knows its boards will not consider for funding.

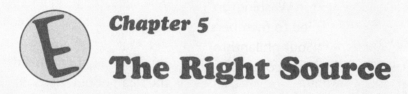

## Chapter 5

# The Right Source

Y ou want to be able to search out funding sources for special projects and, often, for operating funds. In this chapter you'll learn more about sorting through the vast amount of information available and narrowing your field of prospects.

## When Is a Government Grant Appropriate?

Governments cannot be solicited for funds. Instead, you must rely on matching your project with an appropriate RFP. Watch for RFPs not only from the most obvious department—such as Department of Education grants for school districts—but also from other departments. You might find an opportunity from the Department of Justice, for instance, that will allow a school district to apply for funding to provide drug or violence prevention programs.

Also work with others in the community. Federal grant providers nearly always want to know as much as they can about the nonprofit infrastructure in your community. Who's doing what? Where is the potential for duplication? And where is the potential for partnership and cost savings?

While foundations are also interested in large, multiagency approaches to community problems, the most likely source for funding to allow such an undertaking is the federal government.

## When Is a Foundation Grant Appropriate?

Foundation grants are most appropriate for local projects, especially those from organizations the foundations have worked with in the past or for projects in which the foundations have a high interest.

In Maggie's community, for instance, nearly all the foundations support agencies that provide services for young children, including child abuse/neglect prevention, early education, and children's health and nutrition. The community foundation also sponsored a task-force study on issues of children in the community. The study recommended that there should be a new interagency approach to treating child abuse victims. Because of the community foundation's stature, several other funders joined in. Together they launched a new program that, in its ten years of existence, has enjoyed relatively stable funding from all of the original funders and others in the community.

Foundations, unlike government funders, can be solicited for funding and can have their interest piqued by your communications. Often, as you establish relationships with foundation program officers, you can simply pick up the telephone and query the program officers about ideas for new projects.

**ALERT!**

Never submit a grant proposal to a community foundation unless it is targeted to your own community. These foundations are endowed by local people and their intent is that the money be spent on local projects.

Organizations outside the headquarters area of national funders like the W. K. Kellogg Foundation, the Pew Charitable Trusts, Robert Wood Johnson Foundation, or the Rockefeller Fund should only approach these foundations in response to an RFP or by a special invitation from the funder. An exception can be made for projects that promise to have a national reach or effect. Grants from these foundations are difficult to get without a truly strategic and trendsetting project.

## A Checklist of Considerations

You need to consider several things while narrowing your field of prospects:

- Is your organization a qualified 501(c)(3) nonprofit?
- What is the program focus, and where does it match funding programs?
- What type of funding is needed? Use **TABLE 5-1** to direct your attention by type of funding needed.
- How much funding is needed?
- Why would anyone—particularly a funder—be interested in this project?
- What kinds of other projects are going on that might benefit from a partnership or that might be merged as part of a "larger picture" of response?

### Table 5-1: What Type of Funding Do You Need?

| Appropriate for | Government funds | Foundations | Other |
| --- | --- | --- | --- |
| Operations | Only as indirect allocation or from local government | Rarely | United Way; annual fund drive |
| Large, costly projects | Yes | Only in partnership | Community members |
| Small projects | Occasionally | Yes | Internal funding |
| Capital projects | Rarely | Yes | Community |
| Model projects | Yes | Yes (include national) | |
| Products/inventions | Yes, sometimes | No | Private investors |
| Research projects | Yes | Sometimes | By contract |
| Launch new nonprofit | Rarely | Sometimes | Board members, collaborations |
| Endowment | No | No | Community |
| Maintenance endowment | No | As part of capital drive | Community |
| Sustaining new programs | No | Sometimes | Community |

Use systems thinking to resolve difficult social problems. The responses that work best are those in which the entire system mobilizes. It takes businesses, nonprofits, schools, hospitals, communications specialists, community members, and hundreds of others to see the problem—and the potential for change—from every viewpoint.

## Narrowing the Field of Prospects

Sure, it only costs a stamp to write letters to every foundation or government agency listed in a grant-seeking catalog—but it's a waste of postage and of your time if you're unlikely to succeed.

Mass mailings—asking everyone in the world to fund your project—can really damage the credibility of your organization. It's very much like submitting a science fiction novel to the publisher of Harlequin romances. If they remember your name, they are not likely to read any subsequent submissions that you send in—even if you've written the next *Gone with the Wind.*

## A Better Approach

It's much better to target each letter or grant proposal to the individual interests and focus of each grant maker. To do that you have to read the guidelines or the RFP as carefully as a novelist reads through the *Writer's Market.* When you've discovered several likely prospects, target your submissions to those funders and funding sources that are the most appropriate of all.

## Maggie's Case

Maggie tells of an instance in which she had to advise her clients to seek a grant they didn't want to go after. "I had a very small nonprofit organization that wanted to continue to do what they'd always done. They were the only group in town qualified (by virtue of having attended a statewide meeting of interested parties) to seek a grant offered by the state Department of Social Services to develop programs for teenage girls.

"The leaders of the organization had read through the RFP, and they thought it was offered as a grant for providing programs for troubled teenage girls. But when I read through it, I saw that it was a grant to convene all the 'players' in the community and have them develop a systemic, cooperative approach to addressing teen girls' problems. My organization, however, had no experience in collaborating or operating focus groups or any of the things called for in the grant.

"When they understood what the grant was about, they decided against seeking the funding. I had to explain to them that if they received the grant, they could hire another organization with grant money to facilitate the meetings. Moreover, if they were successful in leading the effort, they could gain credibility with the other organizations in town and become a linchpin organization in addressing the needs of problem teens. Besides," Maggie explained, "leading an effort like this would garner the attention of a lot of local funders."

**ALERT!**

If you are a freelance grant writer, think like a consultant advisor. Your clients will be eager to go after every grant that's remotely possible. You should advise them when a grant is inappropriate or when their planned approach is not in keeping with the goals of the program.

Maggie eventually persuaded the nonprofit to apply and as a result, they were acknowledged statewide as the only applicant who addressed the true purpose of the grant. Not only that, three years later they had state senators on the organization's board and now they can raise money easily to support the programs they've developed. Best of all, they are among the first agencies in the community that schools, social services, and juvenile justice call on when teen girls present a problem others can't handle.

## Don't Make Random Attempts

Maybe you've been successful in garnering large federal grants. But don't get too eager and start applying for anything and everything. If you see an RFP that you think you could do something with, but the deadline is in two weeks and you haven't even talked to others in the community about partnering, it's best to get some ideas going and start planning now for the next time that RFP is issued.

## Reading Guidelines

The first place to begin a search of appropriate foundations is with a national or regional catalog of foundations. These catalogs are available from publishing houses, from your regional association of grant makers, and from the Council on Foundations. Catalogs are often available on CD for interactive keyword searches.

Read such listings carefully, beginning with the focus of the foundation. Often, the catalog has an index of lists by program focus (children, the arts, environment, and so on) that you can use to target the list of appropriate funders for your organization.

## Looking at the Profile

Next look at each individual foundation's profile. First read the purpose of the foundation. You want to make sure they share an interest in your project. You also want to check for hints about the best way to approach them. For instance, a foundation that has interests both in education and in environmental protection might be very interested in a summer camp program that provides environmental education and experiences for young people.

Another foundation says it is interested in senior services and civic improvement. You might, in this case, propose your leadership development program but with a focus on recruiting seniors to participate actively in community improvement plans.

**FACT**

Public charities generally do not make grants to nonprofit organizations even though they may have the word "foundation" in their title.

## What's in Their Purpose Statement?

Also check the purpose statement to make sure that your project exactly fits their program interest. For instance, they might be listed as supporting education, but when you turn to the profile you learn that their purpose is to strengthen community colleges in their region. Therefore, your program for a local high school is outside their area of interest and not a good fit.

## Do They Target a Location?

Next, check for geographic priorities. If the foundation only makes local grants and your agency is on the other side of the state, cross its name off your list. If the foundation makes national grants, your project must have national importance if it is to be considered.

## What about Limitations?

Next look at the restrictions or limitations. Often, a listing contains one of three statements that should be used to eliminate the foundation from your list of prospects. The first two of these statements will say, "Grant funds are generally limited to charitable organizations already favorably known to the foundation," and/or "grant funds are committed." Each of those statements means relatively the same thing—that the foundation already is working with established organizations and committing money to those same organizations year after year. When that occurs, the foundation is operating to a large degree as a pass-through agent.

The third statement you might see, "No unsolicited proposals considered," means that if you do not have a means of meeting with the foundation to get a person excited about your proposal idea prior to submitting it, you should scratch this foundation from your cold-call list.

## Other Restrictions

In addition, most catalog lists of foundations provide a paragraph on what each foundation will not fund. Restricted funding might include some or all of the following:

- Operating support
- Program-related investments/loans
- Endorsements
- Publications
- Conferences/seminars
- Underwriting for special events/sponsorships
- Grants to individuals
- Scholarships

- Fellowships
- Educational loans
- Travel or research grants
- Religious purposes

## What Money Is Available?

Finally, look at the range of grants and the typical grant size. This information is published in the catalog but rarely in guidelines received directly from a foundation.

If the grants range from $500 to $10,000 but the typical grant size is $1,000, you probably will approach this funder only when you are at the end of a large fundraising effort or if you have a very small project. If, on the other hand, the range of grants is $200 to $1 million and the typical size is $10 to $20,000, you would look to the funder to provide kickoff funding for a major project or to fund a smaller project in its entirety.

## Develop a Strategy

Be strategic in your approach to foundations. Four or five well-targeted grants will serve you and your organization far better than one letter sent to 200 foundations. Expect to be able to narrow the broad field of prospects to about 10 percent. Then work that 10 percent with everything you have.

# Reading RFPs

The first thing to read in the RFP is the purpose of the legislation and fund. What does the funder hope to accomplish with its money? If the stated purpose matches the purpose or mission of your program, continue reading. If it even somewhat matches, continue reading to see if you can tweak your program to fit more closely.

## Who Qualifies for Money?

Next look at the list of qualified applicants. Often the organization qualified to apply is very specific. For instance, some grants call for the applicant to be a community mental health organization (CMH); others for a local educational agency (LEA); still others for "330" health clinics, as designated by the federal government.

If your agency doesn't fit the qualification, do not give up! For instance, let's say your organization addresses issues surrounding homelessness. You have a food pantry, free kitchen, a store or outlet for inexpensive clothing, shelter services, work-skill development programs, and substance-abuse programs. Your clientele, however, does not have access to health care, and your organization does not qualify to apply for grants that fund health care for the indigent.

## Can You Find a Partner?

In this case, identify the agencies in town that are qualified to provide those services. Call them and suggest a partnership that would enable your organization to receive free or reduced-cost health care.

## What Else to Note

Other important criteria to help you select the right RFP include the following:

- **Deadline and amount of narrative required.** Let's face it, you are not likely to do a good job on a 300-page grant if the deadline is just two or three weeks off.
- **Funding allocation, average amount of awards, and probable number of projects.** When the average grant award is several hundred thousand or a million dollars, you can be sure that thousands of qualified organizations will apply. If the department expects to award only twenty new grants each year, you must calculate the odds of your project being one of them.
- **Match requirements.** Often RFPs are issued for programs that require a certain local match and they will let you know what qualifies as a match or not. For instance, a 50 percent local cash match means that you must already have commitments for half of the money needed for a project before you can apply for the other half. If the RFP states that in-kind money qualifies, you can gather a portion of the required

match in donated space, staff time for coordinating or attending meetings, utilities, existing furnishings and computer equipment, support staff time committed to the project, and other items that are part of your organization's budget.

- **Sustainability requirements.** Many federal grants require that an organization apply for a four-year decreasing amount grant. For instance, it may provide 75 percent of funding needed the first year; 60 percent, the second year; 40 percent, the third year; and 20 percent the fourth. In the first year, the applicant organization must commit to providing increasing amounts of its own money to continuing the program over the four-year term of the grant.

Don't be afraid of the long shots. Even when only five grant awards are planned throughout your entire state, you can help create and "sell" a winning program.

## Chapter 6

# Grant-Seeker Workshops and Conferences

Almost every RFP issued includes announcements of grant-seeker workshops or conferences. Is it worth attending one of these workshops? Does it help you get the grant? In this chapter you'll learn more about these grant-seeker workshops, how they can benefit you, and, what, in some cases, are their drawbacks.

# What Is a Grant-Seeker Workshop?

Grant-seeker workshops are targeted to specific RFPs. They are not intended as a place where you can showcase or have peers review your work. You'd have to go to a grant-writing workshop to receive peer or expert assistance in developing your skills as a grant writer, and they are rare. Occasionally community foundations, local colleges or universities, the United Way, professional grant-writing consultants, or support agencies for the nonprofit sector offer grant-writing workshops. You can expect to pay a fee.

Grant-writing workshops charge a fee and may well be worthwhile for developing and honing grant-writing skills. Fees usually average $150 for a half- or full-day session. Grant-seeker workshops are free and are focused on a specific RFP.

## Grant-Seeker Workshops Are Free

You may be asked to preregister for a grant-seeker workshop, especially if the agency hosting the workshop expects a large turnout of grant seekers. Granting agencies sponsor workshops for grant seekers who plan to submit a proposal for funding in response to a particular RFP. These workshops are learning opportunities and are usually held within sixty days of the deadline for proposals.

If the grantor is a federal agency, the workshop is likely to be held in a central area of your state, its major cities, or in the state capital. If a state agency is sponsoring the workshop, it very likely will be held in the state capital. If the local government or a pass-through agent issues the RFP, you won't have to go out of town to attend the workshop. It's very likely to be held locally at one of the local agencies or a common meeting place such as a library or restaurant banquet room. In some cases you will be provided with a choice of dates and locations for the workshop. Decide early which one you'd like to attend, basing your decision on your availability and the ease of reaching the location.

## Why Should You Go?

A grant-seeker workshop provides additional information about the proposal process that may or may not be available in the RFP. It is often the place where an RFP is released for the first time. You can also count on the workshop leaders to give you pointers or tips on developing programs that respond to the RFP. In addition, the speakers generally are available to answer your questions about individual projects or to respond in general to frequently asked questions.

# Who Holds Workshops?

In most cases, grant-seeker workshops are provided by the granting agency or consultants to that agency or government department. On occasion, however, a central support agency for a large group of similar nonprofit organizations, such as an intermediate school district, will provide grant-seeker conferences for its constituents when new funding opportunities become available.

Grant-seeker workshops are rarely mandatory; however, in a few instances, attendance at the workshop is an absolute prerequisite if you want your project to be considered. So it's essential to read through notices very carefully. If you miss an opportunity because of carelessness, you could disqualify your agency for consideration.

## Federal Workshops

Grant-seeker workshops vary in size, site, and value. It depends on who offers them. Federal grant-seeker workshops are usually held in a convention center or another large site in a state capital. But sometimes to reduce the burden on travelers, the agency will sponsor two workshops in larger or more geographically dispersed states. And they are well attended. You'll find hundreds of people, whose grant-writing skills vary from complete novice to professional writers, attending on behalf of their clients. Federal grant-seeker workshops can last anywhere from a half day to a full day long. Many of them include breakout sessions in which you and other members of the audience can ask more specific questions and get answers from workshop leaders.

Some national foundations will request a preliminary proposal and then invite the "short list" agencies to attend one of two or three workshops (for instance, one East Coast, one West Coast) prior to submitting their final proposal for funding. Such grant-seeker workshops are absolutely mandatory.

If a federal department is issuing an RFP for a brand-new funded program, and if a lot of money has been allocated to the grant program, the department is likely to hold three or four grant-seeker workshops throughout the United States. These trips can provide a pleasant respite from your daily work and climate as they're often planned in cities with warm climates, great scenery, and lots of attractions. But even so, don't count on soaking up a lot of sun or doing a lot of window-shopping or sightseeing. Most of your day will be spent indoors—at the convention center.

## Local Grant-Seeker Workshops

Locally sponsored grant-seeker workshops are usually attended by no more than 100 people. They tend to be more valuable to grant writers for several reasons. The smaller audience allows more time for questions about specific projects, and even when it isn't your project being discussed, you can use the answers to frame your own narrative accordingly.

## Eavesdrop on the Competition

A final benefit to attending local grant-seeker workshops is that it's an opportunity to listen and learn what others are planning. You may hear about another project that meshes well with what your organization wants to do. If you can get together, it would give you an opportunity to collaborate with another agency in a unique and mutually beneficial way. At the very least when you listen to others talking about their projects, you will be able to gauge the strength of your proposal in comparison to what others are submitting for the same funding.

## Who Hosts Local Workshops?

Local grant-seeker workshops are most often provided by large supporting organizations such as city governments, arts councils, or intermediate school districts. Specialized funders such as local Rotary or Variety Clubs that offer once-a-year grants programs may also be hosts.

Grant-seeker workshops are very rarely offered by local foundations and grant sources such as the United Way, not even when they issue an RFP. They deal with agencies and grant writers in a more personal way. They usually provide a telephone number and contact person (a program officer) that you may call to get answers to your questions. Moreover, some foundations are open to having personal meetings with the director of the nonprofit organization and the grant writer to discuss ways to strengthen your program or proposal.

**ALERT!**

If you are invited to attend a personal meeting with a member of the foundation staff, always accept the opportunity. You'll get insight into what the foundation is looking for in proposals, tips on what to include, and the ability to form a professional relationship rewarding for you and your organization.

# When You Should Attend a Workshop

If any one of the following is true, you should plan to attend the grant-seekers workshop:

- The workshop is deemed mandatory by the grantor.
- You have questions about the RFP, funding limits, or the category you wish to apply for.

- You are new to grant writing.
- You have never written a proposal to that particular granting agency or governmental department.
- You're curious about who else is applying for competitive grants.

# What Will You Learn?

Grant-seeker workshops usually begin with an overview of the RFP and announcements of any subsequent changes made to the program or funding allowances since the RFP was issued. You may learn, for instance, that although the RFP suggests funding ranges from $200,000 to $300,000, the granting agency has since determined that more money will be allocated to new projects than was originally anticipated. Therefore, they will either be funding more projects or be giving out larger grant awards.

You are just as likely to learn the opposite, however—that funding is about to be slashed. In that case, you can count on the fact that the competition will be fierce. So if your program doesn't answer the RFP requirements to the letter, you are wasting your time responding. In either case, these last-minute changes are valuable information that you'll find nowhere else, except perhaps in a press release buried somewhere on the Web.

## A Good Source for Tips

You'll also receive tips on developing programs that respond to the RFP, as well as cautions about things that will be more difficult for you to justify as worthy of funding. For instance, a Department of Education grant may call for proposals to reduce the size of large high schools by creating "schools within schools" or by implementing flexible schedules or block scheduling. While the RFP may say no-thing one way or another about constructing a second high school, at the grant-seeker workshop the staff will be able to tell you how you can make a new construction project fit the parameters of the grant. They also may encourage you to try an approach that is more likely to receive funding.

When an RFP has several categories for funding, the workshop often includes breakout sessions you can attend that address each specific category. If you intend to apply in more than one category—and if that option is allowed in the RFP—and if the breakout sessions are being held concurrently, you have one of two choices. You can go to one session and hope to find out afterwards what information was discussed at the other. Or you can plan ahead and bring a colleague to the workshop so you each can cover one of the two sessions.

If a workshop includes breaks, don't be shy about going up to the workshop leader to question him or her privately. It's a golden opportunity to get personalized advice.

Remember there will be fewer people in the breakout sessions than at the introductory sessions. That makes them a valuable opportunity for you to ask questions that may apply specifically to your grant or project.

## Yes, Workshops Get Repetitive

As you become an experienced grant writer, you'll find the workshops become redundant even when a new grant opportunity arises. Depending on who organizes and leads the workshops, the sessions can sometimes make you feel like you're attending a college lecture. That's especially true when the presenter takes on the monotone of a droning professor and covers material that you were assigned to read beforehand. Of course he assumes that you and the others present did not do your homework. In a word—boring.

That's not the worst thing session leaders do. Sometimes they attempt to present a minicourse on grant writing. This apparently is directed at those who have never written a grant before. It's a nice, though somewhat meaningless, gesture. They usually provide the information in a half-hour PowerPoint presentation led by a sociology professor from a local university. Usually the information offers little of real value to a new grant writer. It certainly won't take the place of what you learn in this book or what you'll learn from experience in the field. So, if this type of miniworkshop or breakout session is included on the agenda, we suggest you take a break.

## Good Points about Dull Workshops

Just remember, no matter how boring workshops can be, you are guaranteed to learn at least one vital piece of information. Generally it will be something that has been added to or changed in the RFP since it was issued. Or it may be a piece of information that's entirely new and adds to your own experience as a grant writer. You'll get at least that much from every workshop you attend. And that's a promise.

# Advantages and Disadvantages

There are other advantages to attending a grant-seeker workshop, in addition to those that have been discussed previously in this chapter. They include the following:

- Marketing opportunities for a new grant-writing venture.
- Potential for gaining a competitive advantage over grant seekers not in attendance. You'll get "inside" information or learn about others who intend to apply for the same grant. Then you'll be able to gauge how your proposal stacks up in competition with those proposed by other agencies.
- The opportunity to ask questions and learn from questions asked by others. That also gives you a valuable edge in writing your grant proposal.
- At least one new bit of information that you can use in writing this proposal or another down the line.

Like everything else in life, there is a downside as well and you have to take that into consideration. Disadvantages of attending a grant-seeker workshop include:

- They are time consuming, often taking at least a half-day or more (not including travel).
- You'll be in a crowd that has diverse and wide-ranging skills and experience. So if you're a more experienced grant writer, you'll have to put up with questions that seem downright elementary.

- They tend to be redundant after a while, particularly if you have already participated in workshops offered by the same granting agency or government department.
- Unless the workshop includes breakout sessions or coffee breaks, you may have little or no opportunity to talk to presenters and receive help or advice about specific questions.

Of course, you can't know before you go how good the grant-seeker workshop will be or what it will offer of value. But keep in mind that these can be valuable, especially as you are starting to write your first grant proposal.

*Chapter 7*

# Letters of Intent and Inquiry

Grant writers have to write lots of letters, chief among them letters of inquiry and letters of intent. In this chapter, we'll discuss the difference between the two and provide some guidelines for writing each one.

# What's the Difference?

Many people get confused about letters of intent and letters of inquiry. But you don't have to worry. Just think of a letter of intent as a form stating that you intend to apply for a grant. In contrast, a letter of inquiry is more like a sales pitch.

> Always write a letter to request foundation guidelines. Let the guidelines dictate whether your next step should be to write a letter of intent or a letter of inquiry.

## Letters of Intent

In a letter of intent you are telling the granting agency that you plan to respond to a request for proposals. These letters are most often sent to governments since they are the agencies that most often issue RFPs.

Sometimes the granting agency doesn't request a letter of intent at all. If they don't ask for it, don't send one, because it will naturally confuse people if you do. The agencies that do request letters of intent do so simply to learn how many project proposals they can expect to receive. Sometimes they might also be interested in finding out from which geographical areas potential proposals will be submitted.

## Letters of Inquiry

When you write a letter of inquiry, think of yourself as a sales representative. Rather than just stating that you intend to respond to a request for proposals, your letter of inquiry describes your project and asks for permission to submit a grant proposal. These letters are most often sent to foundation-type funders. They consider this the first step in their grant-proposal cycle.

Use a letter of inquiry when the foundation guidelines request this step and/or when you are unclear about whether the foundation funds the type of project you wish to present.

# When to Send a Letter of Intent

There are three considerations regarding letters of intent. First, you may not be required to write one at all. Second, you may be requested to write the letter but not required to send it. And third, you have no choice. In this case the letter of intent is an absolute necessity, and it will have an absolute deadline for reaching the foundation or government office.

If the instructions say nothing at all about letters of intent, you can be certain it is neither required nor requested. When one is requested, but not required, most often the instructions about a letter of intent say something like, "You are not required to submit a letter of intent, and doing so does not commit you to applying for this grant."

**ALERT!**

Only submit a letter of intent when one is requested or required. Pay attention to the deadline for submission of the letter. Being late is the same as submitting no letter at all.

When a letter of intent is required, the instructions will say something like, "You are required to submit a letter of intent to apply by 5:00 P.M. on January 20. Only those organizations submitting a letter of intent by the indicated deadline will be eligible to apply for funds under this grant program." And make no mistake, you must meet that deadline. If it gets there at 5:01 P.M., the letter will be too late.

# Components of a Strong Letter of Intent

Letters of intent are short and to the point. They should be no longer than one page and should contain the following pertinent information:

- Name of grant program
- Number of grant program (if available)
- Name of applicant
- Contact information for applicant
- Category of funding requested (when the RFP has separate categories)

Do not get chatty in a letter of intent. Think of it as a form (and in many cases, it actually will be a form that you complete and return to the grantor) and include little beyond the required information. Don't use this medium to request additional information or ask questions about your proposal.

## Sample Letter of Intent

Increasingly, government agencies that require a letter of intent are supplying forms that you may complete and fax or submit electronically. They look something like this:

---

### Notice of Intent to Apply for (2003–04) Program Grant

Submit this form no later than January 1, 2003, to assist Department of Education staff in determining the number of reviewers that will be necessary.

Submission of this notice is not a prerequisite for application of grant funds, nor does it obligate the organization to submit an application.

Organization:
Contact Person:
Phone:
Fax:
E-mail:
County(ies) to Be Served:
Mail or fax this form to:
Address:
Fax Number:

---

▲ Sample instruction to supply notice of intent.

Dear Name:

The XYZ Nonprofit in City, State, intends to submit a grant proposal in response to program number 123456.9 in the Federal Register. Of the three categories for projects described in the designated RFP, XYZ plans to submit under category "C": Nonprofit community collaborations to address shortages of affordable housing.

I understand that this grant proposal will be due by 5:00 P.M. on March 31, year, in your offices. If supplementary information becomes available in the interim or if you have reservations about our qualifications to apply for this grant, please contact me by any of the following means:

Phone: 555-5555
Fax: 555-5566
E-mail: xyz@xyz.com
Thank you.

Sincerely,
Executive Director
XYZ Nonprofit

▲ Sample notice of intent from grant seeker.

## When to Use a Letter of Inquiry

A letter of inquiry, as its name implies, asks questions. While you may ask a number of questions, such as the deadline for submission of full proposals, clarification of foundation programs, or available times to meet, there is really only one critical question to ask in a letter of inquiry: Is the funder interested in this project? You can ask the question directly or indirectly, but the whole point is to "pitch" the program and see if the funder responds.

A letter of inquiry, unlike a letter of intent, should be a succinct and compelling summary of your program plans. Include potential links between your program and the goals of the funder, and be sure to request a discussion of the merits of the project.

**FACT**

When you write a letter of inquiry, be sure to ask for the opportunity to submit a full proposal. It's the same thing as closing the sale at the end of a sales meeting.

## Components of a Strong Letter of Inquiry

A letter of inquiry should be addressed to a specific person within the granting agency, most often the program officer. Your letter of inquiry should include the following:

- A summary of the project.
- Potential outcomes of the project.
- A direct or indirect reference to the ways the project fits the goals or guidelines of the foundation.
- A brief budget and breakdown.
- Reference to partners in the project.
- Other places the nonprofit has applied or plans to apply for funding.
- Outcomes of previous fundraising efforts, if any.
- A suggestion of the amount you intend to request and its purpose.
- A request for a meeting or discussion of the merits of the project and a subsequent invitation to submit a full proposal.

## Sample Letter of Inquiry

Here is a letter of inquiry Maggie used when seeking a grant for one of her local nonprofit agencies. She got the results she was hoping for, including an invitation to meet with the executive director of the foundation. Note that in this letter, Maggie links the project outcomes to the stated objectives of the granting agency found in their guidelines. Take care to do the same in your letters of inquiry.

Dear Program Officer:

Last Fall, the XYZ nonprofit launched a mobile media laboratory: a van equipped with laptop computers, digital video cameras, digital video editing software, educational software, and e-learning curricula.

The project was deployed in response to needs for technology education and educational enrichment in several areas of the community. In its scheduled visits to inner-city and other public and parochial schools, and to community and youth centers, the project provides kindergarten-to-twelfth-grade enrichment in the subject areas, and Internet and video production training for children and young adults who would otherwise lack access to equipment or connections.

While the educational outcomes for project participants are not yet available, they do appear promising. The project has been enthusiastically received by teachers, students, community members, and organizational representatives. Students have a natural interest in the cameras and computers and quickly learn to operate the equipment and to edit film. Project staff use that interest to encourage further exploration and study in content-area subjects, as requested by the teaching and administrative staffs of the individual schools.

XYZ now proposes that it use the project not only to enrich academic studies but also to engage children and young adults in the creative process. Through a new program called [project name], staff plan to assist up to thirty at-risk middle- and high-school students in exploring their ranges of talent and in developing the artistic skills needed to support their natural abilities.

Students will participate in the new project five days a week for eight weeks. They will receive several one-act plays written by a local writer, a freelance playwright and director, who will develop four-to-six "starter" plays on various topics of interest to young people. He will guide the students in writing the middle and ends to the plays they select. When they are finished, the group will read all the works and select a person to act as the playwright for the remainder of the project. All students will also study stage production, acting, directing, camera operation, and film editing with the playwright and a staff videographer, and through interactive teaching modules on the Internet accessed with project laptops.

Students may then select or try out for assignments related to producing the play and videotaping it as an artistic film. Some will become actors, others set designers, camera operators, costume designers, film editors, etc. Completed plays will be performed live, and filmed and edited as short features for broadcast on public-access television or streaming to the Internet. Some components of the plays may be made into performing exhibits for display at the local partner agency. The completed curriculum and resulting work will be shared with other school districts that require new or enhanced arts programs.

Project outcomes include:

- Students will engage in the creative process, learn to work as a group, and come to appreciate their own and others' various talents and skills.
- Students will demonstrate a deeper and long-lasting appreciation for the arts.
- Schools struggling with budgets will have improved, rather than reduced, arts curricula and programming.

XYZ requires $___ to launch the project, which will include the following:

| | |
|---|---|
| Curriculum development (2 months); development of interactive curriculum components and deployment to Web | $_____ |
| Vignettes and 8 weeks' program (5 days per week), playwright | $_____ |
| 8 weeks' program, video production and broadcast | $_____ |
| Miscellaneous (costumes, set design, vehicle expenses, etc.) | $_____ |

XYZ is just beginning to explore funding sources for this project. We hope to hear from you soon, not only to learn that you are inviting a full proposal for review by your board, but also so we might hear your ideas for additional partnerships or program refinements. Thank you for your assistance.

Sincerely,
Executive Director

## Chapter 8

# Components of a Grant Proposal

The grant proposal is your response to a request for proposals (RFP). The RFP contains your instructions and, most often, an outline of content. In this chapter, you'll learn what the outline usually looks like and get some tips for "reading between the lines."

# What to Expect

RFPs can range from a single sheet of guidelines to hundreds of pages of instructions and attachments. In nearly every case, the RFP requires that your proposal include a needs section, a project description (with goals and objectives), an evaluation section, and a budget.

The entire RFP package is instructional, and you are expected to read every word in it. Accomplished grant writers turn first to the outline to determine how much work will go into the proposal. Then they also start reading the remainder of the packet to ensure that they are not missing important information.

Freelance grant writers can use the outline to identify the extent of the work required. Based on the outline, they can determine (a) whether they can schedule adequate time to work on the proposal and (b) the cost estimate for their services.

RFPs from the Federal Register are several pages in length. Each page contains up to four columns of very small type. It will probably take approximately one hour to review the contents, highlight those that are promising, and make notes on important information that will help guide your writing process.

The outline for the proposal will be apparent, but additional directions may be scattered throughout the RFP. You'll find other important and relevant information such as the following:

- Paper size and composition. (The Environmental Protection Agency, for instance, requires use of recycled paper.)
- Spacing. (If not specified as double spaced, single-space your documents and double-space between paragraphs or indent the beginning of each paragraph.)
- Minimum size of typeface.
- Deadline for submission (and whether by postmark or arrival date).
- Maximum number of pages.
- Address and phone numbers for contact people and for submissions.

- Formats.
- Qualifications for grantees.
- Purpose and goals of the grant program. (These are critical as you want your program to further the goals of the grantor.)
- Necessary forms and attachments.
- Instructions for completing forms.
- Additional sections required (such as compliance statements, tables of contents, abstracts, etc.).
- Instructions for the order in which you must compile the finished grant proposal packet (sometimes also provided as a checklist).

**ALERT!**

You may find instructions in the back of an RFP for submitting to the State Single Point of Contact, as well as to the granting agency. The State Single Point of Contact is a person or office in your state with the responsibility of cataloging who applies for what grants. The State Single Point of Contact also assists grant writers by responding to questions during the application process. There may be no other mention of the State Single Point of Contact anywhere else in the RFP.

## Follow the Directions

There are three rules to grant writing:

1. Follow the directions.
2. Follow the directions.
3. Follow the directions.

Redundant? Yes! But even though it's been stated several times throughout this book, it bears repeating. The simple truth is that if you forget or ignore directions, or miss something altogether when you've gone through the instructions, your proposal will not be reviewed. Then your work has no value whatsoever.

## There's No Review Criteria?

The directions may or may not include review criteria. If they do not, you can be assured that the questions or headings used in the outline are exactly what the granting agency wants prospective grantees to answer.

## When RFPs Have Review Criteria

Some RFPs replace an outline for your narrative with review criteria or a rubric. Read the questions or qualifications contained in the criteria carefully. Try to determine the gist of each question the grantors are posing. It will clue you in on how to respond. Then respond to each question as completely as you can.

## Sample of Need Section Instructions

Following are instructions, in the form of review criteria, for the need section of an educational grant:

*1. NEED (Ten points) "The proposal provides a brief explanation of why the project is needed. It summarizes the demographics of the district and the selected buildings that will be served by this funding; possible causes for an increase in the number of students requiring special education services or a decrease in state assessment reading scores; and the need for new resources and programs for students who are not achieving in reading or who are at risk of reading failure."*

## Include Relevant Data

In following the instructions, you will provide relevant data, first about the district and then by the building(s) in which you will implement the program. Relevant data in this example would include the number of children and the percentage by building of children failing state assessment and other tests of reading. Other relevant data would point out possible causes for the need.

## Include Programs That Failed

In addressing the last part of the criteria, you'll want to talk about what programs the buildings have tried in the past and why they haven't worked or helped children achieve as much as the principals had hoped. When you complete this section, you'll be set up to begin writing in the project description, addressing just why this project will succeed where others have failed (that is, because it addresses previously unknown or emerging needs cited in the needs section).

# Follow the Outline

Be sure to follow the outline as closely as you can. Don't write a beautiful narrative description of your program—grant proposals are not literature. No matter how good your instincts usually are, if an outline calls for the "need" section to be followed by the description of the program, don't decide that it makes more sense to tell them "what" before you tell them "why."

**ALERT!**

Use the same headings the outline does. If they have a heading marked with "B" or Roman numeral "II," make sure that your heading also says "B" or "II." If they give you subheadings marked "a," "b," and "c," create subheadings marked exactly the same way.

The outline is provided to ensure that you address every single item on which the proposal will be judged. Following it exactly means that you have responded to all the questions.

# There Is No Outline?

Don't panic. A few RFPs don't come with outlines. The Small Business Innovation and Research (SBIR) grant offered by the federal government through several departments—most often the National Institute of Health (NIH)—is one of them.

In these cases, request or look up on the Internet previous grant proposal submissions. Often the contact person will fax or mail you a copy of a successful proposal and you can use its general outline as a guide for your proposal writing.

## A Last Resort

If you cannot locate or acquire a previous submission, base your response on the common elements of a grant proposal or a business plan. Discuss the need (or the potential market for a product). Describe the project or product. Talk about what remains to be done and how you expect to accomplish it. Develop a budget and explain how you derived the numbers you included. Discuss at length the qualifications of the organization and its staff to carry out the project plan.

Finally, discuss an evaluation of the project or product—what you hope to learn from it and what you'll do with the evaluation once it's complete. Be sure to use headings and subheadings as if they were provided in the RFP outline. They will assist readers in navigating the document.

## Review Criteria Can Help

Sometimes you'll receive only review criteria without an outline. In these cases, you are expected to follow the review criteria as outlined in the RFP. Summarize the content of each criteria as your headings and subheadings, rather than writing out the entire statement. For instance, the following are review criteria for the first section, "Statement of Need." You may use one or several subheadings within each criterion:

**FACT**

All grants are competitive in the general sense of the word, though governments and foundations do make a distinction. Grants are called "noncompetitive" when they are awarded to the best proposal. For instance, your grant proposal to the local community foundation for a teen drug abuse program is not competing against a grant proposal for a similar or unlike program. It's merely competing for a grant award from available funds. Grants are "competitive" when the grantor is, for instance, selecting three to ten agencies in the United States to perform a contracted service outlined in the grant.

| Review Criteria | Suggested Subheadings |
|---|---|
| The extent to which the applicant specifies the goals and objectives of the project and describes how implementation will fulfill the purposes of the Early Learning Opportunities Act (ELOA). The applicant must demonstrate a thorough understanding of the importance of early learning services and activities that help parents, caregivers, and child care providers incorporate early learning into the daily lives of young children, as well as programs that directly provide early learning to young children. | Goals and Objectives/Implementation Plan |

| Review Criteria | Suggested Subheadings |
|---|---|
| The extent to which the applicant demonstrates the need for assistance, including identification and discussion of its needs and resources assessment concerning early learning services. Relevant data from the assessment should be included. Participant and beneficiary information must also be included. | Need for Assistance/Target Population |

| Review Criteria | Suggested Subheadings |
|---|---|
| The extent to which the applicant describes its resources assessment and the relevance of the results as the basis for determining its objectives and need for assistance. | Needs Assessment |

| Review Criteria | Suggested Subheadings |
|---|---|
| The extent to which the applicant demonstrates how it will give preference to supporting activities/projects that maximize the use of resources through collaboration with other early learning programs, provide continuity of services for young children across the age spectrum, and help parents and other caregivers promote early learning with their young children. The applicant must provide information about how decisions will be made about who will provide each early learning service and/or activity funded through this grant. | Partners and Their Roles/Maximizing Resources |

| Review Criteria | Suggested Subheadings |
|---|---|
| The extent to which the applicant demonstrates that it has worked with local education agencies to identify cognitive, social, and emotional, and motor developmental abilities that are necessary to support children's readiness for school; that the programs, services, and activities assisted under this title will represent developmentally appropriate steps toward the acquisition of those abilities; and that the programs, services, and activities assisted provide benefits for children cared for in their own homes as well as children placed in the care of others. | Review of Literature/Lessons Learned |

▲ Ways to use review criteria to generate subheads for your proposal.

## Essential Components

A grant proposal must respond to the five W's (and one H) of a good news story: who, what, where, when, why, and how. The primary difference is in how it's laid out. In other words, when you write out a proposal, you're responding to the structure of the document, and that's determined by the names of the sections and the questions asked.

"Who" is both the organization you are describing and the target population whose needs you expect to address with your project. You'll answer that in the needs section of the proposal.

"Where" is a description of the city or region in which the project will take place. You have to address where in the needs section.

"What" describes your project in detail. What will you do? You'll place this in the project-description section.

"When" is your timeline of activities and it also is contained in the project description.

How and why? You'll be answering the hows and whys in various places throughout the RFP, like so:

- How many (people, units of service, hours)?
- How much (change is expected in the population/environment/outcomes)?
- How will you know (evaluation)?
- How much does it cost? (budget)?
- How does your program fit the goals of the grant program?
- Why did you choose this particular program?
- Why do you think it will work?
- Why should the grantor care?

# Other Questions They May Ask

You will be asked to describe all the essential components listed above in every grant proposal. Some RFPs, however, also will ask such things as the history of the organization, the genesis for the project, the roles of partners in the project, and the input by constituents or the target population into the design of the project.

You might be asked to include your plan for disseminating the results of your evaluation. Some agencies want to know what literature you used in developing your project.

A new trend in grant proposals, especially among foundations, is a question about constituent input into program design and/or the evaluation process. This is to help nonprofit-organization staff begin to realize that they are not the final arbiters of someone else's need. Too often in the past, nonprofit organizations have provided too many services to target populations, inadvertently encouraging the population's dependence on social systems rather than engaging them in the change process and thus empowering them to make additional steps to independence.

# Federal Register Instructions Example

The sample RFP shown on the following page is one of the tougher ones, in part because the language of the RFP is that of experts. Maggie suggests that only those who are experts in the field of child care attempt this grant proposal as a first project.

# 20527 Federal Register / Vol. 67, No. 80 / Thursday, April 25, 2002 / Notices

## Part III General Instructions for Preparing the Uniform Project Description

ACF is particularly interested in specific factual information and statements of measurable goals in quantitative terms. Project descriptions are evaluated on the basis of substance, not length. Extensive exhibits are not required. Cross-referencing should be used rather than repetition. Supporting information concerning activities that will not be directly funded by the grant or information that does not directly pertain to an integral part of the grant-funded activity should be placed in an appendix.

## The Project Description Overview Purpose

The project description provides a major means by which an application is evaluated and ranked to compete with other applications for available assistance. The project description should be concise and complete and should address the activity for which federal funds are being requested. Supporting documents should be included where they can present information clearly and succinctly. In preparing your project description, all information requested through each specific evaluation criteria should be provided. Awarding offices use this and other information in making their funding recommendations. It is important, therefore, that this information be included in the application. Pages should be numbered, and a table of contents should be included for easy reference.

## A. Project Summary/Abstract/Geographic Location

Provide a summary of the project description (a page or less) with reference to the funding request. Describe the precise location of the project and boundaries of the area to be served by the proposed project. Maps or other graphic aids may be attached.

## B. Objectives and Need for Assistance

Clearly identify the physical, economic, social, financial, institutional, and/or other problem(s) requiring a solution. The need for assistance must be demonstrated, and the principal and subordinate objectives of the project must be clearly stated; supporting documentation, such as letters of support and testimonials from concerned interests other than the applicant, may be included.

Any relevant data based on planning studies should be included or referred to in the endnotes/footnotes. Incorporate demographic data and participant/beneficiary information, as needed. In developing the project description, the applicant may volunteer or be requested to provide information on the total range of projects currently being conducted and supported (or to be initiated), some of which may be outside the scope of the program announcement.

### C. Results or Benefits Expected

Identify the results and benefits to be derived. For example: specify the number of children and families to be served and how the services to be provided will be funded consistent with the local needs assessment. Or, explain how the expected results will benefit the population to be served in meeting its needs for early learning services and activities.

### D. Approach/Evaluation Approach

Outline a plan of action that describes the scope and detail of how the proposed work will be accomplished. Account for all functions or activities identified in the application. Cite factors that might accelerate or decelerate the work and state your reason for taking the proposed approach rather than others.

Describe any unusual features of the project such as design or technological innovations, reductions in cost or time, or extraordinary social and community involvement.

Provide quantitative monthly or quarterly projections of the accomplishments to be achieved for each function or activity in such terms as the number of people to be served and the number of activities accomplished. When accomplishments cannot be quantified by activity or function, list them in chronological order to show the schedule of accomplishments and their target dates.

If any data is to be collected, maintained, and/or disseminated, clearance may be required from the U.S. Office of Management and Budget (OMB). This clearance pertains to any "collection of information that is conducted or sponsored by ACF."

List organizations, cooperating entities, consultants, or other key individuals who will work on the project along with a short description of the nature of their effort or contribution.

### E. Evaluation

Provide a narrative addressing how the results of the project and the conduct of the project will be evaluated. In addressing the evaluation of results, state how you will determine the extent to which the project has achieved its stated objectives and the extent to which the accomplishment of objectives can be attributed to the project. Discuss the criteria to be used to evaluate results, and explain the methodology that will be used to determine if the needs identified and discussed are being met, and if the project results and benefits are being achieved. With respect to the conduct of the project, define the procedures to be employed to determine whether the project is being conducted in a manner consistent with the work plan presented, and discuss the impact of the project's various activities on the project's effectiveness.

### F. Additional Information

The following are requests for additional information that need to be included in the application:

- Staff and Position Data: Provide a biographical sketch for each key person appointed and a job description for each vacant key position. A biographical sketch will also be required for new key staff as appointed.
- Plan for Continuance Beyond Grant Support: Provide a plan for securing resources and continuing project activities after federal assistance has ceased.
- Organizational Profiles: Provide information on the applicant organization(s) and cooperating partners such as organizational charts, financial statements, audit reports or statements from CPA/licensed public accountants, employer identification numbers, names of bond carriers, contact persons and telephone numbers, child care licenses, and other documentation of professional accreditation, information on compliance with federal/state/local government standards, documentation of experience in the program area, and other pertinent

information. Any nonprofit organization submitting an application must submit proof of its nonprofit status in its application at the time of submission. The nonprofit agency can accomplish this by providing a copy of the applicant's listing in the Internal Revenue Service's (IRS) most recent list of tax-exempt organizations described in section 501(c)(3) of the IRS code, or by providing a copy of the currently valid IRS tax-exemption certificate, or by providing a copy of the articles of incorporation bearing the seal of the state in which the corporation or association is domiciled.

- Third-Party Agreements: Include written agreements between grantees and subgrantees or subcontractors or other cooperating entities. These agreements must detail scope of work to be performed, work schedules, remuneration, and other terms and conditions that structure or define the relationship.
- Letters of Support: Provide statements from community, public, and commercial leaders that support the project proposed for funding. All submissions should be included in the application OR by application deadline.

### G. Budget and Budget Justification

Provide line-item detail and detailed calculations for each budget object class identified on the Budget Information form. Detailed calculations must include estimation methods, quantities, unit costs, and other similar quantitative detail sufficient for the calculation to be duplicated. The detailed budget must also include a breakout by the funding sources identified in Block 15 of the SF–424.

Provide a narrative budget justification that describes how the categorical costs are derived. Discuss the necessity, reasonableness, and allocation of the proposed costs.

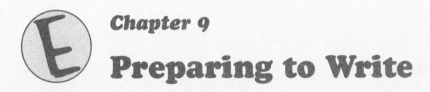

## Chapter 9

# Preparing to Write

Always review the guidelines or RFP closely before you begin writing the first draft. You'll want to be as prepared as possible. Knowing who your audience is and how to address the issues outlined in the RFP is the best way to write a successful grant proposal.

# Know Your Readers

The first rule of all good writing is to know—and understand—your audience. How much do they want to learn from your document? What are their biases? What are their interests? How much do they already know about the subject?

For your purposes, there are two different kinds of grant readers: one reads foundation grants; the other, government responses to RFPs.

## Foundation Readers

Foundation staff and, occasionally, trustees—depending on the structure and size of the foundation—read foundation grants. It helps, therefore, to read the guidelines thoroughly and learn as much as you can about their personal and collective interests before you submit a proposal.

Often you can go to the local foundation to meet staff and discuss your proposal. Then you can revise it before they present it to their trustees. Alternately, program officers may come to your office (called a "site visit"), or ask you to meet in theirs so they can get more information to share with their trustees and to support their recommendations regarding funding.

These program officers are the critical people to impress in the foundation grant-seeking process. Listen to all of their requests for additional information and respond in a timely manner. If they want you to rewrite an entire proposal, do so. They are not the enemy. They know their boards and what the members want covered in proposals. Also, their job is to go before the trustees with solid reasons for recommending funding or declining the proposals. Give them the tools to help you.

## Government Grants

In the case of government grants, the proposal readers are the decision-makers or judges for each proposal. They are the most important figures in the entire process. They award points for each section, total the points, and average them with the scores of the other readers to come up with a final score. That final score must total an established number for the project to be funded. Recommendations of the judges need not be supported by the reviewers or questioned by the funding agency.

In most cases, these proposal readers are experts in their fields who either have responded to a call for readers or been recruited by the issuing department. Proposal readers often represent a cross-section of geography, expertise, and interests. And they are usually peers of those who are submitting proposals.

**FACT**

Very often RFPs will include a supplementary call for readers. That means that any person who receives the RFP may also apply to become a judge. Of course, if the reader also represents an agency that has applied for the grant, he or she will not be assigned to review his or her own organization's proposal.

A research grant submitted to the National Institute of Health, for instance, will be reviewed by a panel of scientists, Ph.D.s, and/or physicians. A proposal submitted to the U.S. Department of Education will be reviewed by educators and curriculum experts. If your proposal asks for funding for computers in schools, you can expect that along with educators, computer software experts, technicians, and others familiar with computers will be reading the proposals.

## A Tight Timeline for Readers

Proposal reviews usually take place in less than a week. Readers are sent ten or more proposals (though there may be hundreds of actual applications) to read and score and return to the funding agency for final tallying. Most often each proposal has three to five judges. Reviewers are provided score sheets to guide their judging, often in the form of rubrics or review criteria identical to that provided in the RFP, and a cover sheet or space to write comments. While they are not required to justify their scoring, they often do provide comments that you can use later to strengthen a failed proposal.

## Scoring an RFP

While grant proposals are competitive in that they compete for the money allocated, the individual proposals are not judged one against another. The final score is the average of all scores awarded by all readers of that proposal. That is the only criterion upon which funding is based, except in cases where the funding agency further ensures geographic equity.

A high score, however, does not always guarantee funding. If, for instance, 1,000 proposals are submitted and 500 of them score 90 out of 100 points, the benchmark for funding will be raised—to 95 or higher. If the grant has limited funds, it means that the grant maker will fund only the best of the best projects, not all of the good projects.

**FACT**

As used in RFPs, a rubric is a chart that contains various classifications and points that may be awarded by readers under each category as they judge individual proposals.

In the case of government grants, it is important to remember that you are writing to your peers (or, in the case of freelance grant writers, to the peers of your clients—so if your clients understand and support the narrative, chances are that the judges will be equally impressed).

## Outlining

Outlining a grant proposal is the easiest thing you have to do. Simply follow the outline provided in the RFP or guidelines and follow it exactly.

Every Roman numeral in the RFP should have a corresponding Roman numeral in your outline. The same is true for all alpha characters and numbers. You also may want to include the point value for each question or some of your notes to the outline. You can delete them later.

## Brainstorming

Once you have an outline and questions, sit down with other members of your organization (and potential collaborators, if they are available) to brainstorm ideas for the program. This is not your typical brainstorming session in which "anything goes."

For this session, you should lay out the program mandates from the grant on one page of a flip chart and the components of programs your organization currently has in place. Begin by comparing the two to see how you can modify existing programs to fit more closely with the program sought in the RFP.

If there is information that you aren't sure of, or areas you know less about, ask other staff members for their assistance, so you can make sure you've got the most complete data possible.

If you're working on a freelance basis, you'll want to schedule a meeting with your clients to gather information. Provide feedback to the group throughout the meeting with comments such as, "I hear you saying that the program should focus on 'a' rather than 'b' . . . is that right? Or are you saying it should offer both, but emphasize 'b'?" Keep the meeting going until most of your questions have been answered and you feel you have enough information to write a fairly solid first draft.

Your brainstorming group can and should become your "grant-seeking team." You'll need help with lots of tasks throughout the writing process; often one or two members of the team can give you a hand. If you're freelancing, make it clear to the potential team members that the more they help, the fewer hours you will have to spend on nonwriting tasks, and therefore, the lower your final invoice for services.

Tasks you can assign the team members include the following:

- Calling other organizations for data
- Locating internal data
- Developing budgets and moving draft budgets through internal approval channels
- Reviewing drafts
- Locating library resources if needed
- Providing anecdotal evidence of need

# Planning Responsive Programs

You are the person most familiar with the requirements outlined in the RFP. And as you gain experience writing grants, you will become very familiar with what local foundations will and will not fund. You'll be able to use this knowledge to guide you as you develop programs and new ideas for collaborations with other groups.

## An Example RFP

One of the family foundations in Maggie's town published guidelines for an environmental program. Its goal is to protect the environment and encourage better land-use planning. According to their guidelines, their grant-making interests include:

- Regional land protection efforts that:
  1. Preserve quality farmland and forests.
  2. Protect ecological corridors and valuable environmental features.
  3. Enhance water quality.
  4. Enhance access to the natural environment by the public.
- Regional or statewide public policy or advocacy that:
  1. Protects or improves the ecological health of natural areas.
  2. Results in the more sensible use of land through farmland preservation and more efficient and sustainable urban development.
- Land use education projects of potential regional significance

To be responsive to these program guidelines, a project that proposes to protect land must work in a geographical area targeted by the foundation and must address the listed criteria.

## What Would You Do?

If you have an idea for a project to preserve and restore inner-city homes, could you make a case for the ways in which such a program would preserve farmland and forests, protect ecological corridors and environmental features, enhance water quality, and enhance access by the public to the natural environment?

Maggie did: "I learned that most often farmland is lost because it's sold to developers for residential centers. Usually these bedroom communities also create long commutes that use additional gasoline and contribute to air pollution and oil runoff into lakes and streams. So I proposed that an effort to improve an inner-city neighborhood would reduce the demand for semi-rural construction and, thus, if successful, save farmlands. It was a tough sell, but we eventually won the foundation over by doing our homework."

## Another Example

Now let's look at a federal grant RFP. In this case, you could not "fit a square peg into a round hole." You must follow all the criteria exactly in planning your program and ensuring that it provides each and every service described.

According to the guidelines, the purposes of the grant program are:

- To increase the availability of voluntary programs, services, and activities that support early childhood development, increase parent effectiveness, and promote the learning readiness of young children so that young children enter school ready to learn.
- To support parents, child care providers, and caregivers who want to incorporate early learning activities into the daily lives of young children.
- To remove barriers to the provision of an accessible system of early childhood learning programs in communities throughout the United States.
- To increase the availability and affordability of professional development activities and compensation for caregivers and child care providers.
- To facilitate the development of community-based systems of collaborative service-delivery models characterized by resource sharing, linkages between appropriate supports, and local planning for services.

**List existing project components with one color ink and suggestions from the team with another.**

## What to Do

List each of the criteria on a large flip-chart sheet and post them in the room during your team's brainstorming session. Have members respond to ways in which the proposed project already does answer these requirements. Then have the team suggest ways that they could strengthen the program to ensure that it meets all the criteria to the highest degree possible.

# What's the Deadline?

Plan backward from the deadline. The closer the deadline, the more you should call on your team to assist you. Work backward from the shipping date (not the deadline for arrival at the grantor's office unless it's a local office where you can drop off the proposal).

Your schedule must include: meetings; time to write at least two drafts; draft review times for team members; time to complete forms and get signatures; time to get and, sometimes, write support letters; and time for gathering attachments, and copying and collating. A typical schedule that Maggie would provide a client looks like this:

| Date | Process/activity | Responsibility |
| --- | --- | --- |
| 2/2 | Complete draft 1 with questions and blanks for first review | writer |
| 2/6–2/9 | Return draft with suggestions for revisions | team |
| | Meet to discuss issues/questions | team and writer |
| Week of 2/9 | Revise draft | writer |
| | Begin preliminary budget | team |
| Week of 2/16 | Review draft 2 | team |
| | Meet to discuss attachments, narrative, potential list of support letters, etc. | team and writer |
| Week of 2/23 | Revise draft | writer |
| | Request support letters, locate additional attachments | team |

*(continued on next page)*

| Date | Process/activity | Responsibility |
|------|------------------|----------------|
| Week of 2/23 *(cont.)* | Finalize budget | team and writer |
| 3/2 | Finalize draft and attachments and submit for approval | writer |
| 3/6 | Compile completed narrative for final review, page allowance, attachments, and forms | writer |
| 3/6–3/9 | Outstanding forms, signatures, letters, etc. | writer and team |
| 3/10 | Ship date for arrival by 3/11 | writer |

## A Checklist of Procedures and Tasks

The following tasks will become second nature as you write more and more grant proposals. Here are some of the things you must be sure to accomplish prior to writing:

- Outline the grant following the outline of the RFP/guidelines.
- Brainstorm and list potential collaborations.
- Contact potential collaborators to participate in project design meetings.
- Develop a calendar of draft submissions and reviews with anyone who has agreed to review the proposal.
- Develop list of outstanding documents. Establish who or where these documents will come from.
- Write letters of support, send them to signers, and set a deadline for return of signed originals.
- Set up a file folder with separate sections for narrative drafts, forms, original letters and attachments, RFP/guidelines, and background materials.
- Make a list of data required and potential sources for data. Include phone numbers and contact names in case you can assign this job to a grant-seeking team member.

## Chapter 10

# (E) Planning for Letters of Support

Experienced grant writers will tell you that if you fail to plan ahead for your letters of support, you'll pay with added stress and travel on proposal-mailing day. You must identify and contact people and sometimes even write their letters of support! You should plan on addressing this early in the process to ensure that all the letters arrive in time to be sent with your grant package.

# What Is a Letter of Support?

There are generally two types of letters of support. One is from an organization that is a partner to the project. Recently, this type of letter has been supplemented or replaced with a formal partnership agreement, which is required by some grantors.

The second type comes from community leaders, program collaborators, or organizational service recipients. These letters of support, as the term implies, validate the need for the program. In addition to providing support for the proposing agency and/or its program, they may also indicate ways in which others in the community are willing to support the project.

# Who Should Write It and Sign It?

The letter of support can be written by anyone. Since the grant writer is most familiar with the program and what has already been stated in the narrative, he or she often writes this letter.

The letter must, however, be signed by the head of the supporting organization. It also must be printed on that organization's letterhead and must be supplied as an original document. You may not rely on faxed copies. Therefore, you must make certain that the originals arrive at your office in time for you to attach them to the proposal.

**FACT**

For the most part, it's not difficult to get people to commit to writing letters of support. Everyone wants to see fellow organizations succeed in securing grants, particularly since they view government grants as a means of returning tax revenue to their community. What is more difficult is ensuring that people follow up on their commitments.

## Don't Procrastinate

Then there's the problem of procrastination. Perhaps because the letter is not a particularly difficult part of the project, it tends to be put off by both grant writers and executive directors until the very end of the process. If either one of you procrastinates, it gives you less time to make certain executives at the supporting organizations write their letters of support, sign the original letterhead copies, and get you the originals.

Your best bet, therefore, is to take charge early in the process, making sure the letters are written (or you have time to write them), signed, and delivered in a timely manner.

## When You Write Them

If you do write all the letters of support as a service to your client or employer, make sure they are all different. The best way to do that is to interview the agencies involved. That way you can learn unique things about each one and incorporate that information into the letter.

## When to Start Soliciting Letters

As soon as you know how many collaborators you'll have on the project, you must begin soliciting their letters of support. If you are writing them, you should e-mail your copy to them so they can print it on the organization's letterhead.

As you develop your schedule for completing the grant, add in a check-back point for those agencies that have agreed to write a letter of support but have not yet sent it in.

Request that the original letters be sent by mail or courier directly to you or to your client's office. Stress that they should be unfolded and sent in a large envelope. Your other option is to pick them up from each agency.

## Writing a Support Letter

Some support letters are overly generic. You don't want the judges to read, "This is a great project, so please fund it." Letters must be specific so that it's clear to the reader what exactly the organization is supporting.

For instance, is the letter-writing organization providing some sort of collaborative service to the project? Is it supporting the need statement and stating that its own constituents would take advantage of the proposed project? Is the letter a letter of agreement to jointly provide services? Or is it a letter from a leader in the community who is vouching for the organization's track record?

Letters of support should not be generic. Encourage your writers to state their commitments specifically. Provide them information or a draft proposal so they can link their commitments to those made in the proposal.

Support letters must state the fundamental components of the program that they are supporting—enough so that the reader knows the agency is familiar with the project and knows what exactly they are committing to doing. You'd be surprised at how often community organizations write letters of support without knowing what they are supporting.

## Sample Support Letters

The following examples show four different types of support letters. Each has a different function. In the first letter, the proposing agency and its primary partners signed the same letter and asked those affected by the program to sign in support of the project:

Date

We, the undersigned, understand that the XYZ project requires a strong network of caring individuals and service providers if it is to help create systemic change, improve the XXX community, and serve as a model of effective practices for reducing prostitution and its resulting social problems. We, therefore, commit ourselves and the organizations and agencies we represent to building and strengthening that network, to participating in the XYZ Advisory Committee, and to providing services judged important to helping prostitutes rebuild their lives.

Sincerely,
Chief of Police Department          University School of Social Work
Neighborhood Association           Social Work Agency

The second sample letter supports a need for services proposed by one agency and states that a local school district would take advantage of such services if they were available. You can tell that the writer has clearly read the proposal and knows what the grant writer has said about the school district and the planned project. She affirms the need for the project in the school district and links program outcomes to the district's student outcomes.

Date
Dear name:
On behalf of XXX Public Schools and our students, I strongly support the Mobile Media Laboratories planned for launch by the XYZ Nonprofit Organization in Fall, 2003. As you already know, our students come from families that range from wealthy to indigent. At one of our ten elementary schools, more than 90 percent of students participate in the Federal Free/Reduced Lunch program; at another, only 22 percent participate. The Mobile Media Lab will help us "level the playing field" for students who don't have access to home computers, high-speed Internet connections, or digital video cameras.

Every graduate of XXX Schools must meet our exit standards which mandate that students are effective communicators (expressing and listening), personal managers, quality producers, global citizens, critical/creative thinkers, and self-directed learners. Our job is to provide the tools that help students meet these standards and to change those tools as students, culture, and future worker requirements change. The Mobile Media Lab will assist us greatly in providing tools that will help our students gather and analyze information, make informed decisions, engage in creative communications, and explore new vehicles for teaching and learning.

The opportunity to link, through the lab's wireless connections, with

XYZ's television and radio stations or directly to the Web, is sure to generate excitement among our students. Media can be a strong motivator for more reluctant scholars, and broadcasting is sure to help some of our students overcome shyness and improve their self esteem.

We look forward to working with you and participating in an ongoing evaluation of the Mobile Media Lab and its programs.

Sincerely,

Assistant Superintendent for Curriculum and Instruction

The third comes from a community leader in support of a local agency. In this case, the author is president of a local foundation and is familiar with the work of the proposing nonprofit. A letter from a community leader or fellow funder has greater importance when sent to a foundation in the state or region—in other words, peer to peer. Such a letter would not be as necessary to a federal grant project.

Date

Dear name:

I strongly encourage the City Foundation to consider XYZ's grant application for improvements to the structure and programming at their Youth Center.

This program is critical to preventing juvenile delinquency and building the self esteem of inner-city youth in our community. When it was conceived nearly sixty years ago, it was the first in the nation to use police officers in the roles of mentors to at-risk youngsters; it remains a model for other communities in the nation for its success, longevity, and unique niche in meeting the needs of young people.

The XXX Foundation, one of the state's largest family foundations, has supported programming at the center despite the fact that the foundation does not generally support programs for teens, but rather, focuses its charitable giving on programs that provide early childhood development. This support is testament to XYZ's importance to prevention services in our community.

If I can answer any questions or provide additional information, please do not hesitate to contact me.

Sincerely,

Foundation President

The fourth sample is really two samples in one. The letters were required by the federal government and are, in essence, an agreement to partner on the project proposed.

Date

Dear name:

The process of grant proposal development is often beneficial, and the FAST opportunity has proved to be perhaps the most beneficial development process ever. As a result of discussions about our various programs, efforts, and goals, the state Small Business Development Center (state-SBDC) and the state Economic Development Corporation (state-EDC) have joined in partnership to focus on commercializing technologies developed by state-based entrepreneurs.

The state-SBDC will continue to work one-on-one with potential and current small business owners, and, with four new staff members, will intensify its efforts and expand its support network for technology innovators. The support network for technology innovators is automatically strengthened by the partnership with state-EDC, which has initiated the state Life Science Corridor, the Emerging Technology Fund, Smart Zones, and Venture Quest, among other of its efforts to strengthen our state's place in the "new economy."

The SBDC operates from twelve regional offices and thirty-one satellite offices throughout the state, each of which is affiliated with a regional college or university. Four technology-resources counselors (two hired by state-SBDC and two hired from grant funds, if we are successful) will cover the entire state, working closely with regional directors, small business counselors, and innovators to deliver the right combination of services needed to develop and commercialize innovative technologies.

We look forward to our working partnership with the state-EDC as we believe this is the best way to identify, reach, and support technology innovators and, ultimately, to bring life-enhancing and, sometimes, life-saving innovations to people who will benefit from them.

Sincerely,

State Director

Date

Dear name:

The state Economic Development Corporation (state-EDC) is proud to announce its newly created working partnership with the state Small Business Development Center (state-SBDC)—a strong addition to the statewide network of initiatives already launched in support of technology innovation and economic development in our state.

The state's economic development entity, the state-EDC has developed several entrepreneurial initiatives, including the state Life Science Corridor, Emerging Technology Challenge Fund, Smart Zones, Venture Quest, and a number of venture- and angel-capital-formation activities, as well as support for SBIR/STTR and other R&D grant seeking.

While we have undertaken creation of this large, statewide support system, we have not had a great deal of one-on-one experience with technology innovators. The partnership with state-SBDC allows us to deploy responses and resources individualized to the needs of each technology innovator.

The two organizations share a goal for commercializing technology innovations and securing the state's place in the "new economy." We are excited about this emerging partnership and its many possibilities.

Thank you for your review of our enclosed grant application. We look forward to your response.

Sincerely,

State-EDC President

# Knowing How Many Letters You Need

You must have letters of support from every formal partner and every organization highlighted as a collaborator in the grant proposal narrative. It sets up red flags if they are not included. Listen to what a program officer at a local foundation says about a grant proposal that did not contain such letters:

"I did a site visit after receipt of a program proposal I thought fit our mission well and held promise for providing early education services through a local college. The proposing college had stated that it was collaborating with three local agencies focused on child care, child abuse/neglect, and systemic services for indigent families.

Some letters of support are really partnership agreements and are required by the grantor. Make sure that, if you write them, you outline the scope of work for both partners.

"Something didn't feel right during the site visit. The proposers were evasive in their answers to some of my questions, particularly regarding the roles of their partners. I decided to investigate further. I called all three collaborating organizations and learned that they had never even heard of this project, let alone been asked to collaborate.

"Needless to say, the trustees of the foundation turned down the proposal."

It's also a good idea to provide as many letters as you can that support the case for need for the service you are proposing. Letters of support from leadership agencies and individuals are simply "icing" and can be attached or not, as you see fit.

Be sure to check the instructions for page limits on attachments. Select from the very best and most critical support letters if you have a limit. Also encourage all support letter writers to keep their missives to one page only. Ⓔ

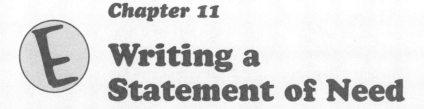

**Chapter 11**

# Writing a Statement of Need

Usually the first section of a grant proposal, the statement of need— also called a "case statement"—is your chance to introduce your organization and community to the proposal judges. Most often grants are awarded to communities where the need is greatest, so use data to support your case for funding.

# Introduce the Organization

The directions usually don't have a section in which you can introduce your organization. So the best place to tell them who you are and what you do is in the needs statement. Not only is the needs statement most often the first section of the proposal, but it's also where you will describe your community and your target population. Use this section to "set the stage" so that readers of the proposal begin to visualize how and why your proposed program will work.

Use data to introduce your organization. Tell the reader how many people you serve, what percentage of the population you reach, how many more people there are that you need to target for services, and any other numbers that help you introduce the organization and state the need for funding its services, such as standardized test scores among students.

# Selecting Appropriate Data

Data are the evidence you present to make your case. Find supporting data from your organization and other nonprofit agencies in your community. Just as in a court case, you must present irrefutable evidence of the need for action—and thus, funding.

The RFP will describe some necessary data, but you must be the judge of what other data you can gather to support your case. Some of the more unusual data Maggie has been asked to supply include the following:

- Rate of suicide or suicide attempts among high school students.
- Blood lead levels among children living in a specific area of the city.
- Rate of volunteerism among alternative education students.
- Purchase date of every piece of computer equipment in a building.
- Number of individuals in the United States who use a prosthetic arm or leg.
- Number of people in a city who speak a language other than English.
- Infant mortality rate by ethnicity, age of mother, family income, and native language of mother.
- Number of active prostitutes in a city.

If you are not confident in your math skills, buy a late-elementary math text to keep on your desk. It's as valuable to a grant writer as a dictionary, thesaurus, or style guide.

You will be asked to supply numbers to support your case and to form your evaluation of the program. Along with being a good writer, you will have to develop your research and mathematics skills. First you have to find the data and then you have to "crunch the numbers." For instance, you will often be given raw numbers when the RFP requests percentages or vice versa.

## Locating Data

Locating appropriate data can be difficult. Census data are helpful, but often they are not current or specific enough to support an emerging need. When a community has a low unemployment rate during the year of the census, for example, but then unemployment rates steadily rise over the next several years, census data can actually harm your case for a job-training program. While your local United Way may collect the data, they often must rely on information provided by member organizations. And generally the United Way organization does not verify those numbers.

### Best Sources for Data

Instead of going to the United Way, you'd be better off going directly to its member organizations. Individual and specific organizations are generally the best source for reliable data. For instance, if you need to know how many students receive the federal lunch program in a school district, you simply have to call the central district office to find out. Or if you need to know the number of AIDS cases in the current year, you could call the health department in your county or region. Call the police department for crime statistics; the juvenile court for teen delinquency rates; or the YWCA for domestic abuse cases.

Sometimes you'll just have to estimate. In those cases, tell the reader how you arrived at your estimate. For instance, to determine the number of prostitutes in a city, first find out the number of men and women arrested for prostitution. Go over the list with the police officers who cover the area where prostitutes are known to hang out. They will tell you which of the arrests are repeat offenders, especially since prostitutes often use different names when they are arrested. The police will also provide you a more accurate estimate than the arrest numbers indicate. You'd write something like, "In 2002, the police made more than 300 arrests of approximately 280 women and 15 men. Officers working with the population estimate that the number of active prostitutes on city streets and in known houses of prostitution is between 500 and 700 people."

Another good source of data can be a local or nearby university. Telephone the social sciences department and ask to speak to a researcher. Some really helpful university departments will assign graduate students to help you update old data or extrapolate pieces of data from aggregates.

### Clip Published Reports

You can also clip newspaper articles that you encounter throughout the year that may be related to the people your organization reaches. You can find stories on such things as increasing infant mortality rates, programs for teenage girls, and homelessness. The reporter has already gathered the data to support his or her article, so you can just clip the information and file it in a notebook, saving it for later so you have a source to go to the next time you need data for a grant proposal.

## Use Data to Support Your Case

It's not enough just to put the data requested in the RFP. Your next step is to use it well so that you can demonstrate that your community needs the particular service or program your organization is proposing.

Analyze why the RFP has asked for certain information and how relevant the data that you've gathered is to your program. For instance, you may have the data on teens who have attempted suicide, but do you use it to justify a case for additional computers in the schools? Typically you would use that data in grants about health or mental health services in the schools, about violence prevention, or about the need for alternative programs for teens who are struggling academically and/or socially, but there are exceptions.

> Don't let the numbers rush you to judgment. For instance, just because a large number of infants are born with HIV, you cannot conclude that a similar large number of them require out-of-home placement and care.

Sometimes your data are counterindicative. In other words, the data suggest that your organization or community does not have an overwhelming need for the services or programs for which you are applying. You can work around this. For instance, in the sample needs statement that you'll find at the end of this chapter, the writer states that the school district scored high on a state assessment of availability of computers in classrooms. But then the writer goes on to say that even though there are computers, test scores haven't improved and the computers are clearly not enhancing or improving learning. Now the writer has used the data to make a case for improved teacher training programs, perhaps for additional or improved software, and for targeted computer-assisted learning programs in the content areas.

## State Your Case

You must pull all the data together to form a "picture" of the situation and to set the stage for your proposed program. Make sure that the data support the program you are proposing. If you tell the reviewers, for instance, that 90 percent of prostitutes are drug abusers, then you should have a drug-abuse treatment or intervention program in your overall program.

If you describe a school district where 60 percent of teens are overweight, you should have built into your program a fitness component or even a weight-loss program that takes place in the schools.

Be coherent. This is where you lay a foundation for understanding why you selected the program you are now proposing. As with the foundation of a building, if you don't make a strong case here, everything you add later is in danger of collapse.

# Use a Gap Analysis

When you don't have a lot of data to support your need statement, you can pull together a team of people who are collaborating on the grant and have them help you perform a gap analysis.

A gap analysis is a means to identify hindrances or other roadblocks that might otherwise prevent you from achieving a desired goal. It forces a realistic look at the current situation and helps identify the things that need to be done to arrive at the desired future/goals.

Use your data (the present state of affairs), your outcomes (the desired future), and the gaps between them (the need). Following is a step-by-step method for a gap analysis.

## Identify the Future State

Where do you want to be? What's the desired outcome? Add detail to your goal statement. List the information and thoughts and details in a box labeled "desired future."

## Identify the Present State

How are things now? Describe the same components featured in the future state, but do so in present terms. For instance, state that you know that 90 percent of prostitutes are drug users. You know that approximately 2 percent of prostitutes are male transvestites. And you know that there are gay male prostitutes but that they are not on the street and you have no way of counting them or analyzing the extent of the problem. Again, be very detailed. Post the ideas generated in a box labeled "present state."

## Focus on the Gaps

Ask teammates and collaborators to talk through the following points:

- What are the gaps?
- What are the barriers to achieving the goals?
- What's missing in already existing services?

## Write a Needs Statement

Use the results of the gaps you focused on to assist in writing your needs statement. In the above example, the teammates found that there were no services that addressed the need for child care while prostitutes were in drug rehabilitation. Although they had other data (such as that regarding male prostitutes), they were more interested in addressing the greatest barrier they found, that relating to prostitutes seeking drug rehabilitation services.

# Citing Resources

While you don't have to cite every source of data or create a research paper with bibliography and footnotes, it is important to cite any experts you quote and to credit published reports from which you take data.

Add just a few resources and citations if they are available. Don't overdo it. For example, if you are writing about prostitution in your city, add some statistics about prostitution in general.

## Using National Stats

*Nationally, police departments are estimated to spend approximately 40 percent of their budgets on enforcing prostitution laws. It is time-consuming police work, requiring in many cases that officers pair up, obtain a solicitation form, and make an arrest of a suspected prostitute. Then they have to transport the woman to the police station or jail, complete fingerprinting and identification, write and file a report, and testify in court. Teams of police officers in other cities are estimated to spend twenty-one officer hours on each prostitution arrest. ("Prostitution Control Costs," Hastings Law Journal, April, 1987.)*

If you are able to cite national statistics and link them to the case in your own community, that's even better. In the above example, you might say: "Here in City, State, the police department receives no special budget allocation for battling prostitution. Instead, it works with courts, social service agencies, and others to share and reduce costs. It also has streamlined the arrest process to reduce the amount of time officers spend completing paperwork. Last year's 300 arrests cost the city only $10,000 (after fines were paid); police officers spent approximately fourteen hours per arrest."

## Sample Needs Statement

Use the first paragraph of the sample needs statement to introduce the organization and the community it serves.

City Public Schools (CPS) is a public school system serving nearly 6,000 children and young adults in kindergarten through twelfth grades, alternative education, preschool, and adult education programs. The district is composed of portions of the cities of City A and City B and of Township A. CPS includes eight elementary, two middle, one alternative, one alternative charter, and two high school buildings.

The predominant service area is the city of City A, which was built as a suburb of City just after World War II and was composed primarily of "tract" housing modeled after Levittown, Pennsylvania, developments. Although City A now has more diverse housing options, some industry, and much retail, according to experts on land-use trends, it is becoming increasingly poorer as upwardly mobile families move to more distant suburbs. Whereas in 1970, city residents earned exactly the average regional median income, by 1990, they earned only 87 percent of the regional median income. This decline is indicated in the City Public Schools as the number of children participating in the federal free/reduced lunch program has increased from approximately 10 percent in 1970 to 26 percent in the 1996–97 school year and to more than 29 percent in 1998–99.

Nevertheless, the City community has a history of supporting educational institutions and initiatives. Although many communities of comparable size have only one high school, City voters have continually approved school-support millages and bond issues that enable support of two high schools of 700–900 students, which Carnegie Institute researchers have found to be the most appropriate size for learning. One elementary school has garnered national attention for its experimentation with a longer school year and nearly 100-percent parental involvement. Parent participation at CPS elementary school conferences regularly exceeds 95 percent.

The community has also supported increased technology resources and learning opportunities for its children. In 1992 and 1997, the CPS community passed two bond issues for a combined total of $57 million ($14 and $43 million respectively). These bonds were used to provide computer connectivity (LAN/WAN network) in and across all CPS educational and support buildings, to purchase computer hardware, and to remodel, repair, and add to existing school buildings. Today, each school building has a twenty-five-station networked computer lab in its media center. One elementary school has an additional three to five computers in each classroom. The two middle schools have a second lab in addition to the one in the media center, and the two high schools have two labs in addition to the computers in their media centers.

Community support has enabled CPS to score "high-tech" on the STaR chart in the areas of connectivity and hardware. Computer-to-student ratios in buildings ranges from twelve-to-one in Elementary 1 to four-to-one in Elementary 2. The eight CPS elementary schools serve nearly 2,600 students (K–5) with approximately 370 computers. The combined ratio of computers to students in the elementary schools is seven-to-one.

To date, the hardware and connectivity have improved only the technological "look" of CPS schools, but they have failed to improve learning as measured on standardized tests. In fact, in all but a very few instances, test scores among CPS elementary students, despite additional tutorial resources and testing strategies, fell dramatically between the 1996–97 and 1997–98 school years.

The following chart indicates the percentage of CPS elementary students scoring satisfactorily on various sections of the 1997–98 State Educational Assessment Program (SEAP) and the percentile change between those scores and 1996–97 school-year scores. As is evident, all building scores declined in math. All but one declined in reading (and in the case of the one building that increased, scores are still less than 60 percent satisfactory). Only three buildings improved writing scores, though all buildings continue to exceed 60 percent satisfactory. Only two buildings improved in science and, in both cases, fewer than half of students scored satisfactorily despite increased annual scores.

| Building | Math 1997–1998 | Percentage Change | Reading 1997–1998 | Percentage Change |
|---|---|---|---|---|
| Elementary 1 | 84.6 | -7.7 | 57.7 | +25.8 |
| Elementary 2 | 92.9 | -8.6 | 60.5 | -33.6 |
| Elementary 3 | 82.9 | -4.8 | 70.7 | -21.9 |
| Elementary 4 | 63.9 | -20 | 38.5 | -21.6 |
| Elementary 5 | 75.4 | -16 | 51.7 | -23 |
| Elementary 6 | 70.2 | -10 | 53.2 | -3.2 |
| Elementary 7 | 50 | -17 | 38.2 | -9.9 |
| Elementary 8 | 88.5 | -11 | 68.5 | -4.8 |

| Building | Writing 1997–1998 | Percentage Change | Science 1997–1998 | Percentage Change |
|---|---|---|---|---|
| Elementary 1 | 78.9 | +30.8 | 47.4 | +9.4 |
| Elementary 2 | 80 | +20.8 | 32.3 | -1.7 |
| Elementary 3 | 63.9 | -40 | 41.7 | -2.9 |
| Elementary 4 | 73.3 | -14 | 49 | +2.7 |
| Elementary 5 | 66.7 | -36 | 46.2 | -16 |
| Elementary 6 | 66.7 | -43 | 36.7 | -1 |
| Elementary 7 | 62.5 | -11 | 17.5 | -20 |
| Elementary 8 | 93.3 | +7 | 57.4 | -21 |

To mitigate the effects of rising poverty levels and improve SEAP scores, CPS must put the hardware and LAN/WAN network to use as the learning tools they are meant to be. All CPS school buildings score "low-tech" in the areas of content/software, professional development, and instructional integration and use. CPS's first technology plan (1997) held outcome objectives for students to become computer proficient, but it did not emphasize the use of technology in content areas as tools to enhance learning. Since that plan was written and filed, CPS has had several changes in administration, including a new technology director and a new assistant superintendent.

The assistant superintendent comes from direct experience in the schools, specifically as principal of a model elementary school, and understands the importance of integrating technology resources to improve academic outcomes. Both new administrators are in the process of revising the long-range technology plan and are committed to acquiring software, providing "just-in-time" training for teaching staff, and integrating the use of technology resources into all areas of instruction.

Note how the grant writer weaves in information about land use and makes it relevant to a grant proposing to address a need for technology resources among school children. Additionally, a STaR chart was used in this case by the state to help schools measure the number of computers they had, the age of the computers, the uses of the technology, and the comfort level of teachers with the equipment. The numbers were then compiled into a final measure of low-tech, medium-tech, and high-tech to demonstrate need in the various categories. Ⓔ

## Chapter 12

# Writing Goals, Objectives, and Outcomes

No part of the proposal is more important than the goals, objectives, and outcomes, which are usually a part of—and integral to—the project description. The granting agency wants to know what their money will achieve, and they want to know what evidence you'll be supplying to ensure them they've made a difference.

## What's the Distinction?

Goals are broad statements about what the program will accomplish or your mission(s) for the project. Outcomes are planned changes in the environment or people. Outcomes should be measurable. Objectives are the things that you'll plan to do in order to affect outcomes. Objectives must also be measurable. Other words you may encounter in describing goals, objectives, and outcomes include these:

- **Benchmarks:** The places along the way that will mark your progress. Think of them as mini-goals.
- **Activities:** The specific steps you will take to achieve objectives in the grant.
- **Indicators:** The measures you will use to determine periodically or at the end of the grant period whether you have met the objectives or outcomes of the grant.
- **Inputs (resources):** The items you'll need to carry out the objectives or activities (such as surveys, money, staff time, volunteer time, etc.).
- **Outputs:** Direct products from program activities (number of service units, number of participants, products developed, curricula developed, etc.).
- **Timeline:** A schedule for completion of objectives/activities.

**FACT**

In the last decade, "measurable outcomes" have taken the place of "goals and objectives" in many RFPs; however, others still ask for all three.

## Writing Goals: What Will You Accomplish?

Goals are the broad, overarching statements of purpose for your program. Ask yourself what the program will accomplish. For instance, a lead-hazard program may state its goal as "reducing the risk of lead hazards to children in inner-city homes." A health clinic may state a goal as "ensuring translation services to all non–English speaking clients."

Goals need not be measurable and can be fairly broad since you must include support for each in the form of objectives, activities, outcomes, benchmarks, and/or indicators. But be practical. A broad goal, such as "to change the world," would be ridiculous. Keep your goals realistic for the time frame of the grant and the money you are requesting. Remember that you must report on progress toward goals and outcomes at the end of the grant period or periodically during the grant period, so you'll want to make sure that the goal statements describe objectives that your organization is relatively sure it can meet.

## Writing Outcomes: What Will Change?

Outcomes are the basis for your evaluation plan. Ask yourself what will change as a result of your project and use the answers as outcomes. Then ask yourself how you will measure the change.

If you are implementing a project to make your local high school safer from school violence, you might plan on the following changes and measures that can be combined into an outcome statement:

- **What will change?** Students will not bring weapons to school.
- **How will we know?** Reduced number of students expelled for weapons; findings of random locker checks.
- **Outcome statement:** As an outcome of the safer schools program, results from four random locker checks will yield fewer weapons and at the end of year one, fewer students will have been expelled for weapons violations on school grounds.
- **What will change?** Teachers will be able to identify behaviors indicative of propensity for school violence and take appropriate intervention measures.
- **How will we know?** Number of teachers attending workshops provided by FBI school-violence specialist; number of teachers scoring high on workshop learning reviews; number of students referred to counseling for suspicious behaviors.
- **Outcome statement:** As a result of workshops conducted by FBI school-violence specialists, teachers will be better equipped to identify behaviors that signal school violence and make appropriate system

referrals for troubled students as indicated by an increased number of teacher referrals to counseling specialists and the reasons for referrals.

- **What will change?** Fighting on school grounds will decrease.
- **How will we know?** Fewer suspensions/expulsions for fighting; referrals for counseling; number of students participating in peer dispute resolution sessions.
- **Outcome statement:** Fighting on school grounds will decrease as indicated by comparative data on school disciplinary actions and by the number and results of student peer-dispute resolution sessions.

Outcomes, goals, and objectives are your answers to four questions: What will you accomplish, how will you accomplish it, what will change, and how will you know?

Some outcomes cannot be achieved during the grant period, even in a three-year funded project. After all, real change is slow. When you report on your outcomes, you should be sure that you report progress toward the outcomes even when you cannot report having achieved the change permanently.

## Writing Objectives: What Will You Do?

Objectives are a running list of activities, projects, seminars, and other events or items you will produce, participate in, and/or use to achieve the goals and outcomes of a project. Objectives must be measurable.

Using the example of a safer schools program, some objectives might include the following:

- At least 80 percent of staff members will attend at least one of three FBI-led seminars focusing on identifying indicators for school violence and possible actions teachers can take.
- At least thirty more students than last year will be referred for counseling services because of indicators for violence.
- At least fifty students will be trained to perform peer mediation.

At least 400 students will participate in peer mediation services in year one.
- Random locker checks will be performed four times during the school year.
- The school will rewrite its policies and procedures for dealing with violence on school grounds. New guidelines will be distributed to all students, signed, and returned to homeroom teachers. New guidelines will be mailed to 40,000 households in the school district that receive the district newsletter.

Note how the objectives are measured so that later you will be able to write a progress report based on how many objectives you have accomplished and to what degree. Unlike outcomes, you must achieve as many of the objectives as possible and to the degree that you state. So while you're writing, be realistic.

Writing objectives is a balancing act. You have to promise to do enough to interest funders, yet not over-promise so you set your organization up to fail.

It's nice to promise, for instance, that 100 percent of the teachers will attend a seminar, but the truth is more likely that at least 10 percent won't. If the teachers are not being reimbursed for their time, you may not be able to expect more than a 50 percent turnout. Discuss these eventualities candidly in your review of the writing to make sure that your client or employer can truly commit to the objectives.

## Putting It All Together

Following is a program outline for Museums Are Fun for Everyone that includes goals, objectives, outcomes, and indicators. Note the differences in language used to respond to an RFP that called for a purpose statement, services, outcomes, and indicators.

## PROGRAM TITLE
Museums Are Fun for Everyone

## PROGRAM PURPOSE (GOAL)
The Museum provides a series of workshops about its programs for mothers and two- to five-year-olds from the Hills High School parenting program and Cabot Park neighborhood to increase visits by local families and to increase the museum comfort level of mothers who rarely or never visit the museum.

## PROGRAM SERVICES (OBJECTIVES)
1. Make outreach visits to Hills High School and Head Start parent meetings.
2. Provide three Saturday workshops for target mothers and children.
3. Provide three after-school workshops for target mothers and children.

## INTENDED OUTCOMES
Mothers from Cabot Park and Hills High will feel more comfortable bringing kids to the museum, and these families will use the museum more.

## INDICATORS
(a) The number of participating mothers who report their comfort in bringing kids to the museum increased to at least four on a five-point scale, and (b) the number of Cabot Park and Hills High visitors in Kids' Week 2002.

## DATA SOURCE(S)
(a) Questionnaire and phone survey for all mothers who participate in a workshop and (b) random exit interviews of adults who visit the Museum with children during Kids' Week 2001, repeated in Kids' Week 2002.

## TARGET FOR CHANGE
(a) Participants' reported comfort level goes up 75 percent or more from workshop one to six weeks after workshop three, and (b) visits by target

families increase from less than 1 percent in Kids' Week 2001 to 10 percent in Kids' Week 2002. In the project described above, the goal is to increase the comfort level of mothers visiting the museum, with the longer term goal of increasing museum visits by families. The project will ask mothers who participate in the workshops to rate their comfort level in the museum on a simple scale ("five equals very comfortable, one equals not at all comfortable") to show that mothers feel more comfortable in the museum after the workshops. During Kids' Weeks 2001 and 2002, it will compare information about where visitors live to see whether the workshop series increased visitors from the target neighborhoods.

▲ Sample outline for a new program.

Questionnaires and interviews can be very short. They provide the opportunity to ask other important planning questions. Of course there might be other explanations for a rise in local Kids' Week attendance, but if the museum did not make major changes in the program or publicity, it will be reasonable to think the workshops made a difference. Outcome-based evaluation has different goals from research or many visitor studies—it simply seeks to document the extent to which a program achieved its purposes.

## It's Measurable, But Is It Important?

Don't get trapped by a common error. In the effort to create measurable objectives and outcomes, some organizations make promises to do something that nobody cares whether they do or not.

In the above example on dealing with school violence, for instance, the fact that the organization is offering three seminars by an FBI specialist means nothing unless people attend. Furthermore, unless attendance and learning in the seminar translates into action on the part of teachers—measurable action—the mere presence of someone from the FBI is not very important either.

# Completing a Project Description

While the goals and objectives and outcomes are the most critical part of the project description, they are not the only components. You also must provide a narrative introduction and explanations, often a timeline of activities, and a rationale for why you've chosen one method or project over another.

You may be asked to address several other issues or requirements within the section, including but not limited to the following:

- Stakeholder involvement in project design
- Partners to the project and their roles
- Research findings regarding the project
- Projected benefits to constituency
- Professional development activities related to the project
- Strategies
- Programmatic divisions and separate goals for each

# Sample Project Description

The following sample is in response to a state Department of Education RFP that required a purpose statement and goals and objectives but that did not request outcomes. The available funds were targeted more toward capital expenses for technology equipment or infrastructure.

In this sample response, the granting agent did not assume that an investment in technology would yield social change, so it did not request outcome-based measurement.

Tell the people reviewing your grant what the need is and make the link between the response and the need statement through measurable objectives. Report local data and use footnotes to support the use of research material that references national studies. Describe how your community's needs are the same or worse than others in the nation.

## PROJECT DESCRIPTION

The purpose of the school district's technology project is to equip the district with a fiber-optic WAN/LAN and to deliver the professional development/training its staff requires to meet the following goals:

- (a) incorporate technology to teach to the state and district outcome standards;
- (b) report student achievement of standards to parents, district, and state officials;
- (c) improve teaching strategies and methodologies for all students; and
- (d) improve communication channels and outreach with parents and community members.

All teachers will be required to attend at least fifteen hours of training in one or more of the following, depending on their proficiencies: CIMS, Word, Excel, PowerPoint, Internet, distance learning, and using e-mail and listservs, Web site development, and multimedia. Teachers will also participate in multimedia training that will enable them to incorporate voice/video/data opportunities into their classrooms.

Four of the elementary buildings, for instance, have environmental projects dealing with plant life, water resources, air quality, and wetlands. Fiber-optic lines would provide video capabilities to enable the teachers to share their school-ground environmental laboratories across the district. Teachers could also use the voice-video-data transfers to address shared concerns, become members of interdistrict learning groups, or communicate with the administrative office or parents of their students.

Classes for teachers on distance learning and maximizing their use of the fiber-optic WAN/LAN will be offered during the school year on release time or on an alternate schedule as proposed by staff.

Within one year, teachers will submit information about curriculum, homework, and standards for addition to the district Web site. Teachers will be encouraged and supported to develop their own Web sites to enhance communication with students, parents, and community members. In addition, teachers will develop e-mail connections between themselves and parents/students so that parents might contact teachers regarding specific questions about their children and students can submit homework or questions electronically.

Students without home computers will be encouraged to access Web sites from the multimedia computer labs in the upper-grade buildings and from the media-room computer in elementary schools. All students, beginning in third grade, will participate in at least one e-mail correspondence with their teacher(s).

### GOALS AND ACTIVITIES

Goals and activities/objectives are summarized here:

1. Incorporate technology to teach to the state and district outcome standards, to report student achievement of standards to parents, district, and state officials, and to improve teaching strategies and methodologies for all district students.
   - Objective 1.1: By December, 2002, install fiber-optic WAN-LAN to intra- and inter-connect all school buildings.
   - Objective 1.2: By August, 2003, connect Student-Report System software for tracking student achievement of standards, attendance, course outlines, and syllabi. Select software that can look for trends among standards and desegregate student achievement by standard.
   - Objective 1.3: By July, 2003, connect all computers to the district's intranet and to the Internet.
   - Objective 1.4: By June, 2004, provide professional development courses in distance-learning and use of VVD lines to share classroom activities.
2. Improve communication channels and outreach with parents and community members.
   - Objective 2.1: By December, 2003, establish a district-wide e-mail system.
   - Objective 2.2: By December, 2003, require teachers to submit information for inclusion on district Web site.
   - Objective 2.3: By June, 2004, establish listservs to facilitate communication between teachers and parents.

Tips that you can learn from this sample include the following:

- Whenever possible, provide concrete examples of program activities or strategies. It makes the project "come alive" for the reader and assures them that you really plan to move from theory to action.
- When neither the grant money nor the organization can ensure equal access to programs or equipment by all the target population, you must provide a solution. In this case, kids without home computers can use the media center at the school in the evening.
- It's not enough to apply for grants to purchase computers because your school needs them. Explain what you'll use them for and how they will improve educational outcomes for all students.

## Chapter 13

# Writing Action Plans and Timelines

**M**ost RFPs request a fully detailed plan of action—a step-by-step explanation of what the grantee organization will do and when. An action plan is the detailed map to achieving your goal. In this chapter you'll learn various ways of developing a detailed plan of action that answers the requirements of the RFP.

# What Are Action Steps?

In the same way that objectives are the steps toward achieving a goal, action steps are the next level of detail, the steps your organization will take to achieve the objective. For each objective you've listed, ask yourself how you will achieve that objective. For instance, following is the list of hypothetical objectives from Chapter 12.

- At least thirty more students will be referred for counseling services because of indicators for violence than were last year.
- At least fifty students will be trained to perform peer mediation. At least 400 students will participate in peer mediation services in year one.
- Random locker checks will be performed four times during the school year.
- The school will rewrite its policies and procedures for dealing with violence on school grounds. New guidelines will be distributed to all students, signed, and returned to homeroom teachers. New guidelines will be mailed to 40,000 households in the school district that receive the district newsletter.

The next step is to develop a plan to describe how you will achieve the objectives. Think about what it will take to do that. What will it take, for instance, for a school to perform four random locker checks during the school year? Obviously, at minimum, they will have to do the following: (a) identify a means for random selection of lockers; (b) plan a schedule to ensure that they perform the inspections four times within the nine-month school year; (c) identify what inspectors should look for during the inspections; (d) communicate the plan and goal to inspectors; and (e) develop a plan for reporting findings.

To fulfill the spirit of the objective, they also must have a plan ready for what they will do if they find drugs, guns, knives, or other contraband in the lockers. This step, however, would be better if made a part of the fourth objective to rewrite the school's policies and procedures for dealing with violence on school grounds.

# Who's Responsible?

An integral part of an action plan is assignment of responsibility, and by definition, accountability. In the example of random locker checks, assignment would likely go to the high school principal. It would be up to the principal then to assign inspectors, help identify the means of random selection, and ensure that the objective is met with no fewer than four locker inspections during the year.

Remember that you are often adding additional responsibilities to someone's job by assigning action steps. Try to have high-level administrators at your organization check with people before redefining or expanding their responsibilities, getting everyone on board up front. Grant money won't be used to increase the pay for their increased work.

Responsibility for training teachers to fulfill the first objective would fall to the district administrators. After training, it would fall to the teachers, and then ultimately, when you address accountability for achieving the objective, to the principal directly in charge of the teachers.

The organization implementing a funded project must assign responsibility for each objective or each step in the action plan, whether requested by the RFP or not. You can do that during the writing process by developing a grid or narrative that assigns responsibility. You can always change those reporting channels later if you need to. For instance, if between application and funding, the principal retires and a new one is hired, the district might want to reassign responsibility to the vice principal because he or she has been in the school longer and is more familiar with personnel and existing procedures.

The granting agent rarely, if ever, cares exactly who is responsible for achieving an objective. But they will care very much if the objective goes unfilled. Ultimately, if the funded organization fails to achieve its objectives, someone will be held accountable!

# How Long It Takes to Achieve Goals

No one has to tell you that nearly everything takes longer than you think it will. It's true about writing the grant narrative, and it's especially true about implementing a project. Grant awards are most often for one year or three years. If you have a one-year grant, you have to be very realistic in writing your plans about what can be accomplished in one year, especially when it's very likely that it will take even longer to meet all of the objectives. With three-year grants, obviously, you have more latitude in planning your timeline and meeting your goals.

## One-Year Projects

With a one-year project, you must make sure that your agency can accomplish what it sets out to do and that it can achieve or make progress toward the outcomes in one year or less. One-year action plans must be very detailed. Think of the year as being the first step in a long process of change—it will take longer than the grant period to reach your desired outcomes. Therefore, action plans should list just those steps your organization can make in one year, not all the effort that will take place later to achieve the outcome.

Assign every step, from developing a job description for a new position, to hiring that person, to sending out product bid requests, to purchasing them. This is a good way to give your organization two or three months early in the action plan to plan and put things into place before you have to launch the project.

One way to handle this task is by structuring the timeline for a year-long funded project by each month of the year, beginning in the month that the organization is likely to receive the grant funding.

## Three-Year Projects

If you are applying for a three-year grant, you must submit a three-year action plan. In three years you can come closer to achieving an outcome for change, so you can use many of your objectives and outcomes as the framework for a three-year action plan.

You do not have to be exact in your timeline. Provide a month-by-month breakdown for year one, and a much more generic timeline for years two and three, incorporating only recurring activities and next steps in the process that began in year one. At the end of the first year, you will write out a detailed action plan for year two. This will help you accomplish your stated goals in the time alloted.

## Detailed Action Plans

If you are asked to write a detailed action plan, it's implied (if not stated) that the grantor wants a timeline of activities. Besides, it's sometimes easier to develop a plan of action by asking yourself what needs to be done first, second, third, and so on, so your thought process becomes the structure of the plan. The third sample at the end of this chapter provides a simple illustration of a timeline-centered plan of action.

# Illustrating Goals

As stated earlier in this chapter, sometimes the questions about action plans, persons responsible, and the time frame of activities are asked as separate questions. More often, the RFP requests "a detailed plan of action that includes objectives, measures, persons responsible, action steps, and a time frame for accomplishments."

## Using Grids

In these cases, a grid is the most efficient way of communicating all the required information in a short amount of pages. Cells or tables available in most word-processing computer programs make such illustrations simple. Remember, however, that you will sometimes have six or more columns if you separate each topic.

Print grids horizontally. Extensively detailed action plans are best constructed on landscape-oriented pages. In fact, you may even want to write the entire grant narrative on landscape-oriented pages if you hate having to turn pages this way and that just to read the entire proposal.

## Using Diagrams

Process-oriented projects often require a diagram to illustrate the steps in planning. Continuous improvement, for instance, is a cyclical rather than a linear process. Grids don't work to illustrate concepts like the process of planning, doing, checking, and acting, which can be ongoing and may start anywhere in the process. Instead, illustrate these concepts with simple diagrams like the one below.

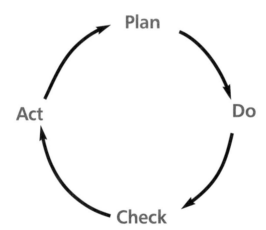

## Using Typeface and Gray-Scale Techniques

Most RFPs will specify that they do not want color graphs or charts. But when illustrating levels of information, you can use various fonts, typefaces, simple black-and-white graphs, gray-scale shading, and tables. Just be sure that your illustrations photocopy well. Copy that's lost in an improperly shaded box, for instance, counters your attempts to be clear and concise in your action plan.

**FACT**

If you choose to set off copy with different type styles, don't get too creative by using too many fonts. Your finished product will look more professional if you keep it simple.

# Sample Action Plans

The first sample action plan was developed for a health-care clinic. Organized by life cycle stages (perinatal, pediatric, adolescent, adult, and geriatric), it begins with a problem statement. Each problem then has a set of goals, objectives, action steps, and evaluation measures.

Note that timelines and the persons responsible for each step are incorporated into the chart. For instance, each objective begins with "by this month" (in correlation with the timeline) and each evaluation statement tells who is responsible for evaluating progress toward the objective. Timelines and responsible persons also may be called out separately in action plans.

These three different ways of presenting a timeline demonstrate the flexibility you'll have for presenting the requested information clearly and concisely, in a form that does not eat up excessive amounts of your page limits.

## Life Cycle–Stage Organization

Problem/Need Statement: "The population of this state ranks highest in the U.S. in incidence of chronic disease illness. 'Healthy County 2000' targets reducing preventable chronic disease incidence and mortality, focusing on cancer (173.8 per 100,000), cardiovascular disease and stroke (231.6 per 100,000), and diabetes (approximately 26,570 individuals). The poverty and cultures of the clinic's geriatric patients contribute to their high risk of developing one or more chronic illnesses. The clinic sees many patients for episodic care only and has developed objectives to increase prevention services to these patients."

Goal (funding): "To increase prevention-education and treatment for clinic's geriatric patients, thereby working to reduce incidence and mortality due to chronic diseases. (CHC funding)"

| Objectives | Action Steps | Evaluation and Data | Comments |
|---|---|---|---|
| J1: By December, 1996, 70 percent of all patients who visit will have had an annual risk assessment completed during an episodic visit in a calendar year. Risk assessments will include, as applicable: offers for health maintenance exam, pap test, immunizations and boosters, cancer screening, anemia testing, cardiovascular screening, prostate screening, mammograms, diabetes screening, and screening for depression, ADL, smoking/ alcohol/substance abuse, oral nutrition, and morbid obesity. | J1.a. Revise risk assessment forms for geriatric life cycles (change colors each year to indicate calendar year in which each risk assessment was completed).<br><br>J1.b. Providers document risk assessments performed.<br><br>J1.c. Providers document risk management plans in place, if indicated. | J1. Quarterly audits of ten randomly selected geriatric patient charts performed by coordinator. Results reported to medical director. | See appendix for sample risk assessment sheets that are currently being revised. |
| J2: By December, 1996, provide medication review for 8 percent of geriatric patients at risk of drug interactions. | J2.a. Add appropriate questions to patient progress note forms; e.g., "Has patient seen other providers since last visit?" "What medicines has patient been prescribed by other providers?" "What over-the-counter medications is patient taking?" Document responses.<br><br>J2.b. Audit progress notes to ensure that providers ask questions. | J2. Revised patient progress notes: clinical coordinator to audit quarterly ten randomly selected geriatric patient charts. Results reported to medical director. | See appendix for same risk assessment sheets, which will be revised. |

▲ Action plan organized under a problem statement, showing a set of goals and objectives for the named problem.

# Horizontal Landscape

The second example is from a community problem-solving organization. This horizontal (landscape) timeline is a good way to graph activities that are scheduled to take place over a period of months, a year, or more. You'll see activities for five months in this sample.

| | Month 1 | Month 2 | Month 3 | Month 4 | Month 5 |
|---|---|---|---|---|---|
| Activity A | Observe funder staff systems thinking workshop<br><br>Hold ABC focus groups | Participate in leadership planning for final visioning retreat | Synthesize learning from previous activities<br><br>Identify and attend at least one community meeting | Identify and attend at least one community meeting | Continue community engagement; triweekly design team meetings.<br><br>Identify and attend at least one community meeting |
| Activity B | Triweekly meetings of design team for community engagement process.<br><br>Identify and attend at least one community meeting. | | Hold first systems thinking workshop for twenty-four diverse leaders as nominated/selected from advisory committee and leadership | Synthesize learning from first systems thinking workshop | Synthesize learning from community meetings |
| Associated Costs | | $3,000 (facilitators, food for activity B) | $12,000 (facilitator materials, food, lodging, logistics, for activity B) | $5,000 (facility, facilitators, publicity, and materials for activity A, which continues for several months) | |

▲ Action plan organized by activity.

# Timeline Example

The last sample is a simple timeline of a year's activities for each of the first twelve months. Begin timeline with the month in which funding is likely to be approved. Whether as dots on a chart or in narrative form (as "monthly" indicates in the timeline sample), be sure to identify recurring activities throughout the project. Also, continuous improvement is, by definition, recurring and continuous. Be sure to illustrate evaluation steps that lend themselves to constant review and program revision.

**JUNE:** Announce to local media memberships of partner organizations and citizens, the grant award, and launch of the commission. Finalize job description and seek applicants for project coordinator.

**JULY:** Interview and select project coordinator.

**MONTHLY:** Convene meetings of commission; select, and schedule speakers and/or expert consultants for gathering information and sharing lessons learned.

**AUGUST–JANUARY:** Gather data from Information Infrastructure providers, businesses, and others needed to identify current infrastructure.

**JANUARY:** Map current public-access sites and disseminate to sites frequented by those who are believed to lack access to computer equipment. (Note: This activity is funded by the Community Foundation.) Hold "town meeting" to encourage input by commission nonmembers on issues regarding technology infrastructure and digital divide.

**JANUARY–APRIL:** With professional facilitator and available data, develop vision, key findings, and recommendations for the Information Infrastructure.

**APRIL:** Perform SWOT on data, findings, and draft recommendations; identify gaps between preferred infrastructure and existing infrastructure.

**MAY:** Begin mapping process for inclusion in commission report. Report evaluation of the planning process and grant expenditures.

▲ Action plan organized by a timeline.

# Balancing Ambition with Realism

Often, once an organization has been granted funding, its members suddenly feel overwhelmed looking at the action plan and think (even though they approved the action plan during the proposal stage), "How are we going to get all this done in a year?"

This is a common struggle. Most nonprofits just don't have the capacity to be ready to launch a new program the minute they are awarded the funding. Often the project implementation schedule is two or three months, sometimes more, behind the schedule (timeline) that was included in the proposal.

The grant writer must strike a balance between setting forth an action plan and schedule that are sufficiently ambitious to get the grant and setting a schedule that is not unrealistic. And it's not only because the organization will struggle to get started. Many grants are turned down because the action plan is unrealistic. Grant reviewers have been there— they know when you overpromise.

**ALERT!**

Set aside the first month or two of your action plan for tasks your organization can accomplish quickly while you prepare to implement the newly funded project.

Be thorough and detailed. Promise on behalf of your client or employer enough work to accomplish the stated goals, but not so much that even the grant readers shake their heads in disbelief.

Also be sure to write a paragraph about the capacity of the organization. Will it need additional staff to lead or carry out the project? Schedule at least thirty days early in the action plan for finding those people. ⓔ

## Chapter 14

# Designing an Evaluation Plan

How will you know if your program is working? Almost no layperson knows how to develop and write an evaluation. Even when they try, they are unsure and tentative. In this chapter, you'll get guidance on the language and approach to evaluation plans and the assurance that you can, indeed, write one with confidence.

# The Language of Evaluators

Evaluators have their own language. It's important that you learn to use this language when writing grant-program evaluations, not only because the evaluation is a critical part of the grant proposal but also because using the language of evaluators adds authority to your grant writing.

This list includes some of the most common terminology:

- **Qualitative:** Means of measuring objectives with "soft" data, including opinion surveys, individual stories from participants and staff, etc. Remember the root word "quality" to determine the difference between qualitative and quantitative.
- **Quantitative:** Means of measuring objectives with "hard" data (that is, numbers). Remember the root word "quantity" to determine the difference between quantitative and qualitative.
- **Operationalize:** Act of forming measurable outcomes from aims and goals of the grant program.
- **Longitudinal study:** Study of change over a specified time period.
- **Anecdotal evidence:** Stories from participants or staff. A part of a qualitative (soft data) measure.
- **Indicators:** Level of measures that will determine success.
- **Learning history:** Particular type of evaluation, useful for projects that are highly process-oriented and do not lend themselves to quantitative evaluation. Formed from written documents such as meeting minutes and interviews of participants.
- **Assessment:** Measurement tool.
- **Continuous improvement:** Use of indicators and evaluation to determine ways the project can improve its services.
- **Benchmarks:** Data on the current status of the problem that the evaluator can use to measure subsequent changes.

You don't have to be a professional evaluator to write an evaluation. You just need to speak the language.

# Types of Evaluations

There are internal, external, and national evaluations. Internal evaluations are those performed by project personnel as a part of the project. External evaluations are performed by a consultant hired by the organization to perform the service.

National evaluations are cross-organizational, cross-project evaluations performed by the granting agency to determine the effectiveness of a particular type of project in its various geographic locations.

**FACT**

National evaluations are strong learning tools for all participants. They share results of all their evaluations as well as plans, remedial efforts to fix what doesn't work, and success stories.

## Mandatory Evaluations

Sometimes an RFP will mandate an external evaluation or both an external and a national evaluation project. If an external evaluator has to be called in, the granting agency will mandate a budget line item that will pay the cost. It's usually a percentage of the overall grant request. If your agency participates in a national evaluation project, there are no extra charges.

## External Evaluations

When an external evaluation is commissioned, it is likely to be performed by a nearby or state university/college department, by the local United Way, or by a national organization under which your organization operates (such as a media-technology support organization, a health studies group, etc.). When the type of evaluation is not predetermined, you and your organization can choose the most appropriate means of evaluating the project, as well as the person who will perform it.

## Evaluating Small Grants

Generally the smaller the grant request, the less stringent the grantor is about the form of the evaluation. Small grants may be evaluated by something as simple as a survey developed by project staff that asks participants about their impressions of a new building façade or what they learned at a seminar or whatever else was funded.

You can write a grant requesting money just for evaluation. If your project is up and running, you might ask the local United Way or community foundation to fund a learning history or a cost-effectiveness study.

## Asking the Right Questions

The best way to begin an evaluation plan is to ask yourself what you and the grantor hope to achieve or learn, then develop a process to identify and measure your success.

The following list of questions was developed for a long-term community improvement project involving public transportation. The agency recognized from the start that it would take a number of years to see any meaningful changes taking place in the use of public transportation and the habits of people in the community. Nevertheless, the agency wanted to measure any small steps taken in that direction. To do it, the agency decided to conduct an annual evaluation.

- Have we developed a shared vision statement for improving transportation that is accepted by the entire community? Is the statement applicable to all social, environmental, and economic issues?
- What has been our work with existing community initiatives? Has there been progress in merging like initiatives, particularly those that are cross-cluster or cross-sector? Is participation in these initiatives increasing and does participation reflect the community's diversity?
- Are participants in events and meetings surrounding the project and its action teams diverse in age, opinion, ethnicity, income, gender, and residence?
- Are problem-solving models and strategies readily available? Are they being requested? Used?

- Have we collected and shared data? To what degree? What is missing?
- What are the agreed-on measures of success? Are benchmarks available for all areas of agreement?
- With what communities have we communicated to share information and lessons? What new connections among individuals, organizations, and/or sectors have grown from the project and its transportation action team?

**FACT**

Remember you can learn what the granting agency wants by reviewing the guidelines or RFPs.

Weigh both the grantor and grantee goals. Be sure to ask both questions: what your organization hopes to learn, and what the granting agent hopes to learn. Blend the questions together to form the basis for your evaluation plan.

## Determining Results

Once the questions are listed, ask yourself how you can find the answers. For instance, in the questions posed above, how will the organization find out if its action teams are diverse? Clearly, the organization must survey participants about their opinions, ages, ethnicity, income, neighborhood, and gender.

If the organization asks about gender, for example, it will become apparent after just a few meetings if it lacks women. Then it can target that group to ensure (the operative word signaling success of the evaluation criteria) that the action teams become a good cross-section of participants.

In the first evaluation sample at the end of this chapter, one of the things the organization wants to learn is the long-term effect of a ninth-grade adventure camp experience. The evaluator, therefore, might be asked to develop a series of surveys and other evaluative tools to test the effects. One could take place at the end of the camping experience, a second at the end of ninth grade, and the others, perhaps, could be scheduled annually thereafter. This might be the best way to determine whether the learning at the adventure camp has changed the lives of its participants, either for better or worse.

An evaluation of a hypothesis (for instance, that ninth graders will have a life-altering experience at an adventure camp) need not be proven true in order to have a successful evaluation. The evaluation is a success even if the hypothesis turns out to be false.

## Linking Evaluation to Goals and Objectives

If you've written strong goals and objectives, half the work of writing the evaluation section is complete. Return to your project plan. Pull out every objective or outcome, and repeat it in this section. Use the indicators you developed for the objectives/outcomes, if any, or establish indicators in the evaluation section as the measures of effectiveness for each of your objectives.

The strongest grant proposals make the link between the project goals and objectives and the evaluation plan. If your goal is to improve the public transportation system and you have objectives regarding marketing, additional stops for buses, new times for bus routes, and similar efforts, you can develop an evaluation plan that addresses the overall success toward reaching your goal. In this case, you would measure ridership both before and after implementation of the objectives. Then you can determine whether the steps the transit authority took had the desired effect on the goal (that is, improving the public transportation system).

It's difficult to establish evaluation criteria or tests of capital projects. If the project has been built, clearly that is success. If it hasn't, the grantee should return any grant funds previously pledged. Nonetheless, foundations (generally the most appropriate funders of capital projects) want an evaluation section in their grant proposals. Keep it simple—say that the project will be judged successful if it is constructed on time and within budget. This is likely to be as detailed as you need to get.

# Sample Evaluation Plans

The following sample was written to address an RFP mandate for a local (external) evaluator to be hired by the project. The RFP also stipulated that the evaluation would be coordinated with a national evaluation process for all similar projects in the United States that were designed and funded by the federal grantor.

This grant proposal lists the numerous components of a program that addresses the entire life cycle (infants to seniors) and, therefore, requires extensive evaluation to address each of the components.

The school district and its local partners to the project agree to participate in a national evaluation of the Safe Schools–Healthy Students Initiative, which will collect data on student-risk indicators and outcomes of the programs implemented across sites on an annual basis. Further, the local evaluator will:

- Help district strategically plan activities that will achieve the program goals and objectives.
- Respond to the direction of the national evaluator to ensure the collection of high-quality core data.
- Design and implement a process evaluation of the local program with assistance from the national evaluator to show results achieved as appropriate.
- Provide district with data that can be used to make adjustments in service delivery and improve the overall program.
- Design and conduct an outcome evaluation to determine whether an intervention is producing its intended effects.

Specifically, the local evaluator, Dr. T. of State University's School of Public Administration and director of the Office of Community Research, will assist the partnership in all forms of interim, annual, and final evaluations. She will teach staff how to gather and log appropriate data to track the progress of the district's Safe Schools–Healthy Students Initiative and all students.

Academic and other appropriate data on all students will be gathered continuously by district staff as advised by the local evaluator and reviewed quarterly in reports to the project partners to ensure immediate responses to weaknesses in the plan.

The Search Institute survey of assets was given to district seventh, ninth, and eleventh graders in 2000 and in 2002 and is scheduled to be given again in 2004. In this way, the district is able to gather comparative data on cohorts of young people (i.e., the ninth graders tested in 2002 were mostly the same seventh graders tested in 2000). The year 2004 asset-survey responses will provide a baseline measure of assets early in the proposed process of involving the entire community in building assets. A fourth survey (second during the grant period) in 2004 will measure the effect of the community process on the youth.

Healthy Communities–Healthy Youth has compiled the following list of fifteen characteristics of asset-building communities. The local evaluator will operationalize these characteristics to establish benchmark measures for the city community in the first year of the grant. By the end of the three-year process, the district and its partners will have demonstrated progressive development in each of the characteristics listed:

1. All residents take personal responsibility for building assets in children and adolescents.
2. The community thinks and acts inter-generationally.
3. The community builds a consensus on values and boundaries that it seeks to articulate and model.
4. All children and teenagers frequently engage in service to others.
5. Families are supported, educated, and equipped to elevate asset-building to top priority.
6. All children and teenagers receive frequent expressions of support in both informal settings and in places where youth gather.
7. Neighborhoods are places of caring, support, and safety.
8. Schools—both elementary and secondary—mobilize to promote caring, clear boundaries and sustained relationships with adults.
9. Businesses establish family-friendly policies and embrace asset-building principles for young employees.

10. Virtually all youth ten to eighteen years old are involved in one or more club, team, or other youth-serving organization that see building assets as central to their mission.
11. The media (print, radio, television) repeatedly communicate the community's vision, support local mobilization efforts, and provide forums for sharing innovative actions taken by individuals and organizations.
12. All professionals and volunteers who work with youth receive training in asset building.
13. Youth have opportunities to serve, lead, and make decisions.
14. Religious institutions mobilize their resources to build assets both within their own programs and in the community.
15. The community-wide commitment to asset building is long-term and sustained.

Within the first six months of the grant period, the local evaluator will design a plan for evaluating all components of the initiative including, but not necessarily limited to:

- A longitudinal study of the effect of ninth-grade-retreat camp on the students' high school careers and number of assets.
- A sample population study of at least thirty toddlers from high-risk families and the effect of parent training/counseling and educational intervention on development and/or kindergarten readiness.
- A comparison of all sociological and academic data gathered in each of the three years of the grant project indicating reductions in such things as truancy/expulsion, dropping out, disputes in schools, teen depression, teen pregnancy, experimentation with alcohol/drugs, juvenile crime, and reports of abuse/neglect, and increases in state assessment test scores and academic performance against district outcome standards.
- A sample study of at least ten high-risk teens identified as potentially violent and the effect of intervention services on behavior and attitude.
- A comparative study on reported feelings of "safety" among students in each of the building levels: elementary, middle, freshman, and high school.

Here's another sample evaluation plan. This one employs what is known as a "log frame" model. A log frame, or logic model, uses the goals and objectives of the organization's work plan as the basis for continuous evaluation and improvement. You can learn more about logic model evaluation from your local United Way.

**Defining and Measuring Success:** This project will employ a Log Frame Model (also known as Logic Model) and Participatory Evaluation Process to evaluate effectiveness against a set of indicators. The methodology employs an independent evaluator working with program participants, ensures that evaluation is continuous, and involves program participants (e.g, family members, staff, and collaboration partners).

The independent evaluator will work with an evaluation team composed of neighborhood captains, family members from affected households, program staff, and members of the collaboration throughout the process. He or she will create the Log Frame Model and meet twice monthly with the evaluation team to track progress on the Logic Model and to measure effectiveness against indicators the team will establish to determine progress toward and effectiveness of the planned outcomes, goals and objectives, and activities of the project plan.

**Evaluation Dissemination and Project Replication:** Quarterly, the evaluator will provide a written report to the collaboration steering committee. The evaluator will provide an annual compilation report that will be made available to the collaboration steering committee and project funders. It will be the responsibility of the collaboration steering committee, working with the staff, to adjust the Logic Model in response to the findings of the evaluation team in order to maximize effectiveness of the project.

Once finalized and launched, the project model will be sent to the national foundation with a request for any information the foundation may have on other models for reducing lead hazard in the nation and for review as a replicable model for other communities.

**Constituency Involvement in Evaluation:** The Logic Model of evaluation includes constituents of the program in all aspects of evaluation.

## Chapter 15

## Developing a Budget and Budget Narrative

As you're developing the program, you'll also need to develop the budget needed to support the objectives. Perhaps there is an accountant within the organization who can work with you, but more often, you will probably be responsible for writing the budget and budget narrative yourself. This chapter gives you the information you need to develop a grant budget.

# How Much Can You Request?

Federal requests for proposals always list the total amount of money the department expects to have available for that project and a ceiling amount that they will grant to each successful project. Foundations, on the other hand, give a range of grant sizes and a typical grant. So they might write in the guidelines or catalog: "Range: $500 to $5,000. Typical grant size: $1,000."

This can be confusing to a new grant writer, especially those who have lived in a community for a long time. They've read or heard about donations made to certain projects and recall grants that don't match the published grant range and typical grant size or what they know about the funder's giving patterns.

When wealthy individuals give, it's based on this formula, in this order:

1. Who asks.
2. How they ask.
3. What they ask for.

## When to Ask for More

Follow your best intuition and best information about previous giving when you want to solicit a local foundation. Or simply ask the program officer directly if he or she can recommend a way to increase your request.

Remember our freelance grant writer, Maggie? She once called a program officer and asked if they'd consider 5 percent of a capital campaign. The program officer told her that if this was for an organization the foundation generally would support for programs, they might consider 10 percent. She said Maggie could apply for ten with the understanding that she might get less.

## When Less Is Better

On federal or state grants, never exceed the highest amount on the range of grant funds. In fact, it's wiser to ask for less. It's also wise to ask for an unusual amount, such as $272,241 if the published cap is $300,000. An unrounded number infers that you are asking only for the funding absolutely necessary to implement the project. It also tells them that you have gone into great detail in your search for pricing on budget line items.

**ALERT!**

Never ask for cents in a grant proposal, such as $272,241.22. And never use cents in your budget presentation. Stick with whole dollar amounts.

# Match Requirements

Match requirements are those monies required to "leverage" or qualify for a grant. That means that the applicant must, through its operations budget or other donations—such as in-kind donations of time, space, products, and/or staffing—offer a certain amount of funds in order to qualify for the grant. Most often, match is required up front by federal and state granting agencies. It also can be stipulated in the grant agreement established by foundations after you have received notice of a successful application.

## Match Tied to Sustainability Plans

Match is also linked to sustainability plans. For instance, the RFP may state that in year one, the applicant must provide a 25 percent match ($25 for every $100 requested); in year two, a 50 percent match; and in year three, a 75 percent match.

**FACT**

One good way to provide part of a cash match, particularly if you are asking for staff salaries in the grant, is to have a willing applicant donate the new staff person's benefits package as a cash match. (Benefits are usually calculated at 20 to 25 percent of the salary.)

These requirements are meant to encourage the applicant to begin planning immediately to incorporate the project into its annual budget by year four, when the grant expires. It also has the result—intended or unintended—of discouraging applications by organizations that are more interested in pursuing grant money than in implementing and sustaining a necessary service.

Read the fine print in the RFP regarding matching requirements. Is it a combination of allowable expenses, or must it be a cash match?

## Federal Financial Match Example

An RFP from the U.S. Department of Education says applicants receiving grant funds must maintain and document local resources at the following ratio:

- **Year one:** at least 10 percent of total project cost
- **Year two:** at least 20 percent of total project cost
- **Year three:** at least 30 percent of total project cost
- **Year four:** at least 40 percent of total project cost
- **Years five through eight:** at least 50 percent of total project cost
- **Years nine through twelve:** at least 65 percent of total project cost

The eligible applicant's share may be obtained from any source, including funds made available for programs under Title I, and may be provided in cash or as in-kind goods and services. All match items must be designated for the purposes of this project and must not be used to provide match to any other project.

To determine match, the requested amount is divided by the percentage that is the federal share of the project. Thus, a first-year project requesting $125,000 in federal funds will need to match with at least $13,888 ($125,000 divided by .90 = $138,888). To maintain that level of funding in the second year, the match would need to be increased to $31,250 ($125,000 divided by .80 = $156,250).

# In-Kind Support

In-kind support refers to those things that the organization and its partners, if any, are offering in addition to or in lieu of money. In-kind support includes such contributions as the following.

Remember, your in-kind donations can be applied to only one grant at a time. For instance, an in-kind donation of existing computer equipment for a newly hired project coordinator cannot also be used by the secretary for an entirely different project.

- **Staff time:** This is necessary when staff participate in such things as collaborative planning with others and are not paid additional wages for that participation.
- **Space and utilities:** If an organization is providing office space for a staff person, space and utilities for the space usually qualifies as an in-kind donation. This amount is usually available from the organization's accountant who has computed the cost of square footage and operational overhead (electricity, gas, etc.) to determine the value of a space donation. Telephone expenses are sometimes also included in the cost per square foot.
- **Volunteer hours:** Volunteer hours can be computed based on the average amount you would pay for comparable services in your community times the number of hours you can guarantee will be allocated to this project.
- **Products:** Existing products (such as desks and computer equipment) that merely have to be moved to an office for a new staff person count as in-kind donations. New product donations (for instance, software donated to a nonprofit organization) can be added as "cash match" if you document the value of the donation. Purchasing new equipment such as computers, furnishings, or telephones to support a staff position may be requested of grant funds or purchased by the applicant and offered in-kind.

## Multiyear Requests

The RFP will define whether the program and the request must cover one or more years. Multiyear projects have their pluses and minuses. First, on the plus side, a project that is funded for three years is pretty much assured of continuation funding at the level it really needs to prove itself.

The only instance in which the grantor will take away second and third year funds is if the grantee does not comply with the grant agreement. Before that happens, however, the grantee is likely to receive a warning and a set of goals it must achieve prior to being given year-two funding.

The negative side of multiyear requests is that it's difficult to plan anything three years in advance, whether for programming or budget. Granting agencies understand this, however, and thus provide some latitude in the level of detail you must provide for second- and third-year budgets and details of the project.

In planning a three-year budget, you will have to accomplish two competing objectives. You often must decrease grant funds over each of the years and at the same time, increase costs, such as salaries, that are likely to go up each year. Here is a sample multiyear budget that Maggie prepared for one of her clients:

| Expense | Year 1 | Year 2 | Year 3 |
| --- | --- | --- | --- |
| Personnel | 114,500 | 214,550 | 226,950 |
| Operating | 45,550 | 35,450 | 38,050 |
| TOTAL | 160,000 | 250,000 | 265,000 |
| Grant funding | 80,000 | 120,000 | 80,000 |
| Match funding | 80,000 | 130,000 | 185,000 |

In Maggie's multiyear budget example, the organization planned to receive grants totaling $80,000 in year one to leverage (qualify for) a state money match of $80,000. In year two, it had to raise $120,000 and in year three, $80,000. Granting agencies are inclined to view grants that leverage other donations favorably.

## Taking Care of Partners

If you are required to have partners in order to qualify for a grant program, then you must make sure that the partners are compensated for the services they provide under the project.

The federal Safe Schools–Healthy Students program grant, for instance, requires partnership among school districts, mental health services, and police. It also requires the school district to be the primary applicant and fiduciary (the "accountant") on the grant.

The successful school district applicant, therefore, must purchase the services of police and mental health organizations in order to fulfill the requirements of the funded program. And while you are writing the grant proposal, costs for these services must be determined and calculated as part of the budget.

Other purchased services, such as evaluation, are also calculated before you submit the proposal, so it's best to ask for estimates when you meet with all the project partners to design the program.

## Planning for Sustainability

Whether or not the RFP requests a narrative about sustainability or a budget that reflects such plans, you will be a greater asset to your clients or employer if you discuss the financial and programmatic needs that the project will have at the end of the grant period.

Often, you can counsel them to request one-time purchases (such as computers, furnishings, supplies, or cars) from a grant and put less of the award toward ongoing costs such as staff salaries and benefits. They'll eventually have to pay staff salaries out of the organization's budget anyway unless the project is abandoned.

## Writing the Budget Narrative

Whether you actually write the budget yourself or you receive one from your executive director or accountant, you do have to write the budget narrative. The narrative is your chance to explain how you developed this budget. Your narrative should include the following details:

- **Calculations:** If the project requires two full-time-equivalent (FTE) counselors, each working forty hours per week at $40,000 per year, you budget $80,000 per year. Over three years they will cost $240,000.

(If you need two half-time staff per year, you should request one FTE.)

- **Other sources of funding** if any, and their use.
- **Distribution of funding for the line item:** "Part from matching funds, part from the grant request."
- **Justification:** "$40,000 annual is the average salary of a certified counselor in this area."
- **Estimated or actual cost:** "The cost of software packages is $222 each if purchased through the state plan for mass purchases. ABC, therefore, requests twenty packages at an actual cost of $4,440." Or you can say, "Software packages are estimated at $225 each times twenty for a request of $4,500."

**ALERT!**

Remember to include only the costs that relate to this particular program and not ongoing administration costs that are not part of this grant proposal, unless you are applying for a general operating grant. In fact, you might even explain what will become of equipment after the project is over. Will it be donated or put to use for future projects?

## Citing Other Sources of Funding

When you are required to provide in-kind or matching funds, you must also indicate where you will be receiving those funds. Take a look at the example at the end of this chapter. It is a budget for launching a project that later received federal funding.

Another example is in the foundation grant proposal in Appendix D. The grant applicant stated in the budget narrative the source of all matching donations, including the $80,000 it received from a previously successful grant cited in the sample budget at the end of this chapter. If a budget narrative is not required, use footnotes in your budget spreadsheet to identify sources and values of other funding.

| Line Item | Total Cost (two years) | Requested of City Foundation | ABC Match | Community Match |
|---|---|---|---|---|
| **Capital Purchases** | | | | |
| Van and conversion equipment to include phone-switching equipment, storage, security, and generator | $30,000 | | | $30,000 |
| Laptop computers and DVD players, server, printer, and scanner | $20,000 | $5,000 | $5,000 | $10,000 |
| **Promotion** | | | | |
| Van printing and signage, posters, press kits, rental promotion, television and radio shots, collaborative planning, and promotion with community partners | $20,000 | $10,000 | | $10,000 |
| **Staff** | | | | |
| Vista/Americorp and Community Volunteers (equivalent) | $40,000 | | $40,000 | |
| One FTE supervisory/teaching staff to develop curriculum, deploy and operate program, and train staff and volunteers | $60,000 | $60,000 | | |
| **Maintenance** | | | | |
| Fuel, upgrades, Internet service fees, etc. | $10,000 | | $5,000 | $5,000 |
| **Overhead** | | | | |
| Staff and volunteer supervision, financial tracking and reporting, program oversight, and evaluation | $15,000 | $5,000 | | $10,000 |
| Totals | $195,000 | $80,000 | $50,000 | $65,000 |

ABC Nonprofit provides $50,000 in-kind and cash match and requests a grant of $80,000 to launch the project described: $65,000 to fully implement the project and achieve the stated outcomes will be sought from ABC's community partners and foundations. Line item detail follows:

**Capital Purchases:** ABC requires a van and equipment to launch the mobile media laboratory. A small portion ($5,000) of the total $50,000 capital expenditures is requested of the XYZ Foundation.

**Promotion:** The Mobile Media Laboratory is an opportunity for both ABC Nonprofit and the XYZ Foundation to build and enhance community relations. ABC, therefore, requests $10,000 from the XYZ Foundation for publicity, promotion, and community awareness. Furthermore, ABC will ensure that the project is called the "XYZ Foundation-sponsored Mobile Media Lab," a tagline that will be printed in all promotional materials and painted on the media van.

**Staff:** ABC has been granted the services of two Americorp volunteers whom it will assign to the project. The equivalent pay of an estimated $40,000 over two years is contributed by ABC to the project. ABC requests $60,000 from the funder to pay for two years' service from a project coordinator.

**Maintenance:** Ongoing maintenance and costs are charged to ABC and its community partners.

**Overhead:** ABC requests $5,000 of the $80,000 grant award to be allocated for fiscal oversight and program reporting.

**Community Match:** ABC Nonprofit and its technology planning partners described in this proposal are in the process of applying to area foundations and corporations for support of a comprehensive project to narrow the digital divide.

As a part of that overall plan, the mobile media lab project will receive portions of support granted to the partners. Other funding sources will include rental revenues and reduced costs for staffing afforded by the use of community and recently granted Americorps/Vista volunteers.

▲ This sample budget narrative can help guide you as you begin to create your own budget for your project.

# Sample Budget and Narrative

In this sample budget for a mobile media laboratory project, note that it has columns for total cost, money allocated to the project from the funder, the nonprofit's contribution, and a "community match."

Community match, in this case, is listed separately. It indicates that ABC nonprofit understands that, in order to completely implement the project, it must identify and apply for additional funding contributions above those requested of the funder and provided by the applicant.

Also note that although purchase of a van and equipment is the first logical step in the process of launching a mobile media laboratory, the funder has already indicated that it does not issue grants to support capital purchases. Therefore, the organization applied for funding based on the stated interests of the grantor and is determined to seek capital funding elsewhere.

A budget narrative is shown following the grid sample and describes the rationale for each line item.

Your most complete program proposal, whether it was created originally for a federal, state, or local funder, can become your "master grant proposal," and is a work in progress. Work on it continuously to break it down, move things around, and improve the narrative flow.

*Chapter 16*

# Other Grant Proposal Sections

Every RFP or set of guidelines has, by one title or another, a section on the community or market need, a project description, an evaluation, and a budget. Beyond that, however, you may be asked to respond to numerous and varied questions. This chapter provides information on responding to these other frequently encountered topics.

# What You May Encounter and Where

Although government grants, particularly federal ones, tend to want more detail in your narrative than foundations, you will find a wider variety of subjects to address among established foundations.

Partly this is because in recent years the Regional Associations of Grantmakers (RAG) have worked with the foundations to establish, in some areas, a standardized common grant proposal format. Since each foundation had input into creating the standard, the hybrid is far more comprehensive in its scope of questions than any one of the individual foundation's guidelines was before the standardization.

Many subject areas (such as educational programs, medical programs, technology transfer, etc.) have special questions asked in no other requests for proposals. For instance, educational grant providers often require a section on professional development to ensure that teachers are prepared to deliver the program described.

Medical grant RFPs may require a section responding to issues uncovered in an annual site visit and particular only to your clinic. You might be asked to address sanitation or safety measures implemented or the availability of foreign language interpreters during medical visits.

Technology transfers, medical grants, and experimentation grants always require sections on testing in human or animal subjects.

We've selected those sections that are most common and more applicable to a number of different types of projects. You are likely to encounter one or all of these at some point in your quest for grants.

Specialized sections that may appear on some more technical RFPs require specialized, and often expert, knowledge of the subject matter. You will know best how to address these; they are too specialized to cover in detail here.

# Collaboration/Partnership

Both government and foundation grantors hold collaboration and partnership in high esteem. They believe there's a cost savings in collaboration. While technically that still has to be proved, it is a cost savings to them since they are, at minimum, not funding two agencies to do similar projects or to address similar needs among identical populations.

Whenever possible, use information about your community to make collaborative links between and among organizations. Local funders know when you don't attempt to partner because they know pretty much everything that is going on in the community. State and national funders will know you aren't talking to others when they receive two RFP responses from the same geographic area. Politically, the worst thing your organization or employer can do is know that another agency in town is developing a project similar to yours and not extend a request for partnership.

## When You Partner

In a section on collaborations and partners, if requested, provide a narrative that:

- Lists the partners to the project.
- Provides a brief description of each partner's role in the project.
- Justifies the existence of the collaborative—why it was formed and "the beauty of it."
- Names a lead agency and/or a fiscal agent: The fiscal agent is the only organization that will receive funds. It will then purchase or pay for services from the other members of the collaborative.
- If appropriate, chronicles the history of collaboration between the organizations.

Stating that the collaborative was formed to respond to an RFP requirement, even if it's true, would be a huge and costly error in judgment.

## What If There's No Partner?

No partners or collaborators? Here's a short sample response from one such agency. Note that it addresses the need to coordinate services even though it does not directly partner with others:

> *"ABC collaborates with hundreds of area agencies to develop and/or deploy the assistance necessary in order to improve the lives of individuals and families in the target areas. ABC's role is to work with neighbors and community-based organizations to identify priority concerns and necessary remedial services, and to secure those services from the existing system rather than to duplicate what already exists. ABC also provides community outreach and public awareness in the target areas for the services provided by other agencies."*

# Review of Literature

A review of the literature will be quite familiar to English and sociology majors and at least understandable to anyone who's ever done a research paper. It is exactly that—a review of the research on a topic, cited and stated to support your case and explain the reason you selected the model for service that you did.

Federal departments and some selected medical-project funders are about the only grantors to require a review of literature. Especially in highly specialized areas such as medicine or electronics, if you are not well versed in the field, it is best to work with a professional researcher and/or expert in the field. It is often critical in specialized areas that you cite all the literature available on a subject. For a layperson, that search can be as exhausting as it is exhaustive.

Following is an abbreviated sample provided by an expert resource to a grant writer.

Lead poisoning has become an increasingly significant public health issue. According to the U.S. Centers for Disease Control and Prevention (CDC), nearly one million children in the United States have levels of lead in their blood high enough to cause irreversible health problems and to produce a variety of developmental challenges.

Research has shown that lead poisoning has a pervasive impact on the human body, impacting most of the physiological systems. Those most affected include the central nervous system, reproductive system, kidneys, and other (organs). At the higher levels, lead poisoning can cause coma, convulsions, and even death. But even at the lower levels, the presence of lead in the blood can severely limit a child's development. Some of the most significant consequences include diminished intelligence, limited neurobehavioral development, diminished physical growth and stature, and impaired hearing.

However, lead poisoning is completely preventable. Unlike many public health challenges, the environmental hazards that contribute to lead exposure can be abated and the threat of lead poisoning reduced. The only requirements are a willingness to invest in at-risk neighborhoods and a commitment on the part of key stakeholders at a national, state, local, and community level.

During the past decade, a variety of efforts have been initiated in neighborhoods across the country to remediate lead hazards and track the impact of these remediation strategies on public health indicators. In the City of Baltimore, for example, the city government has joined with nonprofit and development organizations to address the lead hazards in the home.

The primary weakness of many of these efforts, though, is that they fail to make connections among key stakeholders. Most have very little direct involvement by residents of affected neighborhoods and/or lack the necessary investments on the part of national organizations. Also, many of the initiatives fail to involve stakeholders from the public health or medical communities, or from research institutions which prevents them from tracking the impact of their efforts or advancing knowledge of lead poisoning in the scholarly community.

A review of existing literature on lead hazards results in numerous publications on risk analysis, lead hazard control, primary prevention strategies, and global prevention strategies. Little literature exists on the development of broad-based collaborations to ameliorate exposure and risk or on the potential for effectiveness of such collaborative efforts.

Note that the introductory paragraph states the number of children affected from national data. The author draws on further medical research, detailing why lead poisoning is a cause for concern. And again by drawing on national statistics and a review of literature on lead-abatement projects in other cities, the grant writer makes a case for how the proposed program will be different and why it is likely to be successful.

Reviews of literature for social or educational projects are much easier. Locate materials about the service model to use in your project description. Compare the selected service model with one or two others and tell why the one you selected is more appropriate to the needs of your population than the other. Cite your resources (if possible, four or five) and attach a bibliography to the narrative if requested.

## Staff Qualifications

This is a relatively simple section to respond to. Use the resumes of those working on the project staff to summarize their relevant experience. If their resumes are outdated, interview them briefly about more recent accomplishments. If the staff position is not filled, write a job description and list the responsibilities the person in that position will have.

If you are requesting grant funds for a position, you must not only outline the job responsibilities but also discuss at length the type of person the agency will be seeking (bilingual, degrees, years of experience, etc.). Be sure to include a brief plan for a personnel search and an equal opportunity statement from the bylaws of your organization when requesting funding for staff positions.

# Management Plans

The narrative describing management plans should center on the project rather than the entire organization. Do include, however, an overview of the organization and demonstrate where the proposed project fits into its mission and management structure. Illustrate reporting channels with graphs or organizational charts. Describe who is accountable for what aspect of the programming, and be sure to include a statement about fiscal accountability as a part of the management plan.

Let's look at a sample management plan. The following plan to improve and restructure a high school outlines the roles and duties of various personnel and administrators who will enable the district to meet its goals and objectives.

The high school principal will provide leadership in the high school community by building and maintaining a vision, direction, and focus for student learning. He will foster an atmosphere that encourages teachers to take risks to meet the needs of students. The superintendent and other administrators, with school board members, will exercise leadership in supporting the planning, implementation, and long-range momentum of improvement at the school level. Teachers will provide the leadership essential to the success of reform, collaborating with others in the educational community to redefine the role of the teacher and to identify sources of support for that redefined role.

Planning and implementation for the high school restructuring improvement is under the leadership of sixteen committees composed of community representatives, out-district educators, teachers, parents, students, and administrators.

Each larger grouping of committees (such as "school environment" or "assessment/accountability") has selected one of its committees to participate with a leader to consider requirements for accreditation.

Ultimately, district administrators and the high school principal will be responsible for ensuring the success of the restructuring and its outcomes for student learning. However, the team approach ensures that staff, students, and community are responsible for the success of this effort.

# Competing Programs/Agencies

Here's the Catch-22 on discussing your competition: If you list competing programs and/or agencies, you will have to say why they are not partners to the project. If you don't list them, the funder—particularly if it's a local foundation—likely will surmise that you are creating the project in a vacuum and deny your request.

Of course, the best-case scenario is when you have no competition. But most often that's only true if all of the competitors are part of a collaborative addressing the same issue. That leaves you with only one way to "win" this one.

Acknowledge what others in the community are doing, then describe the ways in which your organization or this particular project is different from what others are doing and/or ways in which the similar organizations remain specialized but are coordinating their efforts.

You can say: "LMNO, RST, and XYZ offer services for youth in the inner city; however, ABC is the only organization in the city to work in conjunction with the city police department and to provide police officers as mentors and coaches for youth in all of its programs.

"ABC's Camp was the first of its kind in the state to provide summer camping for low-income youth. Today, staff know of several camps providing experiences for at-risk and/or low-income children and adolescents, including GEF, LMN, and ZYX. Like the inner-city youth centers, however, ABC's camp has always been unique in that police officers participate with youth at camp as day counselors and coaches." With that, you've set your program apart from the others.

# Constituency Involvement

You may be asked to describe constituency involvement in the design of the program, in its evaluation, in its execution, or even in all three. Also, you may see this same request with different phrasing. For example, schools are asked to describe "parent involvement" and hospitals to describe "patient input."

## Empowerment

Consider this section this way: How would you feel if someone gave you a secondhand pair of shoes without ever asking you if you needed or wanted them? How would you feel if your local phone company came out with a statistic that said it had 100 percent customer satisfaction and you've had nothing but trouble with them? Wouldn't you say, "Well, they didn't ask me!"

## Putting a Face on the Statistics

Agencies should always talk up front with those who have a need to be sure that the statistics indicating need have "a face." That means that the program is designed in consultation with rather than for its beneficiaries. It's humiliating to be "provided for," and it is precisely this factor, many believe, that has spawned the so-called welfare mentality among the indigent and expectation of entitlement among the young.

**FACT**

This is such a critical and politically charged issue that even if the RFP doesn't ask the questions, write about it anyway. Write about the involvement of program beneficiaries in your project description whether you've been asked to or not.

Make certain your client talks to the people who will benefit from the services and finds out if they need the services or even want them. Then write about their participation in the section on constituency involvement.

## Sustainability Plans

Foundations and governments love to fund new and innovative projects. Very few, however, fund ongoing operations of an organization or a program that's more than three years old.

The biggest struggle among leaders in the nonprofit sector is finding operational funding to keep the doors open and the lights on, just so they can continue to do the good work they've already started. Often they'll create additional programs just to provide a portion of the overhead costs. But that puts them in an awkward situation because the more programs you invent—assuming they work—the more you have to maintain.

You can understand, then, that it can get a little tricky when you sit down to talk about how you're going to sustain a project over the long term, after it becomes institutionalized and, as such, a responsibility of an already stretched "operating" budget.

## A Good Plan Is Vital

This section, nonetheless, is the make-or-break point of consideration among foundation trustees and grant readers. Up front you must plan how you will put together the funding to sustain the program. You'll have to decide whether it will be through fees for service, partner funding, future grants or donations, operations, or, most likely, some combination of these income sources.

And most often you'll need a plan for sustaining the project for at least three years after the grant period ends.

The hard truth is that most projects really struggle when launch funding runs out. Often, they become a shadow of what they once were. The plus side of the equation is that the leadership of the organization can review its evaluation and eliminate what doesn't work. The negative side is that if a program works just the way it is, any adjustment will weaken it and the agency that operates it.

All that said, you are left with the responsibility of writing something as realistic as possible under rather unrealistic expectations.

## Sample Sustainability Plan

As you'll see in the following sample budget for sustainability, the agency tries to balance declining grant funds with increased fees for services.

### Year One: $432,500 Budget (grant year includes one-time capital investment)

| 45 percent local funding | ABC annual budget | $75,000 |
|---|---|---|
| | Fees for service | $3,000 |
| | Existing grant | $80,000 |
| | Donations and discounts | $40,000 |

*55 percent federal grant funding requested*

### Year Two: $175,000 Operating Budget

| 100 percent local funding | ABC annual budget | $25,000 |
|---|---|---|
| | Local grants | $100,000 |
| | Fees for occasional services | $5,000 |
| | Fees for regular service | $25,000 |
| | Local underwriters | $20,000 |

### Year Three: $175,000 Operating Budget

| 100 percent local funding | ABC annual budget | $30,000 |
|---|---|---|
| | Local grants | $75,000 |
| | Fees for occasional services | $10,000 |
| | Fees for regular service | $35,000 |
| | Local underwriters | $25,000 |

### Year Four: $175,000 Operating Budget

| 100 percent local funding | ABC annual budget | $50,000 |
|---|---|---|
| | Local grants | $30,000 |
| | Fees for occasional services | $15,000 |
| | Fees for regular service | $50,000 |
| | Local underwriters | $30,000 |

This nonprofit was smart. The minute they were awarded a federal grant, they began meeting with local funders to talk about what they'd need in year two and three. Over the next year, they sent program officers media articles about the project and evaluation results so they were well positioned to seek funding when the time came.

## Status of Fundraising Efforts

This section is often requested in local grants. It is appropriate when you are raising a large total sum from several different sources. For instance, you'll be requesting $100,000 from the community foundation, $200,000 from area corporations and corporate foundations, and $50,000 each from a couple of key donors.

The grantor wants to know whether you have submitted proposals to those identified funders—remember, they know who they are and they talk amongst each other—and the status of those proposals (that is, proposals that are submitted, planned, pending, or funded).

A sample response for a capital project might read like this:

*The state provided $37.1 million toward the center's development; private donors have provided $16 million. The capital campaign became public with $4 million needed. The XYZ Corporation Foundation has since committed $500,000.*

*Grant requests are pending with JJJ Family Foundation ($100,000 requested), NNN Foundation ($50,000 requested), and local philanthropist ($500,000 requested). Remaining corporate naming opportunities and a public "buy a brick" campaign are expected to raise the remainder of necessary funding.*

## Organizational History

Write this once, and you'll never have to write it again! No matter who the funder or what its priorities, the history of your organization is not going to change and neither is the "slant" you put on the story. Be sure to put in highlights of the organization, as you'll note in the following example.

> *The City County Art Association was founded in 1910 by a City Federation of Women's Clubs, which recommended the establishment of an art collection as a basis for a future art museum. In 1911 an initial collection was assembled, and in 1924 the association occupied a Greek Revival residence, which was eventually renamed the City Art Museum (CAM). In 1981 the museum moved to its present site, a Beaux Arts style Federal Building listed on the National Register of Historic Places and located in the city's downtown center.*
>
> *CAM's core collection now consists of more than 6,000 works of art from all cultures and periods, with special strengths in European art from Renaissance to nineteenth century, nineteenth- and twentieth-century regional and American art, and works on paper including prints, drawings, watercolors, and photographs. The museum has always placed the highest importance on its public education programs and continues to expand and diversify its classes, lectures, and events through collaborations and creative partnerships with other city institutions. The city's public sculpture program is supported by the museum's collection, which includes maquettes, drawings, and prints by major sculptors.*

Use the history of the organization as a place to record changes in mission, growth of services, and other interesting and relevant facts. In some ways, the history can be used to justify the project, especially when you can cite continued growth or demand.

## Funding Priorities

This section is the funder's way of asking, "If we can't fund you at the level you want us to, how would you like us to help you with a lesser amount?" There are several ways to handle this, as shown in the following examples.

## When Less Won't Do

In this sample, the organization is steadfast in its request for funding at the level requested and offers only an alternative in the length of the grant period:

> *The project proposed would require an XYZ Foundation grant of $600,000—$143,000 to complete the year-one outcome objectives, $253,000 to achieve the year-two outcome objectives, and $204,000 in the final year—to complete the project as described. An alternative would be to structure a five-year plan which would allow smaller per-year investments toward a slightly slowed developmental process.*

## When Any Amount Will Help

In the following sample response, the writer is saying, in effect, that whatever funding is available will be welcome and that the agency would appreciate the assistance of this funder in helping it get funding from other community sources.

> *Whether or not funding is available at the level requested, the coalition hopes that the foundation staff will consider assisting us in building a partnership of funders to share the three-year financial commitment necessary to achieve the stated objectives.*

## Offering Choices

This final sample offers the grantor some choices.

> *If the XYZ Foundation is unable to grant the full three-year request, ABC Nonprofit offers two alternatives: the first two years' funding at $60,400 and $42,280 respectively for a*

*total grant of $102,680, or the executive director salary only, in decreasing amounts as follows: $45,000 in year one, $31,500 in year two, and $22,050 in year three for a total grant of $98,550.*

# Challenge Grants

This is more likely a question than a whole section in the grant proposal. The funder wants to know if you are applying for a challenge grant, meaning that you want them to put up funds that you can use to challenge or enthuse other potential donors.

For example, if you want to raise $50,000, you could ask for a $25,000 one-to-one matching challenge. A word of caution, however. Under challenge grant agreements, if you don't raise $25,000 from other places, you don't get the $25,000 put up by the challenge funder.

**ALERT!**

Don't propose a challenge grant unless you are fairly certain you can raise the necessary match.

Say yes to a challenge grant opportunity when you are:

- Launching a capital or fundraising campaign and want to use the challenge grant to attract attention among funders.
- Entering the latter stages of a long fundraising campaign and want to challenge community donors to match one last gift.
- Confident of your ability to raise the matching funds.

If none of these is true, turn to a former First Lady for inspiration and "Just say 'no.'" Ⓔ

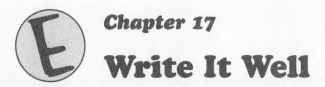

*Chapter 17*

# Write It Well

Good writing won't sell a bad program, but bad writing can sink a good one. You must write clearly, concisely, and simply—without oversimplifying—when writing grant proposals. In this chapter you'll get some tips from the pros on how to get it right.

# Use Everyday Language

Write plainly. You always have limited space, so you have to be brief and thorough. Often the judges must read from twenty to 100 proposals in just a few days. Yours will stand out and be memorable if your proposal is clear, concise, and jargon-free.

Here are some tips for stating it simply:

- Don't add unnecessary adverbs. Use strong action verbs instead.
- Use short sentences.
- Avoid redundancy, particularly within a sentence. (You may note, however, that questions in various sections of an RFP are somewhat similar, and that forces you to be repetitive.)
- Eliminate strings of prepositional phrases.
- Cut the fat from your sentences. Rather than saying, "The project we began last year addressed the needs of at-risk three-year-olds," write, "Last year, we addressed the needs of at-risk three-year-olds."
- Use short and fewer nouns in a sentence.

Consider the difference between these examples taken from *Line by Line,* by Claire Kehrwald Cook (Modern Language Association, Houghton Mifflin Company, 1984).

*"The inference that because high school graduates are more likely to be employed than dropouts, the differences may be attributed to the possession of a diploma is suspect since dropouts and graduates may differ in a variety of ways relevant to both graduation prospects and employment status."*

Compare that paragraph with this:

*"It is not necessarily the diploma that makes high school graduates more employable than dropouts; other differences may affect both their education and their job prospects."*

## Avoid Jargon

We've all been subjected to sociological changes in language. Two decades ago, no one used the word "impact" except as an adjective for a sore tooth or as a noun describing a car crash. Now it's not only accepted as a verb, but also has become overused to the point that it has lost its "impact."

To avoid using "impact," as a verb, learn the difference between "affect," and "effect," and use them appropriately. Usually, if you're tempted to write "impact," you want "affect."

"Proactive" has been done to death, especially when used in the phrase "proactive rather than reactive." Just say your team will be "active" in addressing issues as they arise. It means the same thing. Or even better, "The team will actively address issues as they arise."

Some jargon is specific to an industry or focus and, because it is used among peers only, it tends to put off your reading audience. For instance, if you were to tell someone who hasn't read this book and is unfamiliar with the grant writing process that you are reading the rubrics in an RFP, he or she could very well feel like you were trying to be secretive or trying to exclude them.

Cut the fat from your writing. You'll encounter at least one RFP that allows you ten pages in which to answer completely twenty or thirty questions.

Other forms of jargon are idiosyncratic ways of expressing yourself. While these "tics" are perfectly appropriate in spoken language, they muddy writing. Remember, you have limited space for describing your project, so you want to avoid turns of phrase and redundant words and descriptions. Also avoid too many prepositions—"off of"—and lengthy, redundant phases, such as "the reason is because . . . " or "due to the fact that . . ."

## Be Politically Correct

Using everyday language does not excuse street talk. Be politically correct, particularly when you are discussing individuals. Say "people with disabilities," not "disabled people." (Emphasize the person rather than the disability.)

Don't sensationalize a disability with such phrases as "afflicted with," "unfortunate," "pitiful," or "victim of." And don't use the word "handicap" unless you're writing about golf. You want to emphasize the person's abilities. Say "She walks with crutches," or "He uses a wheelchair" rather than "He is confined to a wheelchair."

Use "able-bodied," rather than "nondisabled" when discussing people who don't have a physical condition that interferes with their ability to walk, see, hear, learn, or lift.

Use "people of color," "minority individuals," or terms such as "African-American," "Hispanic/Latino/Latina," "Native American," and "Asian" when you have to be specific about ethnicity.

## Avoid Sexist Language

Use inclusive, nonsexist language by substituting she/he and his/her. Better yet, you can avoid that awkward structure by changing a single-tense subject and verb to the plural. Then you can use "they are" instead of "he/she is." Avoid words that contain "man." Change "chairman" to "chair," "manpower" to "workforce," or "manmade" to "synthetic."

Another tired phrase is "at-risk youth." Substitute "teens," "adolescents," "young adults," "students," or "boys and girls" for youth whenever you're talking about programs for teens.

# Explain Acronyms and Terms

You cannot assume that readers who will judge your proposal will know the same acronyms or buzzwords that are common to your organization or field of interest. While they may understand that "HUD" refers to the U.S. Department of Housing and Urban Development, what about CAC—Community Advisory Council, or R&D, which can refer to either Research and Design or Research and Development?

Make yourself clear. Give readers the full name or title on first reference, followed by the acronym in parentheses. After, and throughout the document, you can then use the full name or the acronym interchangeably.

## Name Your Project

RFPs often are tagged with explanatory titles—"small business innovation and research," "technology for the twentieth century," "early childhood educational opportunities," or "leadership development for nontraditional leaders." That title appears on the cover sheet and again on assurances attached to the proposal.

Why not set your proposal apart from the others, particularly if it's something unique to your community? Instead of using a ho-hum title, try to find one that's catchy, memorable, or an acronym.

**FACT**

An acronym—always spelled out on the first reference—takes much less space when you're writing the narrative and filling out forms. It also makes a program more memorable for the judges.

A technology planning group, for instance, might be called the electronic technology infrastructure planning commission—and referred to as "e-TIP." For an art project, formally referred to as "public art and community enhancement" (PACE), you could use, "Setting the PACE." And for an early childhood educational program, why not call it a school-time educational program (STEP)? Then you can dub the project "First STEPs."

## Use Strong, Active Verbs

No one likes to read sentences constructed in the passive voice. That's when the subject of a sentence becomes the object or receiver of an action, and the writer uses a weak verb. Passive voice is particularly deadly in grant proposals. Yet, interestingly enough, it's incredibly common to see grants written in the passive voice.

People who work in the nonprofit sector often believe they must be modest and not toot their horns by telling others about their organization's accomplishments. Instead of writing, "We served 750 people," they'll say "750 people received services." When you have lots of that in a proposal, the reader gets the sense that services just occur magically.

Improve your sentences by changing passive sentences into active voice. It usually takes fewer words, and it gives your writing more vigor, as well.

## Present or Past Tense?

Your sentences should have strong present- or past-tense verbs. Don't say things like "XYZ would provide mental-health services for 300 individuals." That sentence implies that XYZ will provide services if, and only if, it gets the grant. Instead, be positive. Say, "XYZ will provide mental health services." This says that the organization intends to address the problem whether or not it receives this particular grant. It also reinforces the idea that XYZ is an active community problem-solver and that it is committed to delivering services people need.

## Give Your Organization Credit

Use its name as the subject/noun of nearly every sentence, or use the pronoun "we." For instance, "Last year, XYZ nonprofit provided food and shelter for more than 750 people."

# First or Third Person?

The voice of the entire proposal is a matter of style and, therefore, completely up to you, the writer. Some people think first person voice is friendlier: "We are planning . . . We served . . . We will . . ." Others stick with the third person throughout the document. "XYZ is planning to . . . XYZ served . . . The agency hopes to . . ."

Another way to look at it is to use the third-person voice for all government proposals, but write local foundation grants in the first person. The friendlier approach in foundation grants can be justified because members of your community will read your proposal. It is, therefore, very likely that a member of your nonprofit board knows at least one of the foundation's trustees.

When using a third person narrative, do not refer to the organization as "they." An organization is an "it" and shouldn't be humanized.

> Whether you choose the formality of the third person or the friendlier first-person voice, make certain you use it consistently throughout the whole proposal.

## Speak with Authority

As in all other types of writing, "writing what you know" results in a stronger, more believable piece of work. You also should write with authority. Proposals are most often judged by peers and you must be able to communicate with them as an equal.

In two sections of the RFP—the evaluation plan and reviews of literature—you must break all the rules about not using jargon and speaking plainly. That's because people who read evaluation sections and reviews of literature are looking for language that not only speaks with authority but also with expertise. In other words, evaluators have a language of their own, and their reviews of literature require the language of a Ph.D. You have to be conversant with it.

Some grants, in particular, require expert language. These are usually in very technical or medical fields, and they will be read by physicians and high-level Ph.D.s. Many of these RFPs are issued by the National Institute of Health (NIH), and they require an entire section on using human beings as subjects of experiments. They also often require scientific explanations for the project you are proposing and a lengthy biography of at least one person, called the Principal Investigator (PI), who will lead all experiments or processes surrounding the project. In cases like this, the grants are typically awarded based on the PI's background, so it is important to make those credentials clear. (E)

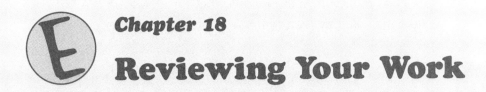

### Chapter 18

# Reviewing Your Work

The little details matter in a grant proposal. You've got the major items taken care of by now—the specifics of the program, the budget, the evaluation criteria. But you're not done yet. It is especially important to go over the proposal, focusing on the aspects that really give it that professional touch. This can make the difference between getting a grant and not.

## Spelling, Grammar, and Punctuation

No matter how good your spelling and grammar skills, you will need good reference books: a dictionary, thesaurus, and a stylebook or two (though no grant requires the use of one particular style over another). The Council on Foundations in Washington, D.C., has a stylebook particular to the philanthropy field, but it is geared more for those writing *about* philanthropy than to those writing *to* philanthropists.

Use, but don't rely on, spell check. You know the perils of words that can be spelled two ways or creating words that, while perfectly correct, are not intended. While either will pass a spell check, only one is correct as it's used in your sentence. What could be more embarrassing than sending in a proposal from a "pubic" rather than a "public" school district?

If your readers are going to judge just the content of the grant, which is their most appropriate role, you must proofread for errors before submitting your first draft. Check tenses, check punctuation and run-on sentences, and check your spelling. In fact, double-check your spelling.

If you have enough time, walk away from your copy for a day or two. Then proofread it again. That's when mistakes will jump out at you.

## Page Counts Count

Instructions in the RFP or grant guidelines almost always provide a page limit and a list of what must be included within the page limits or what is exempt from the limits.

A typical set of instructions regarding page limits might say something like this: "The narrative section must be limited to twenty-five typed pages. The pages must be consecutively numbered in the lower right-hand corner, double-spaced, printed on only one side of 8½" by 11" white paper with one-inch margins on all sides. The font size must be no smaller than twelve-point type. Page limits are for the narrative section only and do not include the title page, table of contents, abstract, assurances, budget form, or appendices."

Be sure to number your pages consecutively and to put the name of the organization and the city and state in all headers or footers.

## Using Headings

Once again, follow the directions. Use the same headings, and be sure to include the numbers, alpha characters, and/or Roman numerals used in the RFP. Do not, however, rewrite the instructions themselves or add the point value for each section.

Make the narrative as clear as you possibly can. Make your headings stand out by using bold, bold italics, underscoring, and other computer-enabled characters to separate sections, subheadings, and points. Do not use color.

Use bullet points for lists of items. However, here's a word of caution about bulleting. If the RFP instructions say to double-space the proposal, everything—including the bulleted items—must be double spaced.

## What Is a Rubric?

A rubric actually is created for the judges of grants, but often is made available to grant writers in the RFP. It's a way of presenting the evaluation criteria that assists the judges in scoring your grant.

Sections of the grant proposal—especially those done for government agencies—are usually assigned a number of points. For instance, a recently released federal grant provided twenty points for the need section; fifteen points for results and benefits expected; thirty-five points for the approach/ evaluation (project description); ten points for budget; and twenty points for attaching the appropriate documentation and letters of agreement.

A more typical grant proposal might provide twenty-five points for need, forty-five points for project description, twenty points for evaluation, and ten points for the reasonableness of the budget. By the way, don't bother adding up the numbers. They are points, not percentages, and don't always come out to 100!

## Evaluation Criteria

Judges use the evaluation criteria as guidelines when they award points to a project. These guidelines can be presented either as a list of criteria or as a rubric.

A rubric provides a scale for determining point awards to each section, according to how well it fits the description for that score. Following is a rubric for the abstract of an education proposal. The abstract in this case is worth up to ten points.

| Not Recommended | Recommended for Funding with Revisions (3–5 points) | Recommended for Funding (6–8 points) | Highly Recommended for Funding (9–10 points) |
| --- | --- | --- | --- |
| The project abstract is not included or is very incomplete. | The project abstract minimally describes the project; portions of the required elements are missing or are labeled "see attached." | The project abstract contains all elements required (content/structure of project; number of students potentially benefiting; student identification process; assessment and evaluation). If ISD applicant, application indicates which local districts will participate in project. | The project abstract contains all required elements and clearly and succinctly gives enough information so that the reader has an understand-ing of the scope, content, and struc-ture of the proposed literacy achievement project and how it will be implemented and evaluated. If ISD applicant, application indicates which local districts will partici-pate in project. |

▲ Sample rubric used to evaluate an abstract.

Now let's look at a list of criteria. This list was established for a federal grant reviewer.

## Criterion 1. Objectives and Need for Assistance (Twenty points)

1.  The extent to which the applicant specifies the goals and objectives of the project and describes how implementation will fulfill the purposes of the Early Learning Opportunities Act (ELOA). The applicant must demonstrate a thorough understanding of the importance of early learning services and activities that help parents, caregivers, and child-care providers incorporate early learning into the daily lives of young children, as well as programs that directly provide early learning to young children.

2.  The extent to which the applicant demonstrates the need for assistance including identification and discussion of its needs and resources assessment concerning early learning services. Relevant data from the assessment should be included. Participant and beneficiary information must also be included.

3.  The extent to which the applicant describes its resources assessment and the relevancy of the results as the basis for determining its objectives and need for assistance.

4.  The extent to which the applicant demonstrates how it will give preference to supporting activities/projects that maximize the use of resources through collaboration with other early learning programs, provide continuity of services for young children across the age spectrum, and help parents and other caregivers promote early learning with their young children. The applicant must provide information about how decisions will be made about who will provide each early learning service and/or activity funded through this grant.

5.  The extent to which the applicant demonstrates that it has worked with local education agencies to identify cognitive, social, emotional, and motor developmental abilities which are necessary to support children's readiness for school; that the programs, services, and activities assisted under this title will represent developmentally appropriate steps toward the acquisition of those abilities; and, that the programs, services, and activities assisted provide benefits for children cared for in their own homes as well as children placed in the care of others.

## Compare the Two

While a grant review can be somewhat subjective, the evaluation criteria—however it is presented—is intended to make it less so. But the two different presentations of criteria somewhat encourage the reviewers to think differently.

For instance, in the rubric form of evaluation, the section begins with no points and earns more as it goes up the scale. Compare that to the criteria list where the need section began with twenty points and then lost points if it did not meet the expectations of the reviewer.

In some cases, the RFP will contain only a list of criteria for selection and no outline for the narrative. Follow the list of criteria exactly, using it as your outline. When you are provided both, use the evaluation criteria as a way of reviewing your work and as a tool for your readers to use to help you strengthen any weaker sections of the proposal.

## Enlist the Aid of Readers

A writer often becomes too close to his or her work and cannot be an objective editor. This is particularly true of grant writing since the audience is unfamiliar with the organization and since you have a limited space for explaining ideas and details.

You need two kinds of readers. First, you need readers with expertise in the field you are writing about. They are most like the final judges and will be ruthless about making sure that you meet the highest level of the rubric with your descriptions and explanations.

You also need readers who are completely unfamiliar with either the field or the organization for whom you are writing the proposal. If they don't "get it," you know you have more work to do. Use their questions or concerns to flesh out ideas.

## Using the Rubric or Evaluation Criteria

The evaluation criteria or rubric helps you and your readers judge your draft. Have others score the proposal just as they would if they were judges. Use their scores to help strengthen sections that need strengthening. Use the criteria to guide your writing, and if you can be objective, score your own proposal when the draft is complete.

In your schedule, be sure to build in enough time for review and revision of at least one draft of the proposal. Ideally, your team will read and judge two drafts before you submit the final.

Once you receive all your scores, add them and divide by the number of readers to come up with an average. If you scored below ninety on a hundred-point proposal, rework the sections in which you scored low. Ask your readers questions if you need more guidance during the revision process.

## Competitive Priority Points

Many grant programs award competitive priority points for certain factors about the agency or its population. Usually five points are available, over and above the score received on the proposal. They are awarded for such things as a high incidence of poverty among the population the organization serves, for being located in a designated economic-enterprise zone, or for some other criteria over which you have little or no control.

Even if you know you'll receive the priority points, do not add them to your evaluation scores. While the additional points can sometimes push you from "almost" to "funded," they don't strengthen your proposal or answer questions of grant judges.

## Novice Applicants

Many federal grant programs are now awarding a competitive advantage to novice applicants. If your organization has never received a federal grant award, check the box on the cover sheet that indicates whether the organization is novice. While the proposal is not awarded additional points for being novice, it is given special consideration by the reviewers. (E)

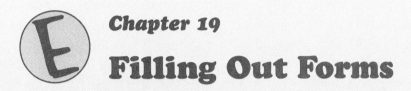

*Chapter 19*

# Filling Out Forms

**W**riting the narrative may be the toughest part of completing the grant proposal process, but the forms cannot be a last-minute task. In this chapter you'll learn what to expect and how to plan to ensure that you're not running around on submission day trying to find an old-fashioned typewriter to complete nonelectronic forms.

# What to Expect

The number and types of forms accompanying a grant package vary, but you will always have at least two: a cover sheet and a budget form. Neither can be entirely completed until the grant package is nearly finished. Budget development takes place concurrently with the program development and is not final until late in the process. The cover sheet usually contains a budget summary section, so that portion will not be ready early. You can and should, however, read the cover sheet much earlier so you can determine what information you will need to gather in order to complete the form in its entirety. Other forms that may accompany grant application packages include the following:

- Assurances
- Checklists
- Project summary form
- Certifications
- Informational grids

Federal grant RFPs usually have a separate packet of forms. If you download the RFP from the Internet, be sure to also download the "application," which will be provided as a separate document.

# Cover Sheets

Cover sheets request all or part of the following information:

- Name of organization
- Name of contact person
- Brief summary of project
- Signature of board chair
- Address of organization
- Telephone, fax, and e-mail address
- Type of organization
- Category of grant
- Federal tax ID and/or other special identity number
- Signatures of CEO/executive director
- Scores of any surveys done to qualify for application
- Budget summary

Most of the information requested can be prepared in advance. You might want to fill out those portions of the form weeks before you have to submit the package.

# XYZ Foundation

Street
Anywhere, USA

## Grant Application (please type or print)

Organizations requesting XYZ Foundation funds **must** submit a Treasury letter certifying 501(c)(3) tax-exempt status.

Date: _____

Organization: _____

Address: _____

Contact person's name: _____ Phone: _____

Contact person's title: _____

Purpose and objectives of your organization: _____

_____

Normal funding/support sources: _____

Geographic area served: _____

Client group served: _____

**Title of project for which funds are sought and brief description of project, its objectives, goals, and benefits to clientele and community.**

_____

_____

_____

_____

_____

_____

_____

_____

Project dates: _____

Total project cost: _____

(continued on next page)

Amount and source of pledges/commitments to date: _____

_____

_____

Other funding sources (and amounts) applied to for this project: _____

_____

_____

Amount requested from XYZ Foundation:_____

Has the XYZ Foundation supported your organization in the past?_____

If yes, specify dates and amounts:_____

If funds requested are for a new or pilot project, how are sustaining operations to be funded?

_____

_____

_____

List XYZ corporate employees (or family) who are members of your board or volunteers in your organization:

_____

_____

_____

_____

List XYZ employees (or family) who are among your clientele: _____

Signed:_____

Date:_____

# Application for Federal
# Education Assistance (ED 424)

**U.S. Department of Education**
Form Approved
OMB No. 1875-0106
Exp. 11/30/2004

## Applicant Information

1. Name and Address

   Legal Name: _____

   Address: _____

   Organizational Unit
   [                    ]

   City _____ State _____ County _____ ZIP Code + 4 _____ - ___

2. Applicant's D-U-N-S Number [ ][ ][ ][ ][ ][ ][ ][ ][ ]

3. Applicant's T-I-N [ ][ ] - [ ][ ][ ][ ][ ][ ][ ]

4. Catalog of Federal Domestic Assistance #: [8][4][ ][ ][ ]

   Title: _____

5. Project Director: _____

   Address: _____

   City _____ State _____ ZIP Code + 4 _____ - ___

   Tel. #: _____ Fax #: _____

   E-Mail Address: _____

6. Novice Applicant ☐ Yes ☐ No

7. Is the applicant delinquent on any Federal debt? ☐ Yes ☐ No

   (If "Yes," attach an explanation.)

8. Type of Applicant (Enter appropriate letter in the box.) [ ]

   A  State
   B  Local
   C  Special District
   D  Indian Tribe
   E  Individual
   F  Independent School
       District

   G  Public College or University
   H  Private, Non-Profit College or University
   I  Non-Profit Organization
   J  Private, Profit-Making Organization
   K  Other (Specify):
       _____
       _____

## Application Information

9. Type of Submission:

   —PreApplication
   ☐ Construction
   ☐ Non-Construction

   —Application
   ☐ Construction
   ☐ Non-Construction

10. Is application subject to review by Executive Order 12372 process?

    ☐ Yes (Date made available to the Executive Order 12372

        process for review): _____

    ☐ No (If "No," check appropriate box below.)

        ☐ Program is not covered by E.O. 12372.

        ☐ Program has not been selected by State for review.

                    Start Date:          End Date:

11. Proposed Project Dates: _____   _____

12. Are any research activities involving human subjects planned at any time during the proposed project period?

    ☐ Yes (Go to 12a.)     ☐ No (Go to item 13.)

    12a. Are all the research activities proposed designated to be exempt from the regulations?

        ☐ Yes (Provide Exemption(s) #): _____

        ☐ No (Provide Assurance #): _____

13. Descriptive Title of Applicant's Project:

## Estimated Funding

| | | |
|---|---|---|
| 14a. Federal | $ | .00 |
| b. Applicant | $ | .00 |
| c. State | $ | .00 |
| d. Local | $ | .00 |
| e. Other | $ | .00 |
| f. Program Income | $ | .00 |
| g. TOTAL | $ | .00 |

## Authorized Representative Information

15. To the best of my knowledge and belief, all data in this preapplication/application are true and correct. The document has been duly authorized by the governing body of the applicant and the applicant will comply with the attached assurances if the assistance is awarded.

    a. Authorized Representative (Please type or print name clearly.)

    b. Title

    c. Tel. #: _____   Fax #: _____

    d. E-Mail Address:

    e. Signature of Authorized Representative          Date: _____

# Identity Numbers

Cover sheets, particularly those supplied by federal and state grantors, request identity numbers. Foundations generally ask only for your 501(c)(3) letter and take the identifying number they need from that document. The identity numbers required by the government include, in some cases, the federal tax ID—as well as a special designation such as the number assigned a school district by the state—or the federal ID of a special health clinic.

# Assurances and Certifications

Assurances are included in most federal application packets. They outline the enabling legislation and its parameters and describe the things that the applicant must already do in order to qualify for a grant. As grant writer, all you have to do is make a copy of the assurance and have it signed by the appropriate person (usually the executive director, chief executive officer, or similar position).

Certifications are similar to assurances, but they also may request additional information. For instance, schools are asked to certify that they are "drug and violence free." The form requests a list of recent expulsions or disciplinary actions for drugs or violence on school grounds as well as the signature of the superintendent assuring the government that the school is addressing the problem.

ASSURANCES AND CERTIFICATIONS
STATE PROGRAMS

Assurance Concerning Materials Developed with Funds Awarded under This Grant

The grantee assures that the following statement will be included on any publication or project materials developed with funds awarded under this program, including reports, films, brochures, and flyers: "These materials were developed under a grant awarded by the Michigan Department of Education."

Certification Regarding Nondiscrimination under Federally and State Assisted Programs

The applicant hereby agrees that it will comply with all federal and Michigan laws and regulations prohibiting discrimination and, in accordance therewith, no person, on the basis of race, color, religion, national origin or ancestry, age, sex, marital status, or handicap, shall be discriminated against, excluded from participation in, denied the benefits of, or otherwise be subjected to discrimination in any program or activity for which it is responsible or for which it receives financial assistance from the U.S. Department of Education or the Michigan Department of Education.

Certification Regarding Title II of the Americans with Disabilities Act (ADA), P.L. 101-336, State and Local Government Services (for Title II applicants only)

The Americans with Disabilities Act (ADA) provides comprehensive civil rights protections for individuals with disabilities. Title II of the ADA covers programs, activities, and services of public entities. Title II requires that "No qualified individual with a disability shall, by reason of such disability, be excluded from participation in or be denied the benefits of the services, programs, or activities of a public entity, or be subjected to discrimination by such entity." In accordance with Title II ADA provisions, the applicant has conducted a review of its employment and program/service delivery processes and has developed solutions to correcting barriers identified in the review.

Certification Regarding Title III of the Americans with Disabilities Act (ADA), P.L. 101-336, Public Accommodations and Commercial Facilities (for Title III applicants only)

The Americans with Disabilities Act (ADA) provides comprehensive civil rights protections for individuals with disabilities. Title III of the ADA covers public accommodations (private entities that affect commerce, such as museums, libraries, private schools, and day care centers) and only addresses existing facilities and readily achievable barrier removal. In accordance with Title III provisions, the applicant has taken the necessary action to ensure that individuals with a disability are provided full and equal access to the goods, services, facilities, privileges, advantages, or accommodations offered by the applicant. In addition, a Title III entity, upon receiving a grant from the Michigan Department of Education, is required to meet the higher standards (i.e., program accessibility standards) as set forth in the Title II of the ADA for the program or service for which it receives a grant.

IN ADDITION:

This project/program will not supplant nor duplicate an existing early childhood development program.

Applicants not operating any component of the project directly must provide a letter of commitment and agreement, including the specifications of terms and conditions for delivery of services.

There is a written agreement between other eligible public nonprofit organizations or programs and the State that outlines provisions for the use of facilities for early childhood development program services (including such use during holidays and vacation periods; the restrictions, if any, on the use of such space; and the times when space will be available for the use of the applicant).

(Competitive Grants Only) The following provisions are understood by the recipients of the grants should it be awarded:

1. Grant award is approved and is not assignable to a third party without specific approval.
2. Funds shall be expended in conformity with the budget. Line item changes and other deviations from the budget as attached to this grant agreement must have prior approval from a School Readiness Consultant of the Michigan Department of Education.
3. The Michigan Department of Education is not liable for any costs incurred by the grantee prior to the issuance of the grant award.
4. Grant recipients will comply with all subsequent legislation pending pertaining to this program.

Signature of Superintendent or authorized official:    Date: _____

_____

# Budget Forms

The federal government issues two types of budget forms: one for construction projects, and one for nonconstruction projects. All social-service projects use the nonconstruction budget form as the federal government does not issue RFPs for construction projects for that sector. The Department of Justice and some other more specialized departments have different forms, but the information requested is mostly consistent from one federal agency to another.

**ALERT!**

Do not substitute your own format for a budget form provided by any federal agency.

Foundations often provide a budget form and a statement saying that if your budget is in a different form, they will accept it.

Most budget forms ask for the following line items:

- Personnel
- Fringe benefits
- Travel
- Equipment
- Supplies
- Contractual services/staff
- Training/professional development
- Indirect costs

Indirect costs are a set percentage (usually 5 to 10 percent of the grant budget) allowed in the grant for the proposing organization's overhead and grant administration. Read the directions to make sure that indirect costs are allowed before completing the budget forms.

The first example shows the budget form for the organization. There is typically a similar (or even identical) one for the specific program or project.

Budget for the period _____ to _____

| INCOME | |
|---|---|
| **SOURCE** | **AMOUNT** |
| *Support* | |
| Government grants and contracts | $ |
| Foundations | $ |
| Corporations | $ |
| United Way or other federated campaigns | $ |
| Individual contributions | $ |
| Fundraising events and products | $ |
| Membership income | $ |
| In-kind support | $ |
| *Revenue* | |
| Earned Income | $ |
| Other (specify) | $ |
| *List Top Five Donors* | |
| | $ |
| | $ |
| | $ |
| | $ |
| | $ |
| *Total Income* | $ |

| EXPENSE | | |
|---|---|---|
| **ITEM** | **Amount** | **%FT/PT** |
| Salaries and wages (for project budgets breakdown by individual position and indicate full- or part-time) | $ | |
| | $ | |
| | $ | |
| | $ | |
| | $ | |
| *Subtotal* | $ | |
| Insurance benefits and other related taxes | $ | |
| | $ | |
| Consultants and professional fees | $ | |
| Travel | $ | |
| Equipment | $ | |
| Supplies | $ | |
| Printing and copying | $ | |
| Telephone and fax | $ | |
| Postage and delivery | $ | |
| Rent and utilities | $ | |
| In-kind expenses | $ | |
| Other (specify) | $ | |
| *Total Expense* | $ | |
| | | |
| *Difference (Income less expense)* | $ | |

▲ Organization Budget: You may reproduce this form on your computer.

# U.S. DEPARTMENT OF EDUCATION

## BUDGET INFORMATION

## NON-CONSTRUCTION PROGRAMS

OMB Control Number: 1890-0004

Expiration Date: 02/28/2003

Name of Institution/Organization

Applicants requesting funding for only one year should complete the column under "Project Year 1." Applicants requesting funding for multi-year grants should complete all applicable columns. Please read all instructions before completing form.

### SECTION A - BUDGET SUMMARY
### U.S. DEPARTMENT OF EDUCATION FUNDS

| Budget Categories | Project Year 1 (a) | Project Year 2 (b) | Project Year 3 (c) | Project Year 4 (d) | Project Year 5 (e) | Total (f) |
|---|---|---|---|---|---|---|
| 1. Personnel | | | | | | |
| 2. Fringe Benefits | | | | | | |
| 3. Travel | | | | | | |
| 4. Equipment | | | | | | |
| 5. Supplies | | | | | | |
| 6. Contractual | | | | | | |
| 7. Construction | | | | | | |
| 8. Other | | | | | | |
| 9. Total Direct Costs (lines 1-8) | | | | | | |
| 10. Indirect Costs | | | | | | |
| 11. Training Stipends | | | | | | |
| 12. Total Costs (lines 9-11) | | | | | | |

ED Form No. 524

▲ Sample budget for U.S. Department of Education (continued on next page).

Name of Institution/Organization

Applicants requesting funding for only one year should complete the column under "Project Year 1." Applicants requesting funding for multi-year grants should complete all applicable columns. Please read all instructions before completing form.

## SECTION B - BUDGET SUMMARY
## NON-FEDERAL FUNDS

| Budget Categories | Project Year 1 (a) | Project Year 2 (b) | Project Year 3 (c) | Project Year 4 (d) | Project Year 5 (e) | Total (f) |
|---|---|---|---|---|---|---|
| 1. Personnel | | | | | | |
| 2. Fringe Benefits | | | | | | |
| 3. Travel | | | | | | |
| 4. Equipment | | | | | | |
| 5. Supplies | | | | | | |
| 6. Contractual | | | | | | |
| 7. Construction | | | | | | |
| 8. Other | | | | | | |
| 9. Total Direct Costs (lines 1-8) | | | | | | |
| 10. Indirect Costs | | | | | | |
| 11. Training Stipends | | | | | | |
| 12. Total Costs (lines 9-11) | | | | | | |

## SECTION C - OTHER BUDGET INFORMATION (see instructions)

ED Form No. 524

▲ Sample budget for U.S. Department of Education (continued).

# Fitting into the Spaces Provided

Increasingly, foundations and government departments are providing interactive electronic forms, which can be filled out and changed at any time. However, many are still available only as hard copies. For these you'll need a typewriter and quite a lot of patience.

It isn't easy to line up all the little boxes and lines with the typewriter's keys and margin allotments. And, because you can vary type size and style only a bit on most typewriters, you'll find less space overall for keying in brief summaries, and even longer job titles, that must fit into the spaces provided.

**You might want to make copies of the forms and complete them by hand first. Once you know what you want to write, then type the responses on the originals last.**

With electronic forms that you get online, you have a bit more flexibility because you can change the size of the type or the font to fit into tight spaces. Forms sometimes allow a fixed amount of space for a brief narrative summary. And when you've entered about 200 or 250 words, you might discover the form simply won't let you write any further. Therefore, before you even get started, you might want to develop a tightly worded, concise narrative summary and then fill out the form.

Use the word or character count function provided in most word-processing programs to make sure your text will fit into the space allotted on electronic forms or submissions.

# Getting Signatures

As with support letters, you must begin planning for forms as soon as you receive the RFP. All of them request the signature of the chief person in charge of the organization, so you must coordinate schedules to get those signatures. Most forms also require the signatures of finance directors, program managers, and/or board presidents. Don't be surprised if you spend an entire day tracking down all of these individuals to get their signatures.

You must always submit one original application and whatever number of copies are requested. The original must contain original signatures from all the parties requested.

ALERT!

Here's a tip: Have officials sign their names in blue ink so you can tell quickly—and so can the granting agency—which is the original copy and which are the duplicates.

## Chapter 20

# Packaging and Submitting Your Proposal

Finally, you're ready to complete the package. Add the finishing touches, compile the last of the forms and attachments and ship it to the funder. Whew! You're almost done! This chapter outlines the last of the steps in the grant-seeking process.

# Writing an Abstract or Summary

Instructions for an abstract will be very succinct. The funder will want a brief description of the project, the need for the project, and the means of delivering the project (such as a collaboration or a qualifying statement about the applicant organization). In other words, they want a one- or two-sentence summary of each of the lengthy sections of your grant proposal.

The directions for the abstract will include a note regarding length either in number of words you are allowed or in terms of a page limit. You're never allowed more than one page, however, and often even less. Sometimes an abstract form is supplied by the granting agency. This will include a header with the name of the organization and its identifying number and sections for summarizing specific parts of your narrative.

Try writing the abstract or project summary last. At that point you've already done the work, and you just have to go into the narrative of the proposal and find some succinct sentences or paragraphs and paste them into the abstract. Then write just a few sentences to "glue" it all together.

Following is a 250-word abstract introducing the applicant and need for the project, describing the project components, and summarizing the budget and request.

The school district is a public school system serving approximately 9,200 children and young adults in kindergarten through twelfth grade, alternative education, preschool, and adult education programs. The secondary (post-middle) schools in the east-state district include High School A (grades ten through twelve), which has a total enrollment of 2,450. The alternative education programs, BB for ages eighteen to twenty who have missed their graduation dates, and CC for ages fourteen to eighteen who have not yet missed their graduation date, enroll approximately 200 students. Approximately 200 students enrolled in the high school program would qualify for alternative education, as indicated by failure rates, state

Educational Assessment Program scores, language barriers, and other indicators of need, but current alternative programs are at capacity.

The district proposes a House School Program that would expand opportunities for failing students in the current ninth- through twelfth-grades buildings (that is, increase enrollment slots from 200 to 250), focus on career pathways, nurture an effective learning environment, and provide additional specialized assistance required by at-risk adolescent students. The restructured program will include student assignments to "learning families" in the House School; focus on career development; a family-liaison worker; on-site security; enhanced opportunities (extended school day and block scheduling) for accumulating necessary credits; socialization opportunities such as anger management; improved teen parenting curricula, the Teen Outreach Program (TOP) curricula; a focus on asset building with adult mentors, and a series of retreats, camping experiences, or other challenges designed to build friendships, individual confidence, teamwork, and leadership skills.

The district provides $__ in-kind and match, and requests a one-year grant of $____ to support the transition.

# Writing Cover Letters

Federal grants and state grants really don't require cover letters, but it's a nice gesture, even if you suspect they may be tossed in the trash by the person who opens the package. Cover letters are very appropriate for local foundations as this is your opportunity to make a personal link between the board or staff of the foundation and the board or staff of the nonprofit organization. After all, people do give to other people—it's "who asks" that matters, more often than what they ask for, especially in local giving.

Start every letter with a "thank you." It's a much nicer greeting than "I have enclosed," because it focuses on the reader rather than the sender.

The cover letter should be signed by the person in the organization who has the closest link to the funder. For instance, if a board member is a close personal friend of a trustee of a family foundation, ask that person to sign the cover letter. If there is no one with a personal link to the foundation, have the letter signed by the CEO or executive director.

Take a look at the sample cover letter below. This organization had previously received a grant from the targeted funder for the same program. Based on evaluation, the organization zeroed in on strategies that worked so they could reduce the cost and present the program for refunding.

Date
Program Officer
ABC Foundation
Street
City, State, ZIP

Dear Program Officer:

Thank you for reviewing the enclosed three-year proposal for XYZ Nonprofit in city, county, state. The model for this program has been revised recently to build on past strengths of the program and to be responsive to community needs. It now calls for one of two services, which will be selected by the parents: telephone-call support from a trained volunteer, or home visits from a paraprofessional provided by one of the collaborating partners. We also have focused our services on first-time parents of infants and plan to provide consistent prevention services for up to three years of home visits or one year of telephone support.

These changes and others, as I've stated, are based first on what works, and second on cost efficiencies. The new model, like the previous one, will ensure that children develop optimally and that parents develop the skills and access the community resources they need to prevent child abuse and neglect. Services will be offered to approximately 1,800 new families each year.

We are respectfully requesting ABC Foundation support of $1 million over three years, which will be used to leverage other private and public funding to support the program's annual $1.2 million budget.

Please contact me with any questions or to set a time to meet for discussion of the project. Thank you for your attention and time.

Sincerely,
Organization Director

## Using Color, Photos, and Other Graphics

Graphic elements are always nice, as long as they can be included in the document and be contained within the page limits. Charts and graphs can be used to illustrate a process, to define the management structure of your organization, or to describe the workings of new inventions. In general, however, avoid the use of color graphics or photos, and try to avoid the need to illustrate your concept in color—use shading or line art instead. There are two reasons for this: First, if you must make copies in color, it is more expensive. Second, even though you've attached the requested number of copies, the funder often makes more copies, and they will not make color copies. In general, consider color prohibited unless you are instructed otherwise in the RFP.

## Using Dividers, Binders, or Bindery

Once again, let the directions dictate your course. Most often, however, especially for federal grants, the grantor will prohibit bindery or special covers. Instead they will direct you to staple the pages together or enclose them in a rubber band.

Stapling can create a problem when you have a lot of pages to fasten together. You can use a heavy-duty stapler that can staple through at least 150 pages. Rather than investing in equipment that you may use only infrequently, go to your local shipper and use one the business provides for customers.

Sometimes the instructions ask you to three-hole punch your original and copies and to secure them with clips or rubber bands. That means that the granting agency intends to create binders for the reviewers. If you want to avoid having to hole-punch dozens or even hundreds of pages, you can buy a ream of prepunched paper for printing your proposal.

> As with the instructions for the narrative, you must follow the binding and copying instructions to the letter.

When a funder is not specific about binding or dividing copies, you are free to package your proposal as you wish. There are a number of different ways to do this:

- A three-ring binder with dividers for each section. (This method is particularly effective when you have large grant proposals of more than 100 pages, such as those for medical or dental programs.)
- Wire or plastic bindery with a full-color cover or a simple cover with titles, logos, and other appropriate information.
- A pocket folder with a cover letter in one pocket and the proposal and attachments in the other.
- Binder clips.

For the most part, keep your packaging simple. Often, even though you send the requisite number of copies, the granting organization must make additional ones. In these cases, they'll have to unbind or unstaple your grant packages.

## Attachments and Appendices

Attachments and appendices are generally allowed (and sometimes required) and rarely count against your page limits. Sometimes the granting agency will limit the number of pages in your appendix and attachments. In this case, select the very best of your optional or limited attachments such as support letters or media stories. Examples of attachments include:

- IRS determination letter—proof of 501(c)(3) status: required by foundations.
- Board roster: required by most foundations.
- Letters of support: required by most grantors, especially when you are proposing a collaborative structure.
- News articles about the program: not required.
- Annual report of organization: not required.
- Organizational charts.

- Maps.
- Most recent audit statement and report.

Appendices might include such things as:

- Progress reports
- Formal needs assessment reports
- Survey results
- Translated materials

Appendices are not required by any foundation. Only some federal grant programs request appendices, and they will be clear about the content.

**ALERT!**

No federal or state grant program has yet allowed attachment of film or video. Most foundations don't appreciate video attachments unless they specifically request them.

# Electronic Submissions

Many federal and state grants are becoming available for electronic completion and submission. They usually accept either a mailed document or the electronic submission, and often you can take an extra day or two on the deadline for the electronic submission. Benefits of submitting your proposal electronically include:

- Additional time for completion
- No cost for mailing/shipping
- Has prompts for missing text or lines

Drawbacks may include the following:

- No record of submission being received
- Unreliable connections to server
- Difficult to send documents for peer reviews

When you work in the electronic submission format, you may go back and change the text as needed. Until you are finished, do not select the button that says "submit."

## Making and Marking Copies

Government grants always tell you in the RFP how many copies to submit. They will also often tell you that the stated number is not required but "will facilitate review." This is really just a nice way of saying, "Send us the exact number of copies we requested." Foundations often do not say how many copies they'd like. Either call the program officer and ask, or submit only one original packet.

Those agencies that require copies also require an original. Be sure that your original document is clearly marked as such. Use one or more of the following ways to indicate the original document:

- Add a sticky note with the word "original" to the original document.
- Sign the original cover sheet in blue or red ink so it's clear on the first page which document is the original.
- Add colored sheets to the top of each proposal, with one color for original and another for all copies.
- Attach a cover letter on organizational letterhead on the original document only. Do not attach a copy of the cover letter to any of the others unless it's requested.
- If binding, add a note to the cover of the package. Or make one color cover for the original and different color covers for the copies.

The Environmental Protection Agency (EPA) and some other departments require you to use recycled paper for all proposals. Be sure that your copies also are printed on recycled paper.

# Shipping and Delivery Options

Other than electronic submission, there are three ways to deliver grants: personally, by mail, or by shipping service. The best choice among the three is the one that guarantees you'll meet the deadline.

For local grants and sometimes state grants (if you live in or near the capital city) the best option is hand delivery.

Federal grants once suggested using the U.S. Postal Service, but since September 11, 2001, and the threat of anthrax for months afterward, they have begun to suggest overnight shipping services instead.

When the grant RFP states that a grant must be "postmarked by" a date, you must use the U.S. Postal Service. Dates entered into a shipping form do not count! When the RFP states that the grant must be received in the grantor's office by 5:00 P.M. on a certain date, you have to select the method that is most certain to get it there.

Since you will often be working on a grant, its forms, or its attachments on the very last day before it's due, you will probably most frequently use overnight shipping as a means of delivery to remote destinations. Use UPS or FedEx for these shipments. Unlike the postal service, these shippers provide a tracking number so you can know for certain when the grant has arrived.

**ALERT!**

When a grant is due on Monday and you are using a shipping service, try to ship on Friday. Cost for pickup and shipping on a Saturday can sometimes be double that of Fridays.

The most critical thing about wrapping up the grant is ensuring that it arrives on time. Know the time of the last mail pickup or how late your overnight shipping service is open. Check to make sure the hours aren't going to change, and keep track of Sundays and holidays that can delay shipping.

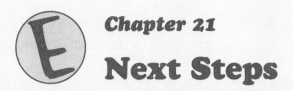

## Chapter 21

# Next Steps

You've met the deadline and shipped the proposal. Big "Whew!" and congratulations! Take a brief breather, then prepare for tackling the next steps. If the grant is awarded to you, congrats! There's lots to do. But even if you don't receive the grant this time, there are steps you can take to ensure you have a better chance the next time.

# What's Next?

Sometimes the RFP will state the process from submission through declination or funding, but more often it won't, especially in the case of federal grants.

You can ask local funders about their grant-making cycles and give a date within a week of the trustee meeting. But federal grantors don't like to be very specific because they want flexibility to respond to acts of Congress that may increase, deny, or reduce the funding allocation for the grant program.

Some grantors like to perform site visits, meeting with someone from the organization at some point after receiving your proposal. Be prepared to respond orally to questions related to the program you're proposing during a site visit.

But don't let the lack of response or the time it takes for the grantor go through its decision-making cycle slow down your efforts. Above all, don't just sit and wait, especially if you have a large program. Since they often require that you find multiple funding sources, immediately begin to refine and reframe your grant proposal so you can submit it to other funders.

Once a major proposal is written, the work gets easier. That's because lots of sections (for instance, the need statement) can be reused again and again. That saves you a lot of time and effort when you are redeveloping a proposal and sending it to different funders.

# Simultaneous Submissions

Unlike in the world of publishing, simultaneous submissions are perfectly all right in grant proposals. In fact, in some cases, it's mandated or at least expected.

In some areas, the major funders meet regularly to discuss what part each wants to play in capital campaigns. In this case, if you haven't submitted proposals to all the major funders, you risk offending one, or worse, being cut out of funding from all of them for lack of planning and communication.

It's also perfectly appropriate to submit portions of a project to various funders all at once or to submit a federal grant proposal at the same time that you are seeking local support. In fact, this too is often expected. You will have to seek funds to sustain a project over its first several years, so why not try to raise as much as you can to see it through the startup? Funders are almost always more interested in new projects than they are in ongoing ones, which they come to see as "continuing operations."

## If the Proposal Is Denied . . .

No one likes to hear the bad news, but the truth is that hundreds, sometimes even thousands, of applications for funding are denied for every one that is granted. Often the funder will tell you in the declination—and for that matter, the congratulatory—letter how many responses they received to the RFP. You'll see statements such as, "Of 378 applications, we were only able to select the twenty-eight that scored ninety-two points and above." That should provide some measure of comfort to you.

The good news is that you can try again—both with another type of proposal and, frequently, by resubmitting the failed proposal when the opportunity presents itself again.

It is possible to get rejected several times by different foundations as you search for funding for a particular program, but don't give up. If you have a good program, you will eventually be able to find the perfect fit between your project and a funder.

## Why Proposals Fail

There are several reasons that a proposal can be denied, including the most obvious and usual—that it did not score high enough to be in the top portion of projects submitted. Other reasons are not so obvious.

For instance, proposals can be turned down because of any of the following:

- The client received a grant recently from the same funder, and the funder wishes to give others a better chance, even though it likes the project you are proposing.
- It's not your turn. Some grants, particularly those that are provided annually by states, appear to be distributed based on a rotating system of every three or four years.
- The organization did poorly on a past evaluation or failed to comply with the grant agreement on a past grant. Even if the grant was for a different funder—don't forget, they often communicate with each other!
- The funder has a political agenda. Unfortunately, this often comes into play, particularly in state grants where one geographic area of the state is continuously favored over another. It may be only because that area has stronger representation or lobbyists.
- The project did not fit the guidelines closely enough.
- Your community does not have the highest incidence of need, compared to most others.
- The funder's priorities shifted or the program emphases changed between the time you submitted the proposal and the time it made grants.
- A similar project was just funded in your specific geographic area. It's unlikely a national funder will invest in two projects to serve the same general population.
- You failed to follow the directions. In this case, of course, you won't be able to help but blame yourself. But stop that right now. Learn from it, and be more careful next time.

## Requesting Reviewer Comments

Local foundations often will tell you what went wrong in the decision-making process during the trustee meeting. There is little you can do unless foundation staff give you some tips about reframing your proposal and invite you to resubmit the proposal.

In the case of state and federal grants especially, the first thing to do about a failed grant is to request reviewer comments if they were not shipped with the declination letter. Send a letter to the granting agency on your organization's letterhead. Include the number of the program, the date of the proposal deadline, and a polite request for reviewer comments and scoring.

Reviewer comments can range from a sheet of criteria with a square for a score and two lines per criteria for comments, to several full pages of narrative reviewer comments on each section of the proposal.

**FACT**

Reviewer comments are critical to helping you improve your grant-writing skills. Even if the organization isn't interested in reapplying, you'll benefit from reviewing the comments on the proposal. It will give you insight on how to improve your chances with other grant requests in the future.

You'll find that if there were three reviewers, scores and comments will differ, sometimes drastically, between them. Where one reviewer might give you full points for a section and make no suggestions for improvement, another may cut your points by half and find fault with nearly everything you've done. Then they seem to switch views in the next section of the proposal. Your final total proposal scores from each reviewer, however, should fall within a few points of each other.

You may not contest low scores—even in the rare instance that only one of your reviewers has scored the proposal poorly. However, these comments are invaluable as a roadmap for strengthening your next attempt.

## Rewrite and Resubmit the Proposal

Following is a compilation of reviewer comments from one Small Business Innovation and Research (SBIR) grant review. Note how some appear contradictory.

Strengths

- Could be a clear advance in prosthetics
- If successful, this work would be significant


Weaknesses

- Idea is not new
- Wide body of literature not addressed
- Literature on specific control devices not referenced
- Market overestimated
- Price seems low
- Unrealistic workload
- Suggest first demonstrate technical feasibility of concept

You will have several months to absorb reviewer comments and contemplate how you will address their concerns in your next attempt. When you sit down to rewrite the proposal, ignore the strengths, or positive comments. Address the weaknesses.

Some very technical grants, like the SBIR, require you, on a second application, to respond directly to reviewer comments and state how you've addressed the concerns they had with the project when it was first presented.

In the example above, a resubmission will require the writer to research further the literature on prosthetics and prosthetic control devices. He or she will have to work closely with a financial expert or business consultant to develop more realistic market estimates and potential pricing. Then, the writer will have to work on the project plan, reducing it to something that can be accomplished in a shorter time. Or, as an alternative, the writer might encourage the inventor to do as much as he or she can prior to resubmitting the grant so the entire experiment is further along and he or she can limit the project plan to a technical feasibility study.

Focus specifically on reviewer comments and address each throughout the revision—even if only one reviewer cited the topic as a weakness and another complimented it. If the evaluation section was weak, take it to the local university and speak with a professional evaluator. If the need section was weak, locate more data to support your case. If the project description requires more detail, work with project staff to strengthen the approach.

As a general rule of thumb, one revision and resubmission is mandatory with the permission of your client or employer. A second, if your revision is denied, is all right. If the second revision is also turned down, however, you may need to look at developing an entirely new project. Clearly, the weaknesses lie with what you are proposing, not how you are proposing it.

## We Got the Grant—Now What?

There's a saying among leaders of nonprofits: "Darn, we didn't get the grant. Darn, we got the grant." Of course, everyone is happy to hear that they submitted a successful proposal. On the other hand, now the real work begins—implementing the project and fulfilling the work plan.

The first thing you, as grant writer, are most likely to need to do when your organization gets the grant is review and possibly revise the project budget. Often six months have passed between submission and the confirmation of funding. Things have changed. The organization may have purchased some requested equipment or implemented some phase of the project with other money. And often, too, the granting agent requests a new budget for final approval.

## You Got Less Than You Wanted

Sometimes you'll get the grant but it's for less than the amount you requested. The funders do this for a number of reasons. They may have decided to fund more projects than they originally anticipated and want all of you to reduce your overall budgets by 10 percent—you choose where. Or maybe they've declined a line item in your budget because they didn't want to fund that particular thing.

Experienced grant seekers understand that they often don't get the full amount they requested and, therefore, they have a backup plan for filling in budget gaps.

You can apply for a local grant to supplement a federal one. You can make up the shortfall from the organization's operating budget. Or, with permission from the grantor, you can reduce the service you intended to provide or the number of people in your target population to compensate financially.

# Writing a Media Announcement

Once you've gotten a grant, you'll want to do a bit of publicity in the local media. Local grants often require a media announcement as part of the grant agreement contract. Just as with grant proposals, media announcements—also called press releases—are formulaic. Always begin with a headline such as "Media Release." Then provide contact information (the name, address, e-mail address, and phone number of the person in the organization who fields questions or can tell the media more about the project).

Also in the heading, you have to say whether the release is immediate or to be held until a certain date so the media knows they may not release the information to the public prior to that stated time. Center a headline that announces the grant and the amount to be received. Then start the story with a dateline just like those in the newspaper that includes today's date and the city and state.

A two-page news release is more than sufficient. And it absolutely should always include at least one quote from project staff or leadership.

If possible, use another quote from the granting agency. Describe the project in a way that makes it sound exciting. Signal the end with three number symbols centered after the last paragraph (# # #).

Following is a sample media release about the federal grant proposal included in Appendix C. Specific identifying information has been deleted or made generic for this example.

30 November 2003
MEDIA RELEASE
For Immediate Release
For More Information:
John Doe at (222) 555-1212
Address
E-mail

ABC Receives $250,000 from U.S. Department of Education
for Mobile Media Lab

November 30, year, City, State. The ABC Nonprofit (ABC) today announced receipt of a $250,000 grant from the U.S. Department of Education for its Mobile Learning Lab for Information Education (MML). MML was planned and launched preliminarily with an $80,000 Ameritech/SBC grant provided earlier this year. The federal grant enables ABC to equip a van with computers, cameras, and wireless connectivity and to develop curriculum for kindergarten through twelfth-grade educational enrichment programs and operation of digital editing software.

MML is a painted van equipped with twenty wireless laptop computers and sixteen video cameras that will travel to city and suburban neighborhoods and schools to provide computer training, Internet access, and video-production training. Audio, video, and computer data can be routed back to the ABC for possible transmission on FM radio, cable television, and streaming on the Internet.

"These funds will allow us to share high-tech resources in low-income neighborhoods, so MML is now one of the foremost projects we have to help us in our effort to close the digital divide," said John Doe, executive director of the ABC.

Under the direction of Americorp VISTA volunteers and staff, MML is piloting programs at a local school and will be ready for full launch in city and suburban schools by the start of second semester. The van and programs also will be provided to neighborhood associations, youth centers, and other programs for homeless or low-income families throughout the city.

ABC is a nonprofit entity with the mission to "Build Community Through Media." Affiliates of the ABC include TV, radio, Internet, and information democracy.

###

# The Progress Report

Many grants require that you submit periodic reports of your organization's progress with the program that has been funded. Take your list of goals and objectives and interview the client about their progress toward each. Include the following topics in all progress reports:

- Progress toward stated goals and objectives.
- Changes in the environment, funding, staffing levels, or other factors that limited progress and the ways in which they did.
- Unanticipated successes and the reasons for them.
- Anecdotal evidence of success (stories from participants).
- Long-term sustainability plans and steps taken in the interim to sustain the project.
- Use of funds.
- Any special terms or conditions of the grant agreement.
- Lessons learned.

## Chapter 22

# Writing Grants as a Career

Are you thinking about becoming a full-time grant writer? Maybe you aren't sure what skills you need and what it takes to be successful. You can make a career out of writing grants, whether as a professional full-time staff member of a large organization or a freelance grant writer.

## Who Writes Grants?

While some individuals, such as inventors, and some businesses—particularly those in product development, research, defense, and construction—apply for grants, nonprofit organizations account for the largest percentage of grant seekers.

That's because nearly all nonprofit organizations must seek grants to develop new programs or sustain operations. In the smaller nonprofit agencies, the work of grant seeking and grant writing is often assigned to the executive director. Larger organizations often hire a fund development officer to do those jobs. On occasion, you'll find program directors assigned responsibility for seeking grants to support the organization's programs or ideas. In many cases a nonprofit's board of directors mandates that staff pursue a specified number of grants or raise a specific amount of money through grant writing in any given year.

**FACT**

In a typical mid-sized city in the United States, there are thousands of nonprofit organizations and only two or three professional grant writers.

As executive directors of nonprofits have become busier and busier, the need for professional grant-writing services has grown rapidly in the past two decades, and it will continue to grow in the next. And that's where you come in.

Whether you're already a freelance writer and want to develop a new market for your work, whether grant writing is one of your job responsibilities, or whether you simply want to assist a favorite charity in a unique way, writing grants can compensate you in two ways. You'll not only be earning a living, but you'll also feel good about the contribution you make in improving your community and the lives of the people in it. And for many grant writers, that's almost as satisfying as the money itself.

## Basic Skills of Grant Writers

You don't need to be a professional writer to write grants. Nor do you need to have a particular style when you write. But you do need to appreciate brevity and simplicity, and you have to be willing to work at refining your writing style in that direction if you come up short. Of course, you can't forget the basic areas of aptitude that any writer should have:

- Sentence structure
- Good grammar
- Correct punctuation
- Accurate spelling

In other words, you need all the skills you learned and have used ever since you completed eighth grade. And when in doubt, like any good writer, you'll know when to consult a dictionary, a thesaurus, or a grammar book.

## Think Like an Entrepreneur

There are a number of other skills a grant writer brings to the profession that you either already have or will develop as you learn more about the field. These skills are almost more important than your ability to write. To be successful, you should be able to think entrepreneurially. That means having the ability to identify an organization's needs and to see how you can use your skills to help them meet their needs. But don't worry too much about whether you actually have those qualifications. You already demonstrated that you do when you purchased and started reading this book. In other words, you saw a need to add grant-writing skills to your resume, and now you are learning how to do it to help fill that void for others as well as for yourself.

Of course, you'll have to be able to develop good client relations and be skilled at negotiating, just as you would in any other business. You'll also want to become a good consultant or advisor to your clients. As you have read in this book, you've noticed that successful grants most often come from making good matches between the funder and the services provided by a nonprofit. In other words, just as you had to decide what you could provide your clients—based on their needs—you have to be able to help them to think strategically and thoughtfully about which grants they should pursue for their service programs. And those choices have to be based on what the grant provider clearly wishes to accomplish with the money it distributes to charitable organizations. You want to help your clients find the best all-around matches for everyone: the charitable organization, funder, and the service population.

**FACT**

The best grant writers think like entrepreneurs, know how to build client relationships, and are able to advise and consult with clients. They know what's going on in their community and who the community players are. They're able to develop programs and keep current on research results. And most important of all, they can meet deadlines and follow directions.

## Keep Track of Your Community and Research

A grant writer who is involved in the community, has helped develop programs for other organizations, or just keeps up to date on what's going on locally is an invaluable asset for his or her client. You will always be able to tap that background and knowledge when you have to put together collaborative proposals or assign project responsibilities. It also helps to know who the movers and shakers in your community are. They are experienced individuals who know how to get things done.

You'll also discover that if you are creative as well as practical when it comes to developing programs, you have another valuable asset your clients need. Sometimes they are just too close to their project or organization to see what seems instantly obvious to you as an outside consultant, if only by virtue of your experience. For example, if a school is designing a program to reduce delinquency, they might not be thinking about how girls fit into that picture and what's important to them in their various developmental stages. If you can remind them of the latest research that demonstrates that young women, especially those in middle school, need programs in which they do not have to "compete" with boys for the attention of their adult mentors, your client might decide to include girls-only clubs or activities in the project that they want funded. In that way you'll be able to help them fill a void.

## Three Absolutely Essential Skills

Above all as a grant writer, you must do three things and do them well and consistently. Always meet your deadlines. If the grant arrives past the given deadline, even an hour late, it will not be reviewed! It will not be returned either. And while you may be able to resubmit the same grant to the same granting organization, it's very likely that the next deadline will be a year or more away. Needless to say, your nonprofit client will not be pleased. The organization was counting on that money for its next budget cycle.

Second, you must be able to read and follow instructions. This is more important than having a good writing style, good client relations, or even a successful grant-writing track record. It boils down to the fact that if you don't follow the instructions contained in the foundation guidelines or in requests for proposals (RFP), the granting organization will throw your proposal into the trash basket—unread, unreviewed, and, needless to say, unfunded. If your client's grant was not considered or was rejected simply because you single-spaced the proposal when the guidelines clearly stated that double-spacing was required, from your client's point of view, there will be very little you can do to redeem yourself.

The three essential skills a grant writer must have are the ability to meet deadlines, follow instructions, and read between the lines.

A third critical skill of grant writers is that of a good "test taker." You must be able to read questions thoroughly, analyze the question for clues to the best answer, and provide the answer that best responds to the core of the question. A common downfall of many grant writers is to answer questions with information they know and want to tell the granting agency, rather than with information the granting agency is requesting. Don't fall into this trap!

Interpreting the questions is the first step in writing a successful grant proposal and a skill that you'll perfect with experience. Focus on your audience, and respond accordingly.

# The Grant Writer's Market

As stated earlier, some individuals and some businesses write grants, but your primary market is the nonprofit sector. Among those applying for grants are the following groups:

- Religious organizations
- Social service agencies of all kinds
- Schools
- Hospitals and clinics
- Governmental units (they often also solicit and fund grant proposals)
- Colleges and universities
- Police/fire departments
- Public-access media
- Arts and cultural organizations

Proposal writers and grant writers perform nearly identical services—one for the for-profit and the other for the nonprofit sectors. Use your grant-writing skills to market proposal writing services in for-profit industries.

## Business and Science Clients

Businesses seek skills similar to those of grant writers. You might see a business in the classified section advertising for a proposal writer, and some individuals market their skills as "proposal," rather than "grant," writers. In general, businesses often must respond to requests for proposals—for services or products—in the same way that nonprofits respond to requests for proposals for new programs that address a particular issue. Occasionally, however, businesses must write grant proposals for specific types of requests made by government agencies or other businesses. Since very few businesses have a grant writer on staff, they will require the services of a professional freelance grant writer. Architectural firms are one exception. Many of the larger firms have proposal writers on staff to provide the narrative description and the other information required that they use to supplement presentation drawings and estimates.

## A Word of Caution

Sometimes individuals apply for a very select grant, such as a Small Business Innovation and Research (SBIR) grant from the federal government. It provides Phase I grants of up to $100,000 and Phase II grants of up to $500,000 to entrepreneurs and inventors so that they can further develop their ideas for products that have some social application (such as a prosthetic device, educational software, or air-filtration system), as well as market promise.

For the most part, however, individuals are not the best market for your business. That's because it is best for them to write the grant proposal themselves. The granting organization is funding the person behind the idea and thus reviews the grant with an eye for that person's level of expertise, experience, and familiarity with the field. There are myriad other criteria, as well, that they use to judge the merit of the applicant and the proposal. The SBIR is judged by Ph.D. reviewers in science, medicine, technology, and/or engineering. The grant writer must be an expert in the field, along with the inventor, if he or she is to write with authority to this audience.

Another factor you should consider before taking on individuals as clients is that individuals often lack the money to pay the professional grant writer. If you want to donate your time and effort, you can easily find projects that are more fun and more interesting than those requested by a struggling inventor or entrepreneur.

## Generalist or Specialist?

Some grant writers specialize. Medical grant writers, for instance, write for hospitals, medical researchers, clinics, and other health-related organizations. Some grant writers specialize in writing only educational grants for schools or colleges. Others focus on issues such as child abuse and neglect. There are grant writers who concentrate on business or scientific research grants and others who prefer to write only one type of grant, perhaps for federal funding. You won't find them interested in taking on foundation grants or vice versa.

**FACT**

Unless you're an expert, you may not have the skills needed to write proposals for professionals in science, medicine, technology, or engineering. Their proposals will be read by peers in these highly specialized professions.

Should you specialize? There are a couple ways you can tell. Which of the two following checklists best describe you and your approach to work?

| | |
|---|---|
| ❒ I like to learn new things. | ❒ I am a master of one or two subjects. |
| ❒ I learn quickly. | ❒ I have an extensive vocabulary in my field. |
| ❒ I enjoy meeting new people. | ❒ I want to work with people who share my interests. |
| ❒ I want a broad market for my work. | ❒ I want to contribute something of value to my field. |
| ❒ I am passionate about my work. | ❒ I am passionate about my subject. |

If you fit best into the left column, you can easily say you're a generalist. You will be embarking on a field in which you'll never want for work. If you agree with the statements in the right column, however, you are a specialist, and there's likely to be a great need for your help in your field of interest.

## Range of Services

Grant writers don't have to limit themselves to grant writing. There's an array of services that you can offer clients that complement the actual writing of proposals. These can include such things as designing programs, planning and facilitating meetings, negotiating collaborations, searching for grant sources, meeting with local funders, writing media releases and packets, planning marketing strategies, and developing other written materials such as progress or evaluation reports. And don't forget, there's always a need for ongoing consulting and advising your client.

Another thing to consider: Grant writers who have established a solid reputation in their communities may find themselves called upon to review proposals written by new writers. That gives them an opportunity to be an editor and mentor to those entering the field. Local foundations may also call on an established grant writer to review proposals before the director presents them to their board of decision makers.

## Potential Earnings

As a grant writer you can earn as much or more than other freelance writers, even though you're working for the nonprofit sector. All clients expect to pay for the things they value the most, and nonprofits truly value grant writers. The more successful grant proposals you write, the more valuable you become to your clients and potential clients.

You are working with organizations that have limited budgets, however, so be fair. Give them a not-to-exceed project fee for every grant proposal. For instance, if you plan to charge by the hour, review the Request for Proposal (RFP) or guidelines, estimate how many hours it will take to completely write, review, and develop the proposal, then add a few more hours to cover contingencies. Using your highest estimate, inform the organization that it will not cost any more than that figure to complete the project. Of course, there may be times you've underestimated a project and make less than you wanted. But as you gain experience with various types of proposals, and get to know your clients and their work, you'll find that as often as not, you'll complete the project in far less time than you had estimated.

Base your fees on your hourly rates, but give clients with limited budgets a guarantee that costs will not exceed a certain level. That should wipe away any hesitation they may feel about an open-ended project.

There is no way to estimate what a grant writer can earn. It depends on whether they are employed full-time as a grant writer or whether they freelance, whether they are specialist or generalist writers, whether they take in several projects a year or just one or two, where they live in the United States, and myriad other considerations. A best guess for full-time employed grant writers within nonprofit organizations is the salary of a mid-level manager. Freelance grant writers can charge their hourly rate, whatever they and their local market dictate, and nearly always earn more than full-time employed grant writers.

## How Long Should It Take?

As a general rule of thumb, you can figure an experienced grant writer will estimate the hours for a project within the ranges listed on the chart below. These estimates include meetings with clients, filling out forms, writing budgets, writing the grant itself and making revisions. Minor expenses such as shipping, mailing, or mileage are not included.

| Item | Time required |
| --- | --- |
| Federal grants (one department) | 40–60 hours |
| Federal grants (more than one department) | 90–120 hours |
| Specialized grants (medical or research science) | 100–180 hours |
| Foundation grants (assets of less than $20 million) | 3–8 hours |
| Foundation grants (assets of more than $20 million) | 10–20 hours |
| Corporate giving program grants | Similar to foundations |
| State/local government grants | 10–20 hours |

Until you become accustomed to the process, you will very likely find that it takes longer to write your first few grants. It's also likely to take more time when you write a grant for a new client. But as you work with them on developing subsequent proposals, you'll find that you accumulate "canned" text that you can use over and over again. For instance, several paragraphs in your need statement must describe the organization and those it serves. Once a client approves what you've said and your first grant for them is successful, there's no need to "reinvent the wheel." It will save you a lot of research and writing time if you plug in those paragraphs when you tackle their next proposals. And you can reuse them again and again!

**ALERT!**

Never accept a grant-writing assignment for a percentage of the final grant award. First, you will not be paid unless the funding is awarded, and second, a financial stipend for grant writers is rarely, if ever, allowed under the terms of the grant award agreement.

## Getting Started

Maggie was a freelance writer looking for a larger market for her work. She read books on grant writing, spoke with a professional grant writer, and even attended a workshop offered by the local United Way organization on writing grants. The problem was that she had only one nonprofit organization among her clientele; the others consisted predominantly of for-profit businesses and local publications. She telephoned her contact at the nonprofit agency but received a cool reception. "It isn't you or your work," the contact said. "It's that these grants are critically important to us. We can't really afford to take a chance."

Maggie wondered how she'd break into a market that she knew would be lucrative when even her nonprofit client refused her assistance. She decided to reduce some of the risk for the nonprofits by offering to write a grant for free. Over the next week, she contacted another nonprofit she knew a bit about. "I'd like to volunteer to write a grant proposal for you," she said. "Do you have experience?" the executive director asked. "No, but I intend to get it by writing one for you," Maggie said. "Sorry," replied the executive director.

Finally, Maggie looked up a Request for Proposals and wrote a grant proposal based on the criteria in that proposal and her information about her client-nonprofit agency. Then she tried again. She telephoned a third nonprofit in the community and volunteered her services.

When the executive director asked if she had experience, Maggie said, "I've only done one, so I'll need your guidance." The executive director was thrilled. "We do have an RFP (Request for Proposals) right now. It's due in thirty days, and yes, we'd love some help! When can we meet?" Maggie was in.

The vignette above is true. It is not easy to break into grant writing for the same reason that the field is lucrative for freelance grant writers. Grant proposals have great value and are taken extremely seriously by nonprofit organizations.

Maggie continued to market her grant-writing services over the following year, and she grew more and more successful at securing clients and work. Before the year was out, she didn't even need to market anymore. Nonprofit directors started passing around her name, and she got as much work as she could handle.

**ALERT!**

Train your clients and staff of nonprofit organizations to send you "heads up" letters announcing upcoming grant opportunities or upcoming RFP releases. Prior notice helps the grant writer advise the client. They also provide ample time to prepare a program and proposal, identify and meet with potential community partners, and sometimes, if the client doesn't meet the qualifications, find someone else in the community who is in position to apply.

## Other Ways to Open Doors

Like Maggie, you may have to donate your services the first time to open the door to your grant writing career. As an alternative, you might subcontract with a professional grant writer in your community who can supervise your work and provide guidance for strengthening the final proposal. Or you may have an existing nonprofit client who is willing to work with you through the first proposal.

If possible, select some of the easier grant formats—usually local foundations or your local government—to get you started. This will limit the total number of hours you volunteer, and it also will provide you with a base of experience that you can use in marketing for more extensive work in the field.

## Meet Funders Periodically

Try to meet annually or biannually with funders. Get to know the people at the local foundations. This can help as you get started with your career, so you'll know better what they're looking for in a proposal. Things change. You may meet with the program officer of a local community foundation who tells you that they based their decision about whether to present a proposal completely on the need section. If the writer didn't prove need right away and have evidence to support that position, they weren't interested. But over time this may change, and you may find that their focus shifts—for example, maybe these days they look for things that approach systems change. Now you'll know that you need to focus your proposals and your client's attention around a framework of systems change.

## Watch for Trends

You are in a perfect position to watch for trends in funding—locally and nationally. For many years, for instance, funders have emphasized, if not mandated, collaborative approaches to projects. They still are. But when that component was first introduced, it could have taken grant writers by surprise.

Recently, funders have emphasized project components such as professional development in educational projects, audience engagement for cultural projects, or systems change for problem solving projects. Outcomes-based workplans and evaluations are another relatively new request from grantors.

If you see two RFPs that ask for information about a new focus or that mandate a new criterion, chances are that other funders will soon be wanting the same thing. Think of those original two requests as being at the forefront of a new trend. Then, when the other funders hop on board—as they will—you and the organization you're working with will be ready to respond. You will be establishing yourself as essential to the clients you're working for, and your business will continue to grow! (E)

 **Appendices**

Appendix A

# Resources

Appendix B

# Glossary

Appendix C

# Sample Federal Grant Proposal

Appendix D

# Sample Foundation Grant Proposal

# Appendix A

# Resources

## Internet Sites for Grant Writers

✑ *www.access.gpo.gov/nara/index.html*
Federal Register and links to federal agency Internet sites. Provides notices of federal funding availability, announces grant opportunities, and gives general information about grant programs. Register does not include information about state or geographically limited grants.

✑ *www.cfda.gov*
Catalog of Federal Domestic Assistance

✑ *www.cof.org*
Council on Foundations. Provides links to other sites such as Government Grant Sources and Private Sector Foundations. Links to Federal Register, Grants and Related Resources from Michigan State University, Resources for Grant Writers, State Grants, Schrock's Guide for Educators, Yahoo!'s Directory of Education Grants. Includes information about such things as Principles and Practices for Effective Grant-Making, Private Independent Foundations, Public Foundations, upcoming conferences and workshops, and Internet resources for nonprofits.

✑ *www.dhhs.gov*
U.S. Department of Health and Human Services. Resource pages and categorized links for such topics as how to find funding, writing grants, and managing grants.

✑ *www.dol.gov*
Department of Labor: grants to help welfare recipients achieve self sufficiency.

✑ *www.fdncenter.org*
Foundation Center. Grant-maker Web sites. Categorized links to private, corporate, grant-making, and public charities, as well as community foundations. Grant-seeker tools, application forms, foundation directory

online. Searches possible by name for information about a foundation. Lists more than 65,000 private and community foundations in United States.

✎ *www.gsa.gov/fdac*
Federal Assistance Program Retrieval System (FAPRS). Electronic database of the Catalog of Federal Domestic Assistance. Access either by category or by keyword. ✆ (262) 708-5126.

✎ *www.fundsnetservices.com*
Sources for grants, fundraising, grant writing, and philanthropy online since 1996. Categorized links to other sites.

✎ *www.fundersonline.com*
Links to European Union institutions, philanthropy, news sites, searchable database of nonprofits, and research information.

✎ *www.grantsbiz.com*
Articles, headlines, and links for grant writers.

✎ *www.lib.msu.edu*
Links to foundations, grant categories, and other useful information for grant writers and nonprofits.

✎ *www.mickeys-place-in-the-sun.com*
Information for grant writers, links by category, and other useful sites.

✎ *www.nonprofits.org*
Internet nonprofit center. News and information for charities and donors.

✎ *www.g2resources.com.80*
Business Service Center (BSC), Chicago. Provides information and assistance with federal contracts and procurement opportunities. ✆ (312) 353-5383.

# Publications for Grant Writers

▶ Catalog of Federal Domestic Assistance (CFDA)

Annual publication describing federal government programs providing funds or nonfinancial assistance to state and local governments, public agencies, organizations, institutions. Includes program's legislative authority, description of program, types of assistance provided, eligibility requirements, etc.

▶ Commerce Business Daily

Publishes procurement and contract opportunities exceeding $10,000. By law, a notice must appear in a publication at least fifteen days before a full RFP can be issued, thirty days before an opening bid can be made, and forty-five days before a job can be awarded.

▶ Federal Information Center (FIC)

Clearinghouse for toll-free numbers. Can be used to obtain contact information contained in the CFDA and Federal Register. Then, to get more information, you must contact the agency's program specialist.

You'll also find many, many catalogs that list grants for particular kinds of agencies. We recommend that instead of purchasing them, you're better off purchasing the foundation lists available from your local RAGs. Or do a computer search on your topic.

# Glossary

**501(c)(3):** IRS designation for nonprofit organizations, including religious, educational, charitable, organizations set up to provide social services. See "nonprofit organization."

**509(a):** IRS designation defining public charities.

**Abstract (also called project summary):** Brief description of project, the need for it, and the means of delivering services.

**Annual report:** Report published by a foundation that describes how grant funds were expended during the fiscal year.

**Application:** Cover sheets and forms that must be completed as a part of the grant package.

**Assets:** Holdings of a foundation in the form of cash, stock, bonds, real estate, etc.

**Assurances:** Forms that must be signed and submitted to the federal government stating that the organization practices equal opportunity, has an environmental policy, or agrees to some other requirement of the granting department.

**Bequest:** Money that is set aside and given to an individual or organization after a person's death.

**Budget forms:** Line item list of items to be funded, including personnel, wages and fringe benefits, projected travel expenses, training, etc. Form usually provided by grantor.

**Budget narrative:** Details pertaining to the budget: explanations and justifications of proposed expenditures, including calculations, other sources of funding, distribution of funding, estimated or actual costs.

**Building campaign:** Fund drive to raise money for construction or repair of buildings.

**Bylaws:** Rules that govern how an organization operates.

**Capital:** Funding sought to support construction or renovation of a building or its infrastructure.

**Capital campaign:** Drive to raise and collect money/funds that will finance an organization's building or renovation project.

**Case statement:** Statement of need.

**Certifications:** See "assurances."

**Challenge grant:** Money that is donated to a nonprofit if other donors contribute a predetermined or matching amount.

**Charity:** Nonprofit organization that operates for the purpose of helping/benefiting a certain segment of society.

**Checklist:** Often funder provided, this lists the components that must be included in the proposal. Sometimes the checklist is submitted and sometimes it isn't. Check instructions.

**Cold calling:** Going to a foundation and describing a need in the community and how your agency would like to address the issue.

**Collaboration/collaborative effort:** Joining of several nonprofit organizations to address a shared goal or develop a joint project.

**Community foundation:** Foundation established by one or two individuals who then enlist the aid of others in the community to contribute to the corpus—fund base—either through direct donations, legacies, or annual donations.

**Community match:** Contributions provided by local donors to support items in a project not covered by primary grant.

**Competing agencies/programs:** Others in the community that may have similar programs but are not partnering in the proposed project.

**Constituency:** In the case of grants, most often the beneficiaries of a project or the target population.

**Corporate donor:** A corporation that makes grants of cash or goods to nonprofit organizations.

**Corporate foundation:** Company-sponsored, private foundation that contributes to the community by using a portion of its profits.

**Corporate-giving program:** A company gift of merchandise or money that came out of the annual budget for charitable giving, not from a separate endowment.

**Corporate grants:** Money or merchandise that is given to nonprofit agencies by a profit-making business.

**Corpus:** Money endowed to a foundation by a wealthy person, family, or corporation to provide funding for agencies that serve the community at large.

**Council on Foundations (COF):** National organization that supports philanthropy throughout the United States and provides services and publications to member foundations.

**Decline/Declination:** Foundation/ government entity denies a request for funding a proposal.

**Direct costs:** Actual cost to operate a proposed project.

**Discretionary funding:** Money allocated to high-level staff or trustees of a foundation that they may grant on their own.

**Endowment:** In the case of foundations, the corpus. Additionally, foundations may "endow" a nonprofit by providing money to be held in trust. The nonprofit then uses earned income from the trust to pay for ongoing maintenance or operations.

**Evaluation component/plan:** Description of how you will assess the project and determine its success or failure.

**Excise tax:** Annual tax that must be paid to the IRS by private foundations.

**Family foundation:** Established by one or two donors/entrepreneurs to ensure that future generations continue to practice philanthropy.

**Federal government departments:** The following federal departments are most often those that make and administer grants for projects:

- DHHS: Department of Health and Human Services
- DOC: Department of Commerce
- DOD: Department of Defense
- DOJ: Department of Justice
- ED: Department of Education
- EPA: Environmental Protection Agency
- NIH: National Institute of Health
- OSHA: Office of Safety and Health Administration

**Federal grants:** Money that U.S. departments grant/give to nonprofits either through direct grants or through another agency, using pass-through funds.

**Federal grant application kits:** A set of forms that accompanies an RFP.

**Federal Register:** Collection of all RFPs expected to be issued by the federal government in a given year. It is published or updated annually.

**Foundation grants:** A source of funding from private or public charitable trusts.

**Funding cycle:** The annual cycle by which foundations make grants (such as annually, tri-annually).

**Fundraising:** Overall effort by an organization to raise funding, including but not limited to grant seeking, special events, year-end requests for support, bequests, and building relationships with major donors.

**Gap analysis:** Used when there is not a lot of data to support need statement; looks at current situation, identifies desired outcome and what's missing, or the barriers to meeting goals.

**Goals:** Broad, overall purposes of a project.

**Government grants:** Tax dollars that the government (usually federal or state) redistributes to communities through programs.

**Grant:** A financial or valued gift made to enable a project.

**Grant proposal:** Documents written and used to apply for funding for a specific project or purpose.

**Grantee:** Organization that receives a grant.

**Grantor:** Organization that awards a grant.

**Grant-seeker workshop:** Workshops targeted to specific RFPs and sponsored by a funding agency to provide additional information about the proposal process.

**Grant seeking:** The process of reviewing possible funding sources and narrowing the field of likely prospects.

**Grant-writers workshop:** Workshop held by a granting agency, usually state or federal government, to receive peer/expert assistance in developing your writing skills.

**Grant writing:** The preparation of narrative, budget, and applications for funding.

**Guidelines:** Usually provided by foundations, the outline of types of projects or categories of projects the funder will and will not be interested in funding. Guidelines provide directions for submitting an application for funding.

**Identity numbers:** Tax identification or other identity number assigned to an organization by the federal or state government.

**Independent foundation:** Usually founded as a family foundation; a large foundation led by a board of trustees nominated from within but generally not composed of remaining family members of the donor.

**Indirect costs:** Costs that a nonprofit may take from project grants to pay a portion of overhead or operational expenses.

Usually awarded as an allowable percentage of the project budget.

**In-kind contribution:** Support offered by agency and partners to project providing such things as staff time, office or other space, utilities, volunteer hours, and products.

**IRS:** Internal Revenue Service.

**IRS Designation:** The letter indicating 501(c)(3) assignment status from the Internal Revenue Service. A copy of this document is most often required by foundations with the grant application.

**LEA:** Local Education Agency (such as school district, intermediate school district, etc.).

**Letter of inquiry:** Describes a project and asks for permission to submit a grant proposal; the first step in the grant proposal cycle.

**Letter of intent:** Tells the granting agency that you plan to respond to an RFP.

**Letter of support:** Written by a partner organization, community leaders, program collaborators, and recipient organizations in support of the proposed project for which you are seeking funding.

**Leverage:** Money or items required to qualify for a grant.

**Management plans:** Narrative supporting plans for managing a project.

**Matching gifts program:** The means by which the match requirement will be met. See "matching grants."

**Matching grant:** A grant that's tied to the requirement that the applicant either use funds from its budget or raise donations of a certain amount in order to qualify for the grant.

**Multiyear requests:** Grants that are applied for once but awarded for several consecutive years of funding.

**Need statement:** Sets the stage for the proposal by describing your community, the target population, grant-seeking organization and what it does, and other relevant data that supports the need for the project.

**NGO:** Nongovernmental organization or a nonprofit organization that is in no way affiliated with government, except in that it might receive funds from government.

**Nonprofit organization:** An organization designated by the Internal Revenue Service (IRS) as meeting the criteria (specifically, does not make a profit out of scale with its costs and performs a necessary function in society) for nonprofit status. Also referred to as a 501(c)(3), its IRS designation.

**Nonsupplanting funds:** Funds that may not take the place of operating costs. For instance, if the organization is paying for a staff position, it may not, if it is prohibited from supplanting, make the position a grant-funded one.

**Objectives:** Measurable means of achieving the goals of a project.

**Operating support:** Support for nonprofit operations (rent, utilities, staffing, etc.).

**Partnerships:** See "**Collaboration.**"

**Pass-through funds:** Funding that is available usually through a federal or state grant that is administered by a local government agency or local foundation.

**Payout requirement:** Amount (usually 5 percent of corpus) that foundations are required to pay out in grants annually.

**Philanthropy/Philanthropist:** An organization/individual who donates money, goods, services, or time to humanitarian efforts.

**Post-grant evaluation:** Project evaluation made at the end of the grant period.

**Preliminary proposal:** Response to an RFP that calls for two papers: The first (preliminary) is used to judge which organizations may submit a full proposal for funding. Usually used for demonstration projects.

**Private foundation:** Also known as a private charitable foundation; it engages in giving to community agencies money that comes from a wealthy person, family, or corporation.

**Private independent foundation:** Often started by a family, but no longer controlled by donor or family members; administered by a board of trustees; the largest foundations in the United States; grants often made worldwide.

**Program officer:** Person who reviews grant requests at a foundation and makes recommendations for funding or not to the board of trustees.

**Project budgets:** Budgets for a specific project. Includes direct costs and indirect costs.

**Project manager:** The lead manager for a project.

**RAG (Regional Association of Grantmakers):** Member organization serving foundations in a given region. Keeps catalogs and electronic databases of member foundations.

**Request for Proposals (RFP):** A document outlining the types of projects the funder might be interested in funding, the criteria a potential applicant must meet in order to qualify for the grant, and the directions for submitting your proposal.

**Review criteria/Evaluation criteria:** Guidelines or the rubric used by judges to judge the strength and value of a proposal and how that proposal will meet the grantor's objectives.

**Review of literature:** Review of research on a topic/issue; cited, and stated to support the case for a grant application and the reason that the model of service was selected; required by federal departments and some medical funders.

**RFP:** See "Request for Proposals (RFP)."

**Rubric:** A chart that presents the evaluation criteria and assists the judges in scoring your grant.

**Seed money:** Initial funds that are used to start a project or fundraising campaign.

**Site visit:** Often a visit by foundation staff to meet the staff and see the operations of a potential grantee.

**Staff qualifications:** Summary of relevant service of staff who will administer proposed project.

**State Single Point of Contact:** Person or office in your state that catalogs who has applied for what grants and assists grant writers by responding to questions during the application process.

**Support letters:** Letters indicating contributions or support for grant applications.

**Sustainability plan:** Applicant's plan for raising money that will continue program after the original grant expires.

**Tax-exempt organizations:** See "501(c)(3)."

**Tipping:** When a nonprofit organization earns more money than allowed over expenses, it may "tip out" of its nonprofit status.

**Trustee:** A member of a foundation's board of decision-makers.

# Appendix C

# Sample Federal Grant Proposal

*The following grant sample proposes a Community Technology Center (CTC) grant project. This grant proposal was funded at approximately $235,000 for one year as requested. The sample follows the outline of the RFP for CTC projects and begins with a request to describe the ways in which the proposed project meets the criteria in the federal statute for authorized Community Technology Centers. All identifying information has been deleted and replaced with more generic information indicated by uppercase type.*

a.     MEETING THE PURPOSES OF THE AUTHORIZING STATUTE

The XYZ NONPROFIT in SOMEWHERE, USA, seeks to equip a mobile Community Technology Center that will respond to needs for technology education from several areas of the community. In its weekly scheduled visits to inner-city and other schools, community centers, and neighborhood associations, XYZ's new Mobile Media Laboratory will provide access to computers and the Internet, to digital video cameras and nonlinear video editing programs, and to e-learning courses on the use of media tools, provided in both English and Spanish.

XYZ has selected a mobile Community Technology Center because it enables the organization to reach into a broader area that could be served by one building site. It also brings media to the people and overcomes transportation and social barriers shared by most targeted service recipients.

The Mobile Media Laboratory (MML) will also be used at meetings of community groups, as a remote broadcast station for public-access television or radio, and as a vehicle for wireless Internet access, particularly in those areas of the City that have either no or outdated technology infrastructure. It will travel to other cities in this or surrounding states, as requested, to demonstrate effective remote routing and switching, and its educational programs on media and technology.

Using an Ameritech grant for that purpose, XYZ has purchased a sixteen-passenger van and has spent six months developing relationships and partnerships with community organizations in need of MML services. Some, most notably three area high schools and an area service center for indigent/homeless adults and families, have requested assistance in improving job skills or facilitating job searches. The State's Small Business Development Center has expressed interest in discussing ways the MML might assist entrepreneurs, particularly those interested in developing and commercializing new life science, computer, or advanced manufacturing technologies. Primarily, however, the organizations that have been most eager to provide MML services to their constituents are local school districts and youth centers. All of these organizations are interested in during school or after-school programs for children, youth and adults, that provide homework help and incentives for learning, academic enrichment programs, Internet access and exploration, e-learning tools and curricula, multimedia activities and tools that link student work with public-access broadcasting systems, and Web page design and deployment. Several of the schools within the districts have requested either special software such as PowerPoint or have asked for English-Spanish curricula and training. On behalf of Spanish-speaking families, these schools have also requested access to e-mail systems so Hispanic families, who feel particularly isolated in the western part of the state, can communicate more regularly and without cost with their relatives in other states or countries.

The MML Project has four overarching goals:

1. To improve literacy skills among school children and low-income adults; build self esteem among users; and introduce isolated populations to the larger network of available services at XYZ and other community sites.
2. To enhance existing school and after-school academic programs and attract additional and regular participation in these programs.
3. To remove barriers and embarrassment for adults who are "technology have-nots" so they can derive benefits from technology such as assisting children with school work, connecting with community resources, online shopping and research, accessing and using data for informed decision-making, and others.
4. To integrate XYZ and MML services into a broader community plan to identify the digital divide locally, to map the existing and changing technology infrastructure on a Regional Geographic Information System

(REGIS), and to develop a five-year technology plan and necessary partnerships to effectively narrow the digital divide in the City/County.

**b.** **NEED FOR THE PROJECT**

**i.** **Local Need**

Somewhere, USA is the state's second largest city with a population in excess of 200,000, and a County population of more than 500,000. According to the updated data from the U.S. Census, one out of every seven children and one out of every nine residents of the county live in poverty ($16,895 or less for a family of four). According to the state's League for Human Services, a family of four in the county would require an income of $34,000 in order to be economically self-sufficient.

Most of the minority population in the county is concentrated in the City of Somewhere, USA. More than 31% of the city's population is African-American, Hispanic-American, Asian-American, or Native-American. Less than 15% of the overall county population is minority. In the past ten years the minority population of the city has increased while the majority population has decreased in the city and increased in the county.

Most of the poverty is also concentrated in the City of Somewhere, USA: 36.5% of households in the County earn less than $25,000 annually, whereas 46.5% of City households earn that amount. In addition, children in the Somewhere, USA, Public Schools are more than twice as likely as those in other County school districts to receive federal free/reduced lunch benefits (66% of children in the 1998–99 school year and rising).

The map on the following page shows a large section of Somewhere, USA (shaded area) that local demographers and social scientists target as having the greatest need for technology infrastructure and access (census tracts 26, 28, 29, 30, 31, 32, 36, and 38). In this area are eight public elementary schools, one branch of the public library, and two neighborhood associations. Also in this area is the highest proportion of minority residents and the greatest rate of poverty: Church's community house serves the population of this area as does one of the Somewhere, USA, Youth Group's centers.

In a 2000 survey of City residents, 59% of the population indicated that they had access to the Internet, while 41% either had no access or were unaware of any points of access.

A study from the previous year showed that only 70% of school children in the County used a computer at school. In a ranking of 20 school districts in the County for technology availability (hardware and software), teacher professional development, connectivity, and other attributes, Somewhere, USA Public Schools ranked 18th, while another District seeking XYZ Nonprofit services ranked 13th.

Low States Educational Assessment Program (the state's standardized test-SEAP) scores correlate with children in poverty: In Somewhere, USA, only 38% of children scored satisfactory on the SEAP of reading. Most other school districts averaged from 50–70% satisfactory scores, while the two districts that scored over 80% both have zero-poverty populations.

Somewhere, USA Public School children struggle on SEAP and other tests of educational achievement. The state's analysis of adequate yearly progress targeted 42 of 57 Somewhere, USA, Public Schools for improvement in reading. An analysis of annual City's Achievement Test (CAT) reading results over the past several years, shows that the majority of Somewhere, USA, Public School students consistently perform below the 50th percentile in reading. When the results are disaggregated, data reveal considerable gaps in achievement between majority and minority students and between low-income and moderate/high-income students. The following table compares the percentage of elementary students performing at or above grade level (50th percentile) in reading in Spring, 2000.

The District's middle school population meets the criteria for at-risk: 71% come from low-income backgrounds; 68% are minority; 22% receive special education services; 15% are bilingual. 1050 middle school students or 36% were on suspension for some time during the 1999–2000 school year. Sixty-three percent (63%) missed over 12 days of school while 29% missed over 30 days of school. Fully ²/₃ of the students are below average (50th percentile) in mathematics, science, and reading as measured by the city's achievement tests. Over 40% are below the 25th percentile. The statistics for later elementary students show similar demographics with again fully ¹/₃ of youngsters below average in reading, mathematics, and science on the city's achievement tests. The only significant difference is suspensions, which are below 5% at the elementary level. Clearly, Somewhere, USA, Public Schools students, particularly those from minority families and/or low-income families, require early intervention to prevent later academic failure and dropping out.

Early intervention must include after-school and summer-school supplemental instruction, particularly geared to increasing literacy skills. To ensure that children attend regularly and often, the program should be safe, entertaining and enriching. More than 40% of families in the inner city do not have home computers. Their children's only access to computers is in their elementary schools, all of which struggle with outdated linkages to the Internet, a high ratio of children to available computers, and limited time and expertise for teaching computer skills or simply allowing children to explore on their own.

Their parents struggle to develop up-to-date work skills or to assist their children with homework. Worse, they are cut off from the flow of information that would enable them to make informed decisions about their and their children's lives, and about school, work, and democracy.

In the past year, several nonprofit, private sector, and governmental representatives have launched the technology planning group around a mission to identify, map, and develop a five-year plan for narrowing the digital divide in the City and County. The XYZ Nonprofit Executive Director sits on the group and is a strong advocate for individuals residing in areas of the community where the technology infrastructure is either nonexistent or out-of-date. Because these areas are not always contiguous and because the need for literacy programs, media literacy training, computer skills training, and other media communications is so great, XYZ Nonprofit is proposing a mobile Community Technology Center that can be deployed to schools, community/youth centers, neighborhood associations, and other centrally located sites throughout the City and nearby suburbs. In this way, XYZ Nonprofit can serve the greatest number of individuals in need of technology assistance, can remove barriers of transportation or unease by bringing media to the people, and can help mobilize public opinion and action around the issue of closing the digital divide. XYZ Nonprofit views the Mobile Media Laboratory

(MML) as a catalyst for deeper community involvement in the issues surrounding the information age.

ii.    **Response to Need**

The XYZ Nonprofit's mission is "Building Community Through Media." XYZ Nonprofit and its affiliates serve most of the county with public-access television, radio, Internet, and Information Democracy services. XYZ Nonprofit provides access to media for citizens and provides media services such as public service announcements, informational video filming and programming, Web page design and deployment, and/or Internet linkages for the nonprofit sector.

Staff and members of XYZ Nonprofit are concerned about equitable access to the Internet, computer training, and media communications and have long provided classes in media tools and media literacy from the XYZ Nonprofit site. However, since many individuals in the inner city are isolated from both information and such services as XYZ Nonprofit provides, staff now propose a mobile training van, which will be equipped with laptop computers, e-learning programs, television cameras, video editing software, and Internet wireless links for communications. The van, Mobile Media Laboratory (MML), will be available anywhere in the county as scheduled, and XYZ Nonprofit is currently developing a rigorous weekly schedule of visits to the following organizations that serve children and/or indigent adults:

- Somewhere, USA, Public Schools (currently scheduling for visits to eight elementary schools and one high school)
- Youth Group's two inner-city youth centers
- Church's Community House and its programs for inner-city children through seniors
- Neighborhood Associations and nearby homeless shelters
- Suburban public schools (The suburb is contiguous to Somewhere, USA, and has similar demographics to the urban core. Its school system serves nearly 9,000 children of varied ethnicity and socio-economic status.) (Currently scheduled to visit weekly one high school and two elementary schools.)

The MML will supplement available computers in after-school programs, allow high-speed Internet access with trained instructors and guides for children, provide cameras for filming activities in the schools and centers, and provide editing software so participants can edit videos and/or stream them directly to the station for airing on public-access television. XYZ Nonprofit plans to develop interactive curriculum on camera and editing equipment use and deploy it to the Web. This will ensure that children and adults wishing to use the video equipment also learn to navigate the Internet. The curricula will be deployed via the software, which allows continuous feedback loops for learners, self-paced learning, and multimedia display. Additionally, with assistance from curriculum specialists at Somewhere, USA, and Suburban public schools, the XYZ Nonprofit will develop eight computer-based units of instruction (four early elementary; four later elementary) in the learning content areas, for enrichment and reading improvement activities.

The television cameras and editing programs are near-universal motivators for learning. The Internet-deployed e-learning program can be geared to age, reading level, or learning style, and will be used to help children and adults improve their literacy skills while learning media skills.

In addition to improving literacy skills, the MML and its programs are integral to a larger community collaborative technology planning initiative that seeks to narrow and close the digital divide. The media lab will be used in that capacity to reach the disenfranchised members of the community, including children, and to provide them voices and vehicles for participating in the technology planning process and numerous other community improvement efforts currently underway.

c. **PROJECT DESIGN**

i. **Goals, Objectives, and Outcomes**

The goals, objectives, and outcomes of the proposed MML community learning project are as follows:

**Goal 1:** Improve literacy skills among school children and indigent adults; build self esteem among users; and introduce isolated populations to the larger network of available services at XYZ Nonprofit and other community sites.

*Objective a:* Write curriculum for e-learning (subjects include video editing, radio hosting and transmission, and Web page development) that is interactive and easy to understand.

*Objective b:* Define reading levels for each separate curriculum according to the skills the student will learn (i.e., higher reading levels for more difficult media skills).

*Objective c:* Train student assistants to assist low-level readers by demonstrating media equipment operation and using e-learning curricula to supplement hands-on training.

*Objective d:* Provide e-learning curricula in Spanish for 15% of the local population that speak and read only that language.

*Objective e:* At end of 2001–2002 school year, hold a city-wide video production competition and honor all participants at an awards dinner.

*Objective f:* With Somewhere, USA, and Suburban public schools, develop eight thematic units of computer-based instruction incorporating the content areas of language arts, science, mathematics, and social studies, focused on reading for comprehension in all content areas.

**Outcome:** Those who participate regularly in the MML program will increase their reading levels by ½ or one grade level (additional beyond that expected through school) by the end of the year.

**Goal 2:** Enhance existing school and after-school academic programs and attract additional and regular participation in these programs.

*Objective a:* Provide laptop computers and digital video cameras during school and after-school programs.

*Objective b:* Train participants to use video equipment and encourage them to explore online learning about video editing, radio hosting and transmission, Web page design, and other computer and/or media skills.

*Objective c:* Provide attractive posters with announcements of MML schedule in individual schools.

**Outcome:** By the end of the year, all Somewhere, USA, and Suburban public schools after-school programs served by MML will increase regular participation by at least 20%.

**Goal 3:** Remove barriers and embarrassment for adults who are "technology have-nots" so they can derive benefits from technology such as assisting children with schoolwork, connecting with community resources, online shopping, research, accessing and using data for informed decision-making, and others.

*Objective a:* Develop and promote a regular schedule of MML stops at inner-city neighborhood organization offices and community centers.

*Objective b:* Introduce media equipment with "thought starters" on how individuals might use the computers, digital video cameras, and/or media training to enhance their lives and their interfamily interactions/activities.

*Objective c:* Provide wireless connection to the Internet for areas of the city that do not have technology infrastructure.

**Outcome:** Participating community residents will report on pre- and post-surveys a greater sense of connection to community services (e.g., library, government, schools, etc.) and a new value for lifelong learning.

**Goal 4:** Identify, map, and develop a five-year technology plan to help narrow the digital divide in the city.

*Objective a:* Program Coordinator and XYZ Nonprofit Executive Director will participate in a government/private/nonprofit-sector led technology planning group

*Objective b:* Commission will identify and map areas of the City according to their respective technology infrastructures. Technology infrastructure maps will be integrated into the Regional Geographic Information System (REGIS) for use by citizens, local government agencies, technology providers, and funders.

**Outcome:** Graphic depiction of digital divide will mobilize public opinion around the issue and encourage technology providers and local funders to address identified issues.

ii. **Linkages**

The Multimedia Training Lab is in the final stages of planning and already has attracted high interest among those agencies and institutions that provide services to children, youth, and low-income adults and families. The following organizations have requested direct services from the MML but have little or no ability to pay for services:

***Neighborhood District:*** An area of the city that provides in a two-block area shelter, clothing, a health clinic, and a food kitchen for indigent/ homeless individuals and families. Neighborhood was among the first areas to request that XYZ Nonprofit establish a minimedia center to allow radio and television training, Internet linkage and computer equipment, and training to those in the neighborhood. The minimedia center has a live television broadcast line and is prepared to expand its program with the addition of supplemental equipment and e-learning opportunities.

***Somewhere, USA, Public Schools (SUPS):*** Serves approximately 22,000 students in K–12. Both the administrators and individual school building staff have requested XYZ Nonprofit services for media training and/or computer assistance. Some of the schools require supplemental computer equipment, some require software availability (e.g., PowerPoint), some wish job training programs, and some schools have media-training programs but lack equipment or up-to-date equipment, particularly for non-linear video editing.

***The Suburban Public Schools (SPS):*** SPS serves approximately 9,000 students in K–12 and has the most diverse range of socioeconomic status among students: Some come from $500,000 homes while others live in rent-subsidized apartment complexes. The District offers media training at the high school building but lacks transmission capabilities and up-to-date editing equipment or facilities.

***Somewhere, USA, Youth Group, Inc.:*** Established more than 65 years ago by then–police chief Mr. Big, it is believed to be the first police-sponsored youth program in the nation. Late last year it completed remodeling and construction of two youth centers on the City's southeast and west sides. Both centers have state-of-the-art computer laboratories that were intended for use by youth members to assist with homework or to improve computer literacy and skills. Neither laboratory is being used fully or wisely. Staff of the centers lack technical training and/or curricular programs; thus, youth use of the computer lab resource is limited. Youth Group has requested XYZ Nonprofit services to assist in developing computer literacy and curricular programming and to supplement activities in the centers with media training.

*Church's Community House:* This full-service center provides day care, job training, senior meals and activities, and after-school programs in one of the City's most economically depressed south-side neighborhoods. It has requested a television broadcast line with links to XYZ Nonprofit public-access broadcasting and seeks to train youth and adults to use media and computer equipment, to develop and air its own television programming around center special events, and to supplement computer training equipment and curricula for its job training program.

In addition, XYZ Nonprofit is linked with numerous organizations and programs throughout the community, including but not limited to the following, which have also expressed interest in at least occasional use of the MML:

*Technology Planning Group (TPG):* A commission composed of representatives from nonprofit organizations, governmental units, and private sector businesses, with a mandate to identify the current technology infrastructure on REGIS maps and develop a five-year plan for closing the digital divide. The TPG will be funded through at least two local grants for the first two years of the program and will seek additional funding as needed to implement its technology plan. The MML will assist in this effort by helping identify areas of the community where the infrastructure does not support technology and by mobilizing public opinion around the digital divide issue.

*The Strategy Group:* TSG was conceived as a way to apply the principles of Continuous Quality Improvement to the larger community. Now in its fifth year, the TSG is focused on a holistic and data-supported approach to problem solving. It models this approach currently by coordinating and enhancing efforts in the community to improve families' economic self sufficiency. TSG holds at least two annual meetings of hundreds of community residents and would use the MML for creating interactive meetings (each table at a work session would have its own computer to enter decisions and comments and link to the server in the van) and to simulcast the meeting for view on public-access television as a means of informing those not in attendance.

*Neighborhood Associations:* XYZ Nonprofit has established relationships with many of the area's neighborhood associations either individually or through its relationships with the Somewhere, USA Police Department and City of Somewhere, USA. XYZ Nonprofit hosts a monthly call-in television program with the mayor of the City and has developed video presentations and other media outreach programming for the police department. XYZ Nonprofit intends to schedule regular visits of the MML to each neighborhood association as a way of reaching into inner-city areas and assisting residents in becoming media and computer literate. This effort will also benefit the neighborhood associations as neighbors will increasingly look to the associations as gathering places and service centers with relevant programs. The neighborhood associations will also use the MML to promote, film, edit, and air media programs about special events such as art fairs, neighborhood clean ups, "take back the night," and others.

*A State University:* ASU is a local university that is involved in numerous community initiatives with XYZ Nonprofit. It is also the site of the State Headquarters for the Small Business Development Centers that are now seeking a technology designation from the federal government. ASU has a well developed community databank and is a source of evaluation tools, training, and processes for many programs in the City. The XYZ Nonprofit will call on ASU to assist in the evaluation of the Mobile Media Lab program, and will provide the MML as requested to assist ASU in its various endeavors.

**d.    PROJECT PERSONNEL**

Mr. Executive Director (ED) is executive director of the XYZ Nonprofit, which oversees the operations of all XYZ Nonprofit affiliates and programs. ED was a founder of XYZ Nonprofit and has been with the organization since 1981. He has been named by the Somewhere, USA, Jaycees as one of the top five leaders in the City and in the State, has been a guest on national morning television programs and has published hundreds of articles on community media, free speech, and/or democratic principles. ED has been keynote speaker at several national and international symposiums and has traveled throughout the world advising Third World nations on issues surrounding democracy and the media. He has worked as a juror for the national art exhibit, and has participated in an arts and Internet project, the Arts Integration Team for the botanical gardens, and the Arts Integration Team for City's Art Academy. ED is chair of the A Media's board and its "Community Media Review" publication and is recipient of the An Award for humanistic communication.

The XYZ Nonprofit employs ten full-time staff, three of whom are racial minorities; three staff members are women. Its Board of Directors is also composed of diverse individuals: ten are majority race; two members are minority; three members are women. The XYZ Nonprofit's personnel policy states: "XYZ Nonprofit provides equal opportunity to all applicants without regard to race, color, religion, age, sex, physical or mental disability, national origin, marital status, sexual orientation, or any other legally protected status. In addition to complying with the letter and spirit of this policy, XYZ Nonprofit practices policies of recruiting, hiring, training, management development, promotion, and compensation based only on an equal opportunity basis."

The MML will be staffed by one full-time project coordinator and two assistants. Equipment repair and linkages will be maintained by Net Services, which has a staff of two. The project coordinator will be responsible for scheduling the training van's stops and visits, for developing curricula and deploying it to the Web, for marketing the services available from the MML with other local nonprofit organizations, particularly those serving at-risk populations, and for reporting progress toward goals to the Executive Director and the XYZ Nonprofit Board of Directors. This person is not yet hired. The XYZ Nonprofit will make every effort to recruit a minority and/or woman for the project coordinator position and will ensure that the person will work well with the population to be served by the MML. At least one of the MML assistants, both of whom will work most closely with program participants, will be of minority race.

e.     **MANAGEMENT PLAN**
i.     **Timeline of Responsibilities and Milestones**
    The following is a chart that provides a timeline.

| Date | Activity | Responsibility |
|------|----------|----------------|
| July–August, 2003 | Purchase MML vehicle | XYZ Exec. Director |
| | Design exterior and have vehicle painted | XYZ Exec. Director |
| | Arrange for e-learning software installation | XYZ Exec. Director |
| August–September, 2003 | Develop written job description and responsibilities for project coordinator position | XYZ Exec. Director |
| | Place advertisements for position in local newspapers (including those serving minorities) | XYZ Exec. Director |

| Date | Activity | Responsibility |
|------|----------|----------------|
| September, 2003 | Screen and interview applicants for project coordinator postion | XYZ Exec. Director |
| | Recruit additional applicants if needed | XYZ Exec. Director with evaluators |
| | Establish evaluation tools and processes for MML and programs | |
| October, 2003 | Receive notification of CTC grant approval | XYZ Exec. Director |
| | Hire program coordinator | XYZ Exec. Director |
| October, 2003 | Develop job descriptions and requirements for program assistants and post/advertise openings | Project Coordinator |
| | Interview and hire two program assistants, at least one of whom will be of a racial minority | Project Coordinator |
| October–November, 2003 | Equip MML with digital video cameras, laptop computers, servers, appropriate software, and wireless connections to XYZ | Exec. Director and Project Coordinator |
| | Develop curriculum for online program teaching video camera operation and editing software | Project Coordinator and TV Affiliate Director |
| | Develop schedule of regular stops and programs for MML throughout city | Project Coordinator |
| November, 2003 | Develop curriculum for online teaching of Web page design and deployment | Project Coordinator |
| | Begin MML scheduled visits to schools, community centers, and other sites | Project Coordinator |
| December, 2003 | Develop curriculum for online teaching of radio hosting, transmission | Project Coordinator and Radio Affiliate Director |

| Date | Activity | Responsibility |
|---|---|---|
| January–February, 2004 | Formally evaluate program and revise offerings, curricula, and/or schedules as recommended for improvement | Project Coordinator, Exec. Director, and evaluators |
| October, 2003– October, 2004 | Continue regular visits to arranged sites and respond to requests for occasional visits to community, meetings, events, etc. | Project Coordinator |
| | Continue ongoing evaluation and program improvements | Project Coordinator |
| | Continue participation in planning commission to identify and map digital divide | Project Coordinator and Exec. Director |
| | As program demonstrates success toward objectives, encourage agencies receiving services to become more independent (i.e., to develop permanent on-site mini-media centers) | |
| July–October, 2004 | Identify year-two and beyond need for support and solicit support from local funders on behalf of agencies and/or XYZ and MML | Project Coordinator, Exec. Director, and participating agencies |
| September–October, 2004 | Formally evaluate program and progress toward year-one goals and objectives for reporting to agency participants, federal government, other communities and local funders as justification for continuation and/or expansion | Project Coordinator, evaluators, Exec. Director |
| | Hold community celebration acknowledging student video productions | Project Coordinator |

### ii. Community Involvement In Program Operations

Monthly, XYZ Nonprofit will host discussion groups of representatives from all user agencies and schools where the MML is deployed regularly.

Members will have open opportunities to suggest improvements or to request additional services or improvements to existing services. For instance, SUPS has already requested that the laptops be programmed with PowerPoint for one of its high school programs that requires a PowerPoint presentation before graduation. The school lacks both hardware and software to enable all students to fulfill this requirement, and even though some of the students have home computers, many of them do not have PowerPoint software. SPS has a high school class on television but lacks updated video editing capabilities and software and has no means of airing students' work. If sites wish additional regular program visits by the MML, the project coordinator will arrange them to the extent possible.

In addition, the two educational organizations will advise on curriculum development in the content areas and for the media instruction and assist in determining appropriate reading levels of curriculum materials and e-learning tools. Curricula will be designed in the Software by the Project Coordinator with assistance from courseware developers at the Software Company prior to review and improvement by the school districts.

Twice during the year (midyear and end of year) all regular and some occasional agency users of the MML will be surveyed and/or interviewed by the outside evaluator from ASU to determine levels of satisfaction with the service, suggestions for improvement, need for continuation or expansion of services, and qualitative data on the Mobile Media Lab program's progress toward stated goals and objectives.

The community will be invited to a year-end event that is the culmination of an all-city student video production competition. The event will include entertainment, video clips of all entries, full viewing of the winning entries, and food and will be held at a centrally located site.

**f.**    **RESOURCES**

**i.**    **Facilities, Equipment, and Supplies**

The Mobile Media Lab van will be equipped with 20 laptop computers, most likely Macintosh G4 PowerBooks, which have easy-to-learn and easy-to-use nonlinear video editing software. The laptops will also contain desktop publishing software for development of Web pages, announcements, or other activities; I-Movie and Moviemaker; Netscape, or another navigational tool,

PowerPoint; and word-processing software. Each computer will be equipped with a wireless modem that interfaces with a wireless relay station on the van. Signals can be sent from any remote site to the XYZ Nonprofit for deployment to the Web, television, or other medium. The Software will be used to develop curricula that can be deployed to the XYZ Nonprofit Web site for interactive e-learning about media tools; however, because it is being donated by the developer to XYZ Nonprofit and requires licensing, the course-development software will not be directly available on the laptops. Other curricula will be developed to reflect early and late elementary learning content areas and will be downloaded to the laptops for use in enrichment programs.

The MML will carry 15 digital video cameras. Completed video can be fed directly, via Firewall, into the computer for real-time viewing and editing or for transmission to XYZ Nonprofit.

The XYZ Nonprofit occupies the second story of the west side Library. It houses Net Services, a computer service provider for nonprofit organizations; a computer laboratory that provides both scheduled classes and free use of computer equipment; the station television studio and video editing offices; a public-access music radio station; and the Somewhere, USA, a program that teaches media literacy around social issues (e.g., treatment of gender, race, cigarette smoking promotion, etc.) and that logs local media election coverage and reports findings to the community. XYZ Nonprofit currently owns and operates a mobile television production vehicle that can be plugged into various television feed sites (b-lines) around the City. The MML will use the same and additional lines to deliver training and programs.

XYZ has received a grant to purchase the MML and to begin program development with an outside consultant. It has good relationships and a history of accountability with local funders and has already discussed potential for continuation funding with several local foundations. Pending evaluation of the year-one program and continued need, three of these foundations have encouraged the project startup and are willing to review subsequent requests for funding.

XYZ has a history of developing programs that are a progressive blend of social welfare and entrepreneurial response. This history has placed XYZ in good standing with local businesses, several of which have expressed interest in leasing the MML for events and training at their locations.

ii.      **Number of People Served and Cost Justification**

Besides providing a vehicle and tools for transmitting community meetings and events to thousands of individuals in the community who are unable to attend such events, and besides its impact on the overall awareness of the community about issues and services surrounding information technology, XYZ anticipates providing regularly scheduled, direct multimedia training for a minimum of 800 individuals from the following sites:

- 320 students from SPS at one or more of the schools
- 80 students from SUPS High School
- 20 students from two OCPS elementary schools after-school programs, including an elementary school where more than 80% of students are very low income
- 100 members of Youth Center
- 60 program participants from Church Community House (various ages)
- 20 Homeless District residents
- 200 community members from Neighborhood Association stops

Training for these individuals, who are expected to increase reading levels, decrease isolation, participate more fully in the social network of the community or school, and/or develop or improve media and computer skills will cost approximately $565 each (calculated by dividing the total program cost by 800 regular students).

iii.     **Project Continuation**

Much of the cost of launching the MML and its programs is requested from the year-one grant. Ongoing costs include maintenance and fuel for the van, staffing, software/hardware upgrades, and an annual student video production competition.

XYZ is prepared to incorporate the estimated annual cost of maintenance, repair, storage, and gasoline for the MML into its annual budget and has already done so for year-one programs. The cable franchise fee recently negotiated provides XYZ with both cable-access television support and some Internet support for the next 15 years. Because part of the cable franchise fee will come from a portion of the cable company's "At

Home" Internet subscribers, the money may be used to sustain the cost of operating and maintaining the MML.

The remaining ongoing costs come to approximately $120,000 (staffing and awards dinner) and approximately $20,000 to $30,000 annually for equipment/software purchase/upgrades or a total of $150,000 needed each year to operate the MML and its programs. XYZ will encourage agencies and schools that use the MML regularly to include in year two and beyond budgets a fee for service based on the number of hours requested and based on positive evaluation and need for continuation. It will also charge fees for service at large community meetings and events, as hosting organizations have the ability to pay, and will seek local funding of ongoing costs until the program is subsidized primarily by fees for service.

XYZ plans the following mix of funding sources for years one through five:

| **Year One:** | **$432,500 Budget** |
|---|---|
| 45% local funding: | XYZ annual budget: $75,000 |
| | Fees for service: $3,000 |
| | Existing grant: $80,000 |
| | Donations and discounts: $40,000 |
| **Year Two:** | **$175,000 Budget** |
| 100% local funding: | XYZ annual budget: $25,000 |
| | Local grants: $100,000 |
| | Fees for occasional services: $5,000 |
| | Fees for regular service: $25,000 |
| | Local underwriters (competition/awards): $20,000 |
| **Year Three:** | **$175,000 Budget** |
| 100% local funding: | XYZ annual budget: $30,000 |
| | Local grants: $75,000 |
| | Fees for occasional services: $10,000 |

|  |  |
|---|---|
|  | Fees for regular service: $35,000 |
|  | Local underwriters: $25,000 |
| **Year Four:** | **$175,000 Budget** |
| 100% local funding: | XYZ annual budget: $50,000 |
|  | Local grants: $35,000 |
|  | Fees for occasional services: $15,000 |
|  | Fees for regular service: $50,000 |
|  | Local underwriters: $30,000 |
| **Year Five:** | **$175,000 Budget** |
| 100% local funding | XYZ annual budget: $50,000 |
|  | Local grants: $0 |
|  | Fees for occasional service: $20,000 |
|  | Fees for regular service: $50,000 |
|  | Local underwriters/donations: $55,000 |

**g.    PROJECT EVALUATION**

**i.    Performance Measures**

XYZ will contract with ASU's School of Public Administration for outside evaluation of the one-year pilot for the Mobile Media Lab program. The local evaluator will help XYZ strategically plan activities that will achieve the program goals and objectives; provide XYZ with data that can be used to make adjustments in service delivery and improve the overall program; and design and conduct an outcome evaluation to determine whether the program is achieving its intended goals.

Specifically, ASU evaluators will gather data (qualitative and quantitative) to measure the following:

- Number of individuals served at each site.
- Rate of repeat use by individuals.
- Baseline and year-end reading levels of users, correlated with repeat users.
- Qualitative data regarding increased self esteem among regular users.

- Survey questionnaires for adult users to ascertain important uses for technology among the population and to gauge differences in feelings of isolation before and after using technology.
- Qualitative data regarding increased community interest in the digital divide and other issues surrounding information technology.
- Qualitative data on reasons and number of other agencies requesting regular services from the MML.
- Qualitative data from teacher interviews on effect of computer-based enrichment classes in the learning content areas.
- Student data from the Software indicating levels of proficiency and understanding of the information presented (e.g., Web page design, using video cameras, nonlinear editing software use, etc.).

Formal midyear and year-end evaluations will be posted on the XYZ Web site and distributed to all program participants and funders. Both evaluations will contain suggestions for improvement of the program based on interviews and data compiled by the local evaluator.

### ii. Feedback and Ongoing Assessment

The evaluator will meet in January, 2003, with students, directors/administrators, users, and teachers to gather their input on the MML program and its progress toward shared goals. He or she will meet again with program participants at the end of the program to share evaluation findings and seek informal validation of the findings. In addition, XYZ will host monthly discussion groups of program participants to generate informal and regular feedback on the program and to report progress toward suggested improvements.

Note: The grant proposal included letters of support indicating the need for the project from all listed partners.

# Sample Foundation Grant Proposal

*The following grant sample proposes developing a countywide pediatric asthma network that will help educate health-care providers, parents, and children about asthma management, using National Institutes of Health (NIH) materials. It also would provide intensive case-management for low-income children who have moderate to severe asthma. The goal would be to reduce morbidity and mortality associated with pediatric asthma.*

### 1. Executive Summary

The County Pediatric Asthma Network (CPAN) is a consortium of individuals from area health-care institutions and related agencies who, since 1993, have collaborated to improve pediatric asthma management among children. With pilot funding from 1996 to 1998, CPAN provided education for more than 5,800 physicians, nurses, school personnel, parents, and others who care for children with asthma, and intensively case-managed fifty children (ages five to nineteen) from low-income families.

The pilot project resulted in statistically significant changes: CPAN findings for 1997 indicate measurable improvements in knowledge about asthma, changes in behavior, and clinical outcomes for children. School personnel, children, and physicians increased their knowledge about asthma significantly as indicated on pre- and post-education tests. Children in the program significantly improved their use of metered dose inhalers and other treatments. Perhaps the most dramatic improvement came in the clinical area where the number of hospitalizations in one year fell from twenty to eight among the thirty-four youth who completed a full year of intervention; the number of days hospitalized dropped from fifty-seven to eighteen, and the number of school days missed went from 718 to 612.

These results were the motivation behind a recent CPAN long-range strategic plan developed with the assistance of the Direction Center. The plan calls for formalizing and strengthening the collaborative partnership, increasing public and health-care provider awareness and knowledge about asthma and asthma management, strengthening and expanding services to reach more and younger children from low-income families, and increasing research activities and dissemination of findings.

CPAN requests the assistance of the community foundation in formalizing and expanding the collaborative partnership to ensure that more low-income families that have infants or children with asthma will benefit from CPAN services.

## 2. Purpose

### A. Needs/Problem Statement

Asthma is the most prevalent chronic pediatric disease, affecting approximately 4.9 million children and adolescents in the United States. The prevalence of asthma in the pediatric age group is increasing more than in any other age group as evidenced by a 56 percent rise from 1982 to 1991. Over this same period, the prevalence of asthma in those under eighteen years of age rose from 4 percent to 6.3 percent (National Center for Health Statistics, 1982–91).

Asthma is the most frequent reason for hospitalization due to chronic disease in children and teens, with an estimated annual cost of treating asthma in those under eighteen years of age of $712 million. That figure increases to $1.3 billion when parents' missed work days and outpatient visits and medications are added. In addition, asthma is the leading cause of school absenteeism with ten million school days lost annually (American Lung Association of Michigan, 1994).

Asthma more commonly affects minorities and with greater mortality too. African-Americans have a prevalence of asthma that is 22 percent greater than whites, while age-adjusted asthma mortality data show that death rates in African-Americans are three times greater than in whites. Asthma also more commonly afflicts those in urban settings and those from poor households (Centers for Disease Control, 1986–90).

Eighty-three percent of the county's half-million population live in urban settings. In 1989, the county had 8,599 children and adolescents with asthma. Of these children, we can expect 7,149 to be from an urban area, 1,092 to be of minority background, and 791 to be from low-income families (United States Census Bureau, 1990). About 2,700 of the nearly 8,600 children have moderate to severe asthma. At least 2,400 live in households where they breathe second-hand smoke. These children are all at great risk. The estimated annual pediatric asthma costs in the county alone exceed $2.5 million.

ABC Children's Hospital, the regional tertiary and primary care pediatric hospital and one of four hospitals that admit children in City, admitted 404 children with the diagnosis of asthma in 1996. Their illness generated a total of 1,141 hospital days and $1,276,895 in hospital charges, or an average of $3,161 per child. Of the 404 admitted children, 50.7 percent received Medicaid insurance and 2.3 percent were private pay (ABC Children's Hospital data, 1996). Finally, of those admitted children for whom ethnic data were available, 29.6 percent were of minority ethnicity.

During its pilot, CPAN provided asthma-management education for more than 4,000 parents, teachers and school personnel, health-care providers, and children with asthma, which proved valuable, statistically successful, and cost efficient. Staff also case-managed fifty children ranging in age from five years to nineteen years with very successful results, particularly in the areas of reduced hospitalization, improved overall health as evidenced by a reduction in school days missed, and improved asthma-management behaviors, particularly among the children, though also among some parents.

CPAN plans to continue its educational outreach and seeks funding to add fifty children per year to its case-management roster (100 children in 2003, 150 in 2004, and 200 in 2005). All qualifying children will be from low-income families (using WIC standards for poverty). Qualifying age range will be expanded to include children younger than age five and their families. More than 50 percent of program participants have been of minority ethnic background, predominately African-American; it is anticipated that this involvement with the ethnic community will continue at the same or greater level.

### B. Goals and Objectives

CPAN has two overarching goals: 1) to educate those caring for children with asthma—the physicians, nurses, school personnel, parents, and the children themselves—using National Institutes of Health (NIH) materials and 2) to intensively case-manage low-income children with moderate to severe asthma. Achieving these goals will reduce morbidity and mortality associated with pediatric asthma.

Achieving the first goal consumes approximately 25 percent of CPAN's resources; accomplishing the latter requires the remaining 75 percent. CPAN believes it can best accomplish its two primary goals by implementing its long-range strategic plan. The plan outlines several goals and specific objectives; however, only those goals for which funding is sought from the community foundation, are described below:

*Goal 1: Formalize and expand partnerships and collaborations with other agencies that interact with the same population. Establish adequate staffing and communication channels to ensure formal, long-term partnerships that are in the best interest of the children served.*

*Objectives*

- Maintain and strengthen linkages between and among CPAN, the County Health Department, City Public Schools, area hospitals and clinics, neighborhood organizations, home health-care agencies, pharmaceutical companies, the American Lung Association of State, State University, health maintenance organizations, private practices, visiting nurse services, area pharmacies, and family members of children with asthma.

- Expand beyond these partners to other agencies and school districts. The City and City Public Schools, among others, have expressed a strong interest in using CPAN's resources, both to in-service their personnel and for the case management of their students.

- Create and increase executive director staff to 0.5 full-time employees (FTE), 0.5 FTE, and 1 FTE for 2003, 2004, and 2005, respectively. The executive director will be expected to oversee the entire operation, including deployment of resources (including the CPAN Speakers' Bureau), maintaining the service and educational missions, seeking future sources of revenue, and contracting with institutions and third-party payors.

- Create and increase medical social worker staff to 1 FTE, 1.5 FTE, and 2 FTEs for 2003, 2004, and 2005, respectively. The use of a medical social work intern for the past six months has proved invaluable. A social assessment tool is being developed by CPAN to identify those families at highest risk.

- Create and increase clerical/data support staff to 0.5 FTE, 0.5 FTE, and 1 FTE for 2003, 2004, and 2005, respectively. As the case-management and data collection—for research purposes—increases, so does the importance of these positions.

*Goal 2: Reduce pediatric asthma morbidity and mortality within a targeted urban, low-income population with moderate-to-severe asthma through case-managed intervention.*

*Objectives*

- Increase the case-managed population to 100 children per year, 150 children per year, and 200 children per year for 2003, 2004, and 2005, respectively.

- Establish protocols for identifying qualifying infants and toddlers for the program and share protocols with area practitioners, social service agencies, and others who can refer pre-schoolage children to program. By the end of year one at least twenty-five infants/toddlers will be enrolled in the program; by the end of year two, at least one-third of participants will be under age five.
- Increase nursing staff to two FTEs, three FTEs, and four FTEs for 2003, 2004, and 2005, respectively. (The current CPAN budget allows for one FTE through June 30, 2004.) A priority in this objective is a nurse-educator with a specialty in infant/toddler asthma management.
- Achieve measurable outcomes within this targeted population: reduce school absences by 20 percent, reduce hospital admissions by 50 percent, reduce days hospitalized by 50 percent, and reduce emergency department visits by 20 percent.

### C. Timeline

All objectives are established for the course of the next three years (2003–2005); most timeframes for completion are included in the objectives. CPAN is currently seeking funding from a number of sources to establish itself as a well-known, successful provider of asthma-management for children from low-income families. Funding for the next three years is necessary until CPAN develops the linkages necessary to obtain government or insurance funding.

### D. Partners

CPAN has enjoyed since its inception as a pilot project great inter-institutional and -disciplinary collaboration. Indeed, CPAN consists of individuals from all four (now three) acute care hospitals in City as well as staff from the American Lung Association of State, the County Health Department, State University, Health Organization, private practices, and visiting nurse services. Physicians, nurses, respiratory therapists, social workers, pharmacologists, managed care providers, educators, and family members of children with asthma are included in CPAN's membership.

Among its strongest and most consistent collaborators have been: 1) the Local Children's Hospital and Health Organization, which have supplied CPAN with health-care professional expertise, direction, and clerical support; 2) The American Lung Association of State, which has supplied CPAN with expertise, clerical support, and physical space; 3) Hospital Health Services, which has supplied CPAN with administrative and accounting expertise and a home; and 4) The City Public Schools, which has partnered with CPAN to educate City Public School personnel—principals, classroom and physical education teachers, school nurses, and school secretaries—to learn the optimal asthma care for their students.

As CPAN seeks to expand its services, new potential partners have been identified. Among those that have expressed an interest in participation are the County Intermediate School District, the City A Public Schools, City B Public Schools, City C Public Schools, and City D Public Schools.

### E. Similar Programs/Agencies

There are no programs or agencies similar to CPAN in County and only a handful of such programs in the nation. In fact, at a recent convention for health-care professionals who specialize in asthma management, the City program was highlighted for several of its features: its broad partnerships, which cross the entire spectrum of health-care providers in the community; its focus on research, education, treatment, and evaluation; and its statistically significant results achieved in a relatively brief time.

It is the vision of CPAN's Board to become the "Region's model organization for asthma care, offering education, professional expertise, and advocacy resources to control this serious illness. Through stronger collaboration with institutions of higher education and health care, CPAN will improve the lives of infants, children, and adolescents with asthma," and to "become a nationwide model making its experience in research, education, and treatment available for replication by any and all interested professionals and organizations" (Long-Range Strategic Plan).

### F. Constituent Involvement

Collaborating partners' specific contributions are described above. Individually, school personnel, health-care professionals, and parents of children with asthma frequently share specific problems related to the management of asthma for review and assistance from CPAN staff; however, most overall planning for services is done by the CPAN Board of Directors. The board at this time is composed primarily of health-care providers and representatives from other partner organizations, such as schools. Another goal of the long-range strategic plan is to diversify and broaden board membership to reflect community constituencies and represent program participants.

### G. Staff Qualifications

Current staff are licensed medical practitioners. CPAN seeks to hire an executive director with a background in social services and/or health care to establish cross-partner communication linkages and quality assurance procedures, and to establish and strengthen new linkages with other agencies that work with the same population group. Further, this person must be knowledgeable about managed care and insurance providers as he or she will be required to negotiate with these providers and with Medicaid to approve CPAN for reimbursement.

The nurse educator to be hired under the grant proposal will have a specialty in infant and toddler asthma management and treatment and will report directly to the Respiratory Department Manager at ABC's Health Services, as well as to the CPAN Medical Director and the CPAN board. He or she must be a registered nurse (RN) or registered respiratory therapist (RRT) with a bachelor's degree in nursing or related field necessary and a master's preferred. Past experience in community health, case management, and patient advocacy are important criteria.

CPAN will make every effort to recruit and hire qualified minority candidates for these positions.

### H. Long-Term Funding Strategies

Once CPAN has an executive director, the organization can begin the lengthy process of identifying insurance and managed care agencies and developing and presenting contracts for care. It will be critical to share with these organizations CPAN's clinical and behavioral outcomes; naturally, it will enhance CPAN's position to have more than one year's data, significant as the year's data are. The executive director will also be charged with identifying a contact within Medicaid and exploring the feasibility of a proposal to the government for Medicaid reimbursement.

While these processes are put in place to ensure future funding, CPAN must continue to seek corporate and individual support. The executive director is important to this process as well and will be asked to identify potential donors, share our clinical outcomes data, and solicit interim and permanent funding to expand services.

CPAN is also seeking funding from national and local foundations and from Local Hospital Health's Community Benefit Fund.

## 3. Evaluation
### A. Defining and Measuring Success

Previous studies of asthma have cited improvements in educational, behavioral, or clinical outcomes when using educational interventions. CPAN is the first such study in the nation to demonstrate all three among its participating children. The children, their parents, school personnel, and primary-care physicians were taught about the effects, triggers, medications, equipment care and techniques, and management plans of asthma. These outcomes are provided below. Those that are statistically significant are indicated in italics.

**Education Outcomes**

| Subject | Pre-test Scores | Post-test Scores | P |
|---|---|---|---|
| *Children* | *73 percent* | *93 percent* | *0.040* |
| Parents | 78 percent | 84 percent | 0.328 |
| *School personnel* | *80 percent* | *91 percent* | *0.001* |
| *Physicians* | *79 percent* | *94 percent* | *0.001* |

**Behavior Outcomes**

| Behavior | Pre-study | Post-study | P |
|---|---|---|---|
| *Inhaled steroid use* | *19* | *28* | *0.004* |
| *Inhaled non-steroidal anti-inflammatory use* | *.16* | *9* | *0.016* |
| *Long-acting beta2 use* | *2* | *8* | *0.031* |
| *Short-acting beta2 use reduction* | | *10* | *0.002* |
| *Tobacco exposure* | *23 no change; 3 increased* | *8 reduced* | *0.227* |
| *MDI/Spacer technique* | | *30 improved* | *0.001* |

**Clinical Outcomes**

| Criteria | Pre-study | Study period | P |
|---|---|---|---|
| *Hospitalizations* | *20* | *8* | *0.008* |
| *Days hospitalized* | *57* | *18* | *0.008* |
| *ER visits* | *58* | *50* | *0.470* |
| *School days missed* | *718* | *612* | *0.260* |

The difference CPAN makes in the quality and duration of these children's lives is the measure of the program's success. CPAN, therefore, will continue to collect data with the use of group-specific pre- and post-education tests, pre- and post-study behavioral criteria, and measurement of clinical outcomes.

### B. Dissemination

Results of the 1998 study have been compiled for presentation at the annual Academy of Allergy, Asthma, and Immunology and American Thoracic Society meetings. In addition, CPAN is preparing the data for sharing with area health-care professionals and the community.

### C. Constituent Involvement

Constituents participate as members of pre- and post-test and study groups. CPAN staff have learned a great deal from their constituents. Clients of the program have been candid with CPAN about how to work in their neighborhoods and how to work with diverse populations. As a result, CPAN has twice modified its enrollment form to be easier to complete and more sensitive to constituent issues and has shaped its methods of approaching and assessing families based on the advice of early program participants.

The most common request of CPAN from constituents is to expand the program to encompass younger children; in fact, many program participants have younger siblings with asthma. Clients also require that staff re-order their asthma lessons to deal with more immediate problems. In many cases, staff work with clients to establish priorities before beginning educational plans.

## 4. Budget Form and Narrative

### A. Grant Budget Form

A. Organizational fiscal year: <u>July 1 through June 30</u>

B. Time period this budget covers: <u>Jan. 1, 2003 - Dec. 31, 2005</u>

C. Expenses: include a description and the total amount for each of the budget categories, in this order:

| | Amount requested from the Local Foundation | Total project expenses (2003, 2004, and 2005) |
|---|---|---|
| Salaries | $169,293 | $626,642 |
| Payroll Taxes | | |
| Fringe Benefits | $42,323 | $156,660 |
| Consultants and Professional Fees | | $21,750 |
| Insurance | | |
| Travel | $4,836 | $10,881 |
| Equipment (Office) | | $4,500 |
| Supplies (Office) | | $2,300 |
| Printing and Copying | | $15,000 |
| Telephone and Fax | | $1,500 |
| Postage and Delivery | | $1,750 |
| Rent | | $18,000 |
| Utilities | | |
| Maintenance | | |
| Evaluation | | |
| Marketing | | $1,000 |
| Other (specify) | | |
|   Reference materials for library | | $1,000 |

| | | |
|---|---|---|
| Peak low meters for each enrolled child | | $3,600 |
| Spacer systems for each enrolled child | | $2,700 |
| Professional development | $1,500 | $3,000 |
| **TOTAL EXPENSES** | **$217,952** | **$870,283** |

D. Revenue: include a description and the total amount for each of the following budget categories, in this order; please indicate which sources of revenue are committed and which are pending.

| | Committed 2003–2005 | Pending 2003–2005 |
|---|---|---|
| 1. Grants/Contracts/ | | |
| Contributions | | |
| Local Government | | |
| State Government | | |
| Federal Government | | |
| Foundations | | |
| QRS Fdn. | | $50,000 |
| ABC Fdn. | | $150,000 |
| The City Foundation | | $217,952 |
| LMN | $24,451* | $90,000 |
| Family Foundation | $20,000* | |
| Health Department | $75,000* | $100,000 |
| Corporations | | |
| Individuals | | |
| 2. Earned Income | | |
| Events | | |
| Publications and Products | | |

3. Membership Income

4. In-Kind Support                    $120,505

5. Other (specify)

**TOTAL REVENUE**            **$239,956**                        **$607,952**

* Committed only for 2003

## B. Explanation

CPAN's request of the Community Foundation is for three years' funding for
the following:

|  | 2003 | 2004 | 2005 |
|---|---|---|---|
| **Salaries** | | | |
| Executive director @ $50,000/year | $25,000 | $20,000 | $15,000 |
| Nurse educator with early-pediatric emphasis | $35,360 | $36,420 | $37,513 |
| Benefits/taxes (25 percent of wages) | $15,090 | $14,105 | $13,128 |
| **Travel** | | | |
| Local mileage for nurse educator | $1,612 | $1,612 | $1,612 |
| **Professional Development** | | | |
| Attendance at professional seminars and meetings for nurse educator and/or executive director as necessary | $500 | $500 | $500 |
| **TOTAL REQUEST** | **$77,562** | **$72,637** | **$67,753** |

*Staffing*

Adequate staffing is critical to achieving CPAN's objectives and goals for
improving the health and outcomes of low-income children with asthma.

Cost for full staffing is calculated on market-rate salaries and includes payroll
taxes. The Community Foundation is asked in this request for decreasing amounts
over the next three years to support a .5-FTE executive director: $25,000 in 2003,
$20,000 in 2004, and $15,000 in 2005. The person hired in this position will be

responsible, with assistance from the board of directors, for establishing contracts with Medicaid and other insurance payors and for seeking alternate sources of funding until the position is self sustaining. Base salary for this position is $50,000/year.

Also included in the grant request is three-years' salary for a nurse/asthma educator with a specialty in early pediatrics (infants and toddlers). CPAN plans to add this position first and to increase nursing staff by another FTE nurse/educator in 2004 and two nurse/educators in 2005 (total four new positions by the end of the grant period). Base salary for each FTE is $17 per hour or approximately $35,500 per year. Currently, CPAN's only nurse educator is supported by a grant from the Local Foundation, for which CPAN intends to apply annually.

Staffing positions not requested of the grant include a clerical/data management coordinator @ $25,709/year (beginning half-time and increasing to full-time by 2005), and a medical social worker at $16 per hour or approximately $33,200 annually (beginning with one FTE and increasing to two FTE by 2005). A medical director's services are donated by Local Children's Hospital at a value of $75/hr for 200 hours/year.

All positions assume a 3 percent cost-of-living increase annually. Fringe benefits include FICA, health insurance, disability, workers' compensation, etc., and are calculated at 25 percent of salaries.

### Professional Fees

Professional fees are donated by the partners and include meeting expenses for the advisory council ($1,000 per year), administrative oversight provided by hospital's Health Services ($35/hour for 100 hours in 2003, 150 hours in 2004 and 200 hours in 2005), and accounting services at $1,000 per year for three years.

### Travel

Local travel is mandatory for the case managers/nurse educators. Mileage for the funded position of early-pediatric nurse educator is requested of the grant at $.31/mile, 100 mi./wk. x 52 weeks. Mileage not included in the grant is calculated by the same formula and applicable to the current nurse educator and additional nurse educators as they are hired.

### Office Supplies and Equipment

Office equipment includes computer hardware and software for the executive director and is not requested of the grant; supplies also are not requested.

### Office Services

Copying and duplication is important to ensure seamless communications and to share information with parents and others charged with the care of children with asthma. This service is not charged to the grant request. Telephone and fax charges are expected to increase with the addition of another line at participants' request. This increase is not reflected in the grant request. Postage costs are estimated based on past experience.

### Rent

Space for staff and program equipment is donated by the partners and is calculated at a rate of $12 per square foot for 400 square feet in 2003, 500 square feet in 2004, and 600 square feet in 2005. Utilities and maintenance are included in the cost per square foot.

### Evaluation

Evaluation is ongoing and integral to the program. It is not calculated separately.

### Marketing

CPAN plans a quarterly newsletter for participants and will seek the estimated $1,000 per year cost for producing the newsletter from other grant sources.

### Reference Library

CPAN hopes in year three to establish a small reference library for staff, other health-care professionals, and program participants at an estimated one-time cost of $1,000.

### Health-Care Supplies

CPAN provides each child with a new peak flow meter (approximately $20/each with 20 percent allocated for loss) and a spacer system (approximately $15 each with 20 percent allocated for loss) upon enrollment. CPAN is seeking assistance with these costs or donated supplies from pharmaceutical companies and manufacturers.

### Professional Development

It is important to remain abreast of changes in asthma treatment methods, educational information, and asthma management techniques, and to attend meetings of professional affiliations. Therefore, CPAN requests of the grant half of the $3,000 allocated for professional development over three years to ensure that the executive director and early-pediatric nurse/educator attend appropriate educational or networking conferences and seminars.

### B. Other Requests

CPAN completed its long-range strategic plan in July, 2002, and immediately contracted with a local fundraising expert to assist it in establishing funding for formalizing the partnerships and expanding outreach and participation opportunities to children under five. Since then, CPAN has submitted requests on the invitation of John Doe to the ABC and XYZ foundations. Those requests are expected to be decided by the end of 2002. Plans also call for an application to the LMN Foundation and, pending responses from larger foundations, requests of several smaller foundations.

In addition, CPAN successfully applied for a hospital Health Community Benefits grant, which will provide $75,000 from October 15, 2002 to October 14, 2003 and may be renewable each year thereafter. It has also recently received a one-year $20,000 grant from the private Foundation at hospital's Health Services and a $48,903 grant from the LMN Foundation, which covers half of this year's and half of 2003's salary for the current nurse educator. CPAN intends to continue to apply to LMN for funding as needed when the current grant expires in July, 2002. An application for special program assistance to purchase new bedding for children in the program was made to one of the trustees of the private Foundation.

### C. Priority Items

If the entire amount cannot be granted, CPAN requests that the Community Foundation consider one of two alternatives: First, that it grant first-year funding and perhaps a portion of the second-year funding request to enable CPAN to begin formalizing its partnerships and expanding services.

Alternately, CPAN most urgently needs an executive director who can oversee daily management, communications, fundraising, marketing/public relations, and data gathering activities and ensure quality control across the partnering organizations.

## 5. Organization Information
### A. History

CPAN was founded in 1993 as a consortium of individuals from area health-care institutions and related agencies who sought to collaborate to improve pediatric asthma management. Pilot funding came from the Community Foundation, Hospital Foundation, Corporate Foundation, Private Foundation, ABC Hospital, and XYZ Memorial Medical Center.

In addition to providing in 2002 successful public education about asthma management to more than 5,800 parents, children with asthma, school personnel, and health-care practitioners and providing asthma case-management for as many as ninety-three children from low-income families, CPAN began community and professional awareness programs, data analysis and outcomes, a professional certification project, and patient educational resources.

Results from its 2002 program indicate significant success in most objectives and demonstrated the need to formalize the partnership so that CPAN can expand its services.

### B. Mission and Goals

The mission of ABC County Pediatric Asthma Network is "to improve the lives of all infants, children, and adolescents with asthma by providing educational and professional expertise."

Goals in support of this mission were developed during long-range strategic planning and include:

- Stabilizing and strengthening the organization
- Increasing public awareness of CPAN and its programs
- Strengthening and expanding services
- Expanding and strengthening working relationships with agencies that serve urban, ethnic-minority children
- Stabilizing and broadening funding
- Increasing research activities and dissemination

### C. Current Programs, Activities, and Accomplishments

Current programs, activities, and accomplishments are described in the proposal narrative. Selected additional planned activities include:

- Diversifying community representation on the CPAN Board of Directors and in its membership.
- Establishing an advisory panel or ad-hoc focus groups composed of customers, providers, and community representatives.

- Creating an organizational marketing plan.
- Developing and providing certification standard for educators and health-care professionals.
- Increasing access to insurance coverage and inclusion in managed care.
- Developing and implementing a CPAN patient/practitioner satisfaction evaluation program.
- Disseminating the results of outcome management programs through community and national professional media.

### D. Organizational Chart

The current partnership structure does not lend itself to the traditional organizational chart. Such a chart has not been developed and awaits adequate staffing.

### Attachments:

Previous grants made to CPAN were handled by Hospital's Health Services, which acted as fiduciary agent. CPAN, therefore, cannot submit an audited financial report with this request. If the community foundation requests, it will supply an audited financial statement from the agent.

# Index

# A

abstract, of proposal, 216–217

accountability, in action plan, 137

acronyms, explaining, 188–189

action plan section, of grant proposal
accountability in, 137
being realistic about, 145
graphics in, 139–141
sample, 141–144
steps in, 136
timeline for, 138–139

active voice, 189–190

"activities," used in goals, objectives, outcome statement, 124

"anecdotal evidence," used in evaluation section, 148

appendices, of proposal, 220–221

"assessment," used in evaluation section, 148

assurances, in grant proposal, 206–208

attachments, to proposal, 220–221

# B

"benchmarks"
used in evaluation section, 148

used in goals, objectives, outcomes section, 124

beneficiaries of programs, *see* constituents

benefits package, in-kind donation of, 159

binding, of proposal, 219–220

block grants, 30

brainstorming, 94–95

budget forms, 209
sample, 210–212

budget section, of grant proposal, 78, 158–167
gifts-in-kind support and, 160–161, 164
how much money to request, 158–159
implementation and, 231–232
matching requirements and, 159–160, 164
multiyear requests and, 159–160, 161–162
partners and, 162–163
sample, 165–167
sustainability and, 163
writing narrative for, 163–164

businesses, as clients of freelancer, 240–241

# C

capital projects

evaluation criteria, 152
funding for, 2
status report in proposal, 180

Carnegie, Andrew, 10–11

catalogs, of foundations, 52–55

certifications, in grant proposal, 206–208

challenge grant section, of grant proposal, 183

charitable giving, history of, 10–11

Cleveland Foundation, 40

"cold calling", 25–26

collaboration, 5. *See also* partnerships

Community Development Block Grants (CDBG), 30

community foundations, 38, 40–42
grant applications and, 41, 49

competing programs/ agencies section, of grant proposal, 176

competitive grants, 82

competitive priority points, 199

conferences, *see* grant-seeker workshops

Congress, local member as resource, 36

constituents
program design and, 85

# Notes:

# Notes:

# THE EVERYTHING SERIES!

## BUSINESS

Everything® Business Planning Book
Everything® Coaching and Mentoring Book
Everything® Fundraising Book
Everything® Home-Based Business Book
Everything® Landlording Book
Everything® Leadership Book
Everything® Managing People Book
Everything® Negotiating Book
Everything® Online Business Book
Everything® Project Management Book
Everything® Robert's Rules Book, $7.95
Everything® Selling Book
Everything® Start Your Own Business Book
Everything® Time Management Book

## COMPUTERS

Everything® Computer Book

## COOKBOOKS

Everything® Barbecue Cookbook
Everything® Bartender's Book, $9.95
Everything® Chinese Cookbook
Everything® Chocolate Cookbook
Everything® Cookbook
Everything® Dessert Cookbook
Everything® Diabetes Cookbook
Everything® Fondue Cookbook
Everything® Grilling Cookbook
Everything® Holiday Cookbook
Everything® Indian Cookbook
Everything® Low-Carb Cookbook
Everything® Low-Fat High-Flavor Cookbook
Everything® Low-Salt Cookbook
Everything® Mediterranean Cookbook
Everything® Mexican Cookbook
Everything® One-Pot Cookbook
Everything® Pasta Cookbook
Everything® Quick Meals Cookbook
Everything® Slow Cooker Cookbook
Everything® Soup Cookbook

Everything® Thai Cookbook
Everything® Vegetarian Cookbook
Everything® Wine Book

## HEALTH

Everything® Alzheimer's Book
Everything® Anti-Aging Book
Everything® Diabetes Book
Everything® Dieting Book
Everything® Hypnosis Book
Everything® Low Cholesterol Book
Everything® Massage Book
Everything® Menopause Book
Everything® Nutrition Book
Everything® Reflexology Book
Everything® Reiki Book
Everything® Stress Management Book
Everything® Vitamins, Minerals, and
       Nutritional Supplements Book

## HISTORY

Everything® American Government Book
Everything® American History Book
Everything® Civil War Book
Everything® Irish History & Heritage Book
Everything® Mafia Book
Everything® Middle East Book

## HOBBIES & GAMES

Everything® Bridge Book
Everything® Candlemaking Book
Everything® Card Games Book
Everything® Cartooning Book
Everything® Casino Gambling Book, 2nd Ed.
Everything® Chess Basics Book
Everything® Crossword and Puzzle Book
Everything® Crossword Challenge Book
Everything® Drawing Book
Everything® Digital Photography Book
Everything® Easy Crosswords Book
Everything® Family Tree Book

Everything® Games Book
Everything® Knitting Book
Everything® Magic Book
Everything® Motorcycle Book
Everything® Online Genealogy Book
Everything® Photography Book
Everything® Poker Strategy Book
Everything® Pool & Billiards Book
Everything® Quilting Book
Everything® Scrapbooking Book
Everything® Sewing Book
Everything® Soapmaking Book

## HOME IMPROVEMENT

Everything® Feng Shui Book
Everything® Feng Shui Decluttering Book, $9.95
Everything® Fix-It Book
Everything® Homebuilding Book
Everything® Home Decorating Book
Everything® Landscaping Book
Everything® Lawn Care Book
Everything® Organize Your Home Book

## EVERYTHING®
## KIDS' BOOKS

**All titles are $6.95**

Everything® Kids' Baseball Book, 3rd Ed.
Everything® Kids' Bible Trivia Book
Everything® Kids' Bugs Book
Everything® Kids' Christmas Puzzle
      & Activity Book
Everything® Kids' Cookbook
Everything® Kids' Halloween Puzzle
      & Activity Book
Everything® Kids' Hidden Pictures Book
      Everything® Kids' Joke Book
Everything® Kids' Knock Knock Book
Everything® Kids' Math Puzzles Book
Everything® Kids' Mazes Book
Everything® Kids' Money Book

All Everything® books are priced at $12.95 or $14.95, unless otherwise stated. Prices subject to change without notice.

Everything® Kids' Monsters Book
Everything® Kids' Nature Book
Everything® Kids' Puzzle Book
Everything® Kids' Riddles & Brain Teasers Book
Everything® Kids' Science Experiments Book
Everything® Kids' Soccer Book
Everything® Kids' Travel Activity Book

## KIDS' STORY BOOKS

Everything® Bedtime Story Book
Everything® Bible Stories Book
Everything® Fairy Tales Book

## LANGUAGE

Everything® Conversational Japanese Book
    (with CD), $19.95
Everything® Inglés Book
Everything® French Phrase Book, $9.95
Everything® Learning French Book
Everything® Learning German Book
Everything® Learning Italian Book
Everything® Learning Latin Book
Everything® Learning Spanish Book
Everything® Sign Language Book
Everything® Spanish Phrase Book, $9.95
Everything® Spanish Verb Book, $9.95

## MUSIC

Everything® Drums Book (with CD), $19.95
Everything® Guitar Book
Everything® Home Recording Book
Everything® Playing Piano and Keyboards Book
Everything® Rock & Blues Guitar Book
    (with CD), $19.95
Everything® Songwriting Book

## NEW AGE

Everything® Astrology Book
Everything® Dreams Book
Everything® Ghost Book
Everything® Love Signs Book, $9.95
Everything® Meditation Book
Everything® Numerology Book
Everything® Paganism Book
Everything® Palmistry Book
Everything® Psychic Book
Everything® Spells & Charms Book
Everything® Tarot Book
Everything® Wicca and Witchcraft Book

## PARENTING

Everything® Baby Names Book
Everything® Baby Shower Book
Everything® Baby's First Food Book
Everything® Baby's First Year Book
Everything® Birthing Book
Everything® Breastfeeding Book
Everything® Father-to-Be Book
Everything® Get Ready for Baby Book
Everything® Getting Pregnant Book
Everything® Homeschooling Book
Everything® Parent's Guide to Children
    with Asperger's Syndrome
Everything® Parent's Guide to Children
    with Autism
Everything® Parent's Guide to Children
    with Dyslexia
Everything® Parent's Guide to Positive Discipline
Everything® Parent's Guide to Raising a
    Successful Child
Everything® Parenting a Teenager Book
Everything® Potty Training Book, $9.95
Everything® Pregnancy Book, 2nd Ed.
Everything® Pregnancy Fitness Book
Everything® Pregnancy Nutrition Book
Everything® Pregnancy Organizer, $15.00
Everything® Toddler Book
Everything® Tween Book

## PERSONAL FINANCE

Everything® Budgeting Book
Everything® Get Out of Debt Book
Everything® Homebuying Book, 2nd Ed.
Everything® Homeselling Book
Everything® Investing Book
Everything® Online Business Book
Everything® Personal Finance Book
Everything® Personal Finance in Your
    20s & 30s Book
Everything® Real Estate Investing Book
Everything® Wills & Estate Planning Book

## PETS

Everything® Cat Book
Everything® Dog Book
Everything® Dog Training and Tricks Book
Everything® Golden Retriever Book
Everything® Horse Book
Everything® Labrador Retriever Book
Everything® Poodle Book

Everything® Puppy Book
Everything® Rottweiler Book
Everything® Tropical Fish Book

## REFERENCE

Everything® Car Care Book
Everything® Classical Mythology Book
Everything® Einstein Book
Everything® Etiquette Book
Everything® Great Thinkers Book
Everything® Philosophy Book
Everything® Psychology Book
Everything® Shakespeare Book
Everything® Toasts Book

## RELIGION

Everything® Angels Book
Everything® Bible Book
Everything® Buddhism Book
Everything® Catholicism Book
Everything® Christianity Book
Everything® Jewish History & Heritage Book
Everything® Judaism Book
Everything® Koran Book
Everything® Prayer Book
Everything® Saints Book
Everything® Understanding Islam Book
Everything® World's Religions Book
Everything® Zen Book

## SCHOOL & CAREERS

Everything® After College Book
Everything® Alternative Careers Book
Everything® College Survival Book
Everything® Cover Letter Book
Everything® Get-a-Job Book
Everything® Job Interview Book
Everything® New Teacher Book
Everything® Online Job Search Book
Everything® Personal Finance Book
Everything® Practice Interview Book
Everything® Resume Book, 2nd Ed.
Everything® Study Book

## SELF-HELP/
## RELATIONSHIPS

Everything® Dating Book
Everything® Divorce Book
Everything® Great Sex Book

All Everything® books are priced at $12.95 or $14.95, unless otherwise stated. Prices subject to change without notice.

Everything® Kama Sutra Book
Everything® Self-Esteem Book

## SPORTS & FITNESS

Everything® Body Shaping Book
Everything® Fishing Book
Everything® Fly-Fishing Book
Everything® Golf Book
Everything® Golf Instruction Book
Everything® Knots Book
Everything® Pilates Book
Everything® Running Book
Everything® T'ai Chi and QiGong Book
Everything® Total Fitness Book
Everything® Weight Training Book
Everything® Yoga Book

## TRAVEL

Everything® Family Guide to Hawaii
Everything® Family Guide to New York City,
    2nd Ed.

Everything® Family Guide to Washington D.C.,
    2nd Ed.
Everything® Family Guide to the Walt Disney
    World Resort®, Universal Studios®,
    and Greater Orlando, 4th Ed.
Everything® Guide to Las Vegas
Everything® Guide to New England
Everything® Travel Guide to the Disneyland
    Resort®, California Adventure®,
    Universal Studios®, and the
    Anaheim Area

## WEDDINGS

Everything® Bachelorette Party Book, $9.95
Everything® Bridesmaid Book, $9.95
Everything® Creative Wedding Ideas Book
Everything® Elopement Book, $9.95
Everything® Father of the Bride Book, $9.95
Everything® Groom Book, $9.95
Everything® Jewish Wedding Book
Everything® Mother of the Bride Book, $9.95
Everything® Wedding Book, 3rd Ed.

Everything® Wedding Checklist, $7.95
Everything® Wedding Etiquette Book, $7.95
Everything® Wedding Organizer, $15.00
Everything® Wedding Shower Book, $7.95
Everything® Wedding Vows Book, $7.95
Everything® Weddings on a Budget Book, $9.95

## WRITING

Everything® Creative Writing Book
Everything® Get Published Book
Everything® Grammar and Style Book
Everything® Grant Writing Book
Everything® Guide to Writing a Novel
Everything® Guide to Writing Children's Books
Everything® Screenwriting Book
Everything® Writing Well Book